DATE DUE

OCT 3 0 1990 2019	
DEC - 7 1990	
MAR 1 8 1991	
MAY - 9 1991	
NOV 2 4 1992	
NOV 1 2 1994	
DEC 0 8 1994	
MAR 2 8 1995	
BRODART, INC.	Cat. No. 23-221

THE CANADIAN
GREEN
CONSUMER GUIDE

Like most human artefacts, books have an impact on our environment. Inks, bindings, colour dyes, the types of paper used – whatever the choices, they can have a neutral or a negative effect on the health of this planet. When McClelland & Stewart Inc. made the commitment to publish *The Canadian Green Consumer Guide* it was agreed that the book's production methods and materials should be as environment- friendly as technology and costs would allow.

For this printing several changes have been made from the first two printings to enhance the *Guide*'s environment friendliness:

• The text has been printed on Glatfelter Restorecote stock, a completely acid–free paper. Stock is rated on a 14–point acid–to–basic pH scale, a rating of 7 being neutral. Previously editions of the *Guide* were printed on stock with a slightly acidic rating (6.1).

• The Restorecote stock is also 50% post–consumer recycled. Recycled paper falls into two broad categories — secondary fibre and post–consumer. The former refers to those paper remnants which are created during the production process and re–used at the mill. Post–consumer means a product has left the paper mill as newsprint, stationery or another finished good, then been returned for recycling. First printings of *The Canadian Green Consumer Guide* in 1989 were done on new, biodegradable stock. Since the *Guide*'s publication, manufacturers have been producing more kinds of recycled paper stock in greater quantities.

• All inks used in the text are biodegradable Inmont inks. The cover has been treated with a UV (ultra–violet) finish. The cover paper stock, while recyclable, is not acid–free as manufacturers are just beginning to provide adequate quantities of economical acid–free, coated cover stock.

• All media kits and promotional material for the book have been printed on recyclable stock.

• The text stock and cover of the guide are 100% recyclable.

The Canadian Green Consumer Guide is designed to make readers of all ages, occupations, and lifestyles aware of the ways in which they can make the world a safer, healthier, greener place. McClelland & Stewart Inc. already has taken some of its messages to heart:

• The majority of our trade titles are now being published on recyclable acid-free paper.

• With the exception of fax material, all paper used internally at the company's Toronto offices is being reused.

• Boxed shipments of books are being sent with non-CFC (chlorofluorocarbon) packing materials. Smaller shipments are being packaged with recyclable newsprint.

• Booksellers are being encouraged to save and reuse boxes shipped from publishers.

• Plans are being drafted at McClelland and Stewart House in Toronto for the implementation of a Blue Box program that would involve not just the M&S offices but the other tenants as well. This will be one of the first such programs for a multiple-tenant building in Canada.

We hope this book will provide similar inspiration to other Canadian companies as well as to the individual consumer. Everyone can make a contribution to better the health of our planet, our home.

THE CANADIAN
GREEN
CONSUMER GUIDE

Prepared by
The Pollution Probe Foundation

In consultation with
Warner Troyer and Glenys Moss

Based on the book by
John Elkington and Julia Hailes

Preface by
Margaret Atwood

M&S

Canadian Cataloguing in Publication Data

Main entry under title: The Canadian green consumer guide
"Based on the book by John Elkington and Julia Hailes." ISBN 0-7710-7162-0
1. Consumer education - Canada.
2. Shopping - Environmental aspects - Canada.
I. Pollution Probe Foundation. II. Troyer, Warner, 1932- . III. Moss, Glenys.
IV. Elkington, John. The green consumer guide.
TX335.C35 1989   640.73'0971   C89-095378-3

Based on *The Green Consumer Guide* by John Elkington and Julia Hailes. First published in
Great Britain September 1988 by Victor Gollancz Ltd. Copyright ©1988
by John Elkington and Julia Hailes

Recipes in Chapter 3 reprinted from THE NATURAL FORMULA BOOK FOR
HOME AND YARD. Copyright ©1982 by Rodale Press. Permission granted by Rodale
Press, Inc. Emmaus, PA 18098

Cover and book design: The Watt Group   Cover illustration: Robert Meecham
Printed and bound in the United States

McClelland & Stewart
The Canadian Publishers
481 University Avenue
Toronto, Ontario M5G 2E9

CONTENTS

Preface *by Margaret Atwood*...............2

Foreword *edited from essays by Warner Troyer*...............4

Introduction *by the Pollution Probe Foundation*...............10

1 Costing the Earth 16

2 Food and Drink 30

3 Cleaners...............48

4 Clothing and Toiletries 58

5 The Home...............66

6 Gardening...............90

7 Waste Management 102

8 Transportation 116

9 Working and Investing 126

10 Travel and Leisure...............138

Further Reading 156

Environmental Organizations 158

Acknowledgements...............160

Index 161

BY NOW, MOST PEOPLE KNOW WE'RE IN DANGER.

We've heard about the thinning ozone layer, the greenhouse effect, acid rain, the destruction of the world's forests, arable lands, and drinkable water. The danger we're in is enormous:

if we don't do something about it, its results could be as devastating as those of a world-wide nuclear catastrophe. We have finally realized that we cannot continue to dump toxic chemicals and garbage into the water, air, and earth of this planet without eventually killing both it and ourselves – because everything we eat, drink, and grow has its ultimate source in the natural world.

However, most people don't know what to do. In the face of such an enormous global problem, they feel helpless. But although the problem is global, the solutions must be local. Unless we begin somewhere, we will never begin at all. An absence of small beginnings will spell the end.

During the depression and the war, conservation was a way of life. It wasn't called that. It was called saving, or salvaging, or rationing. People saved things and reused them because materials were expensive or scarce. They saved string, rubber bands, bacon fat, newspapers, tin cans and glass bottles, old clothes. They made new things out of old things; they darned socks, turned shirt collars. They grew Victory Gardens. "Waste not, want not" was their motto.

Then came the end of the war, a new affluence, and the Disposable Society. We were encouraged to spend and waste; it was supposed to be good for the economy. Throwing things out became a luxury. We indulged.

We can no longer afford our wasteful habits. It's Back to the Basics, time for a return to the Three Rs: *Reduce. Reuse. Recycle. Refuse,* too, to buy polluting products, and *rethink* your behaviour. For instance, use less energy: cut your overhead and increase profits, and stave off a tax hike. Dry your clothes on a rack: humidify your home and lower your hydro bill. Leave excess packaging at the store: let *them* dispose of it. Manufacturers will get the message pretty quick, not just from you but from disgruntled retailers. Start a compost heap. Vote for politicians with the best environmental platforms. Choose non-disposables: razors with real blades instead of the plastic chuck-it-out kind, fountain pens rather than toss-outs. Shop for organic veggies; do it using a shopping basket so you won't have to cart home all those annoying plastic bags that pile up under the sink. Lobby for country-of-origin labels on all food, so you know you aren't eating destroyed Amazonian rainforest with every hamburger bite.

Pollution control, like charity, must begin at home. It's true that industries are major polluters, but industries, in the final analysis, are market- and therefore consumer-driven. If enough of us refuse to buy polluting products, the manufacturers will go out of business. Even a small percentage swing in buying patterns can mean the difference between profit and loss.

This is wartime. Right now we're losing; but it's a war we can still win, with some good luck, a lot of good will, and a great many intelligent choices. This book is a guide to some of those choices. Although they are about familiar, harmless-looking, everyday objects, they are, in the final analysis, life-or-death choices.

And the choice is yours.

Margaret Atwood
Toronto
July 1989

"THE TIME HAS COME FOR HIGHER EXPECTATIONS...

The environment does not exist as a sphere separate from human actions, ambitions, and needs, and attempts to defend it in isolation from human concerns have given the very word 'environment' a connotation of naivety in some political circles... But the 'environment' is where we all live... The downward spiral of poverty and environmental degradation is a waste of opportunities and of resources. In particular, it is a waste of human resources... If we do not succeed in putting our message of urgency through to today's parents and decision makers, we risk undermining our children's fundamental right to a healthy, life-enhancing environment."

Gro Harlem Brundtland,
*Chairman of the United Nations World Commission
on Environment and Development*

Concern about our environment can seem overwhelming. Faced with constant warnings of such global issues as ozone depletion, the greenhouse effect, acid rain, deforestation, and pollution of our air, water, and soil, it would be easy to despair. *What can I do?*

The answer is, quite simply, a lot. All of us have the opportunity – the responsibility – to guarantee a safe environment for our children and their children. We have the skills to diagnose our planet's ills, and the ways, among us, to cure them. What we need is the will.

The World Health Organization now estimates 90% of all cancer is triggered by environmental pollutants (including, of course, cigarette smoke). The bulk of cancer, says WHO, can be directly traced to pollution from industry and at home. The chemicals in our environment – you'll meet many of them in this book – affect our circulatory systems, livers, kidneys, skin, lungs, central nervous system, and more. They make us sick in the short term – what's now called "environmental illness" – while the long-term carcinogenic or mutagenic consequences may kill us. Or our unborn children.

It's true a single act by one individual will not end the problems that plague this earth we share. But as Winston Churchill remarked: "It is better to be frightened now than killed hereafter." Each of us can perform many acts that will make a difference.

We influence the protection – or destruction – of our environment every day. We do it when we go grocery shopping; when we clean our house; when we take out the garbage; when we take pictures of our kid's first birthday in to be developed; when we drop clothes off at the dry cleaners. If you have the will to make environment-friendly choices, this book will arm you with much of the information you need to do it.

It's our view that much of life resembles a hunt for wild mushrooms: nothing one can't definitely identify as both safe and tasty should be picked or cooked. Sometimes, in a shady forest grove, it may be difficult to see which mushrooms are really toadstools. Environmental hazards are like that. They often come in monochromes, in shades of grey. There are no crimson warnings sky-written on the air we breathe, no cautionary dye in the fluids we drink, no scary, skull-and-crossbones labels on the food we buy.

Worse, our enemies and hazards, the environmental "bandits," are akin to the many-headed Hydra monster of Greek mythology. No sooner is one problem solved than another seems to crop up. Today's high-risk substances – CFCs, tropical oils, PCBs, even dioxins – may be taken off the shelves and out of the marketplace later this month, this year, this decade. Apple growers may stop using cancer-causing Alar to preserve their fruit and enhance its colour; some papermakers are starting to market coffee filters, milk cartons, disposable diapers, and sanitary napkins free of the most poisonous chemical invented by modern science, dioxin. (Dioxin is reckoned to be second only to plutonium in deadliness. Enough plutonium to cover the head of a straight pin, held in the palm of your hand, can kill.) But for every poison removed from our air, water, soil, and food chains, a dozen others appear. The Sorcerer's Apprentice was a piker compared to modern chemical manufacturers!

There are between 60,000 and 100,000 chemicals now being used commercially. The appalling fact is that no one – including the government agencies we pay to protect us – knows precisely how many there are, let alone how dangerous they may be! Add to this the estimated 1,000 new chemicals introduced to our environment each year. We don't even know the potential dangers of a majority of those 100,000 chemicals, let alone their "synergistic effects" when they are combined in our bodies.

Synergy is a common chemistry term used to describe an action "where the total effect of two [or more] active components in a mixture is greater than the sum of their individual effects." As applied to the environment, we don't know what, if any, synergistic effects are being created by the witches' brew of chemicals we all ingest (in our food, air, water) every day. We do know chemicals react with one another. We know, too, metals react with chemicals (for example, salt rusts the steel in your car; oxygen tarnishes the coins in your pockets). Metals react with one another, too. That's why a mixture of tin and copper (we call it bronze) is much stronger and more corrosion-resistant than either metal alone.

FOREWORD

What we don't know (and science can't tell us) is how these and the other chemicals in the environment and in our lives – our bodies – react with one another. We know dioxin, for example, suppresses our immunity system; we don't know whether, when mixed with other chemicals in our body, it acts more quickly, or more powerfully.

Now consider how many of those "other chemicals" are in our diet, water, air. Canada's government permits or has licensed:

- 1,500 different flavours to be added to foods;
- more than 1,000 flavours to be added to cigarettes;
- 330 "food additives";
- 103 types of pesticide residues on food;
- 32 food colourings.

And there are 1,400 pesticides out there, all finding their way into our water or food chain. There are at least 15,000 identified toxic (poisonous) chemicals in Canadian workplaces. There are at least a million tonnes of toxic waste being dumped in Canada every year. A lot of it goes straight through our sewage treatment every year; a lot goes back into the water we drink. Some goes into landfill garbage dumps, and thence into our groundwater, and so on into our drinking water – if it isn't absorbed by the farm crops we'll eat next year.

A major and salient point here is simply that we cannot rely exclusively on our scientists for protection. First, they really don't know how great the risks may be – most are afraid even to open the Pandora's box of metal and chemical synergism.

More critically, most efficient researchers have tunnel vision. In an era where specialization spells s-u-c-c-e-s-s, don't expect your local research chemists to find all the answers we need, before we even know which questions to ask. They are too busy with finer and more immediately rewarding detail. At the same time, reasonable, reflective, socially conscious folk aren't always the best researchers.

In short, it's the job of the politicians and their masters, the voters and consumers, to help set research priorities and question research applications. *Our job.*

We're largely on our own in this dangerous carnival house of mirrors, jerry-built by our manufacturers, our chemists, our government bureaucrats and politicians. Only by acting as individuals, and groups of individuals, can we ensure our future, and our children's. It means being sceptical, demanding answers. It means reading labels carefully and insisting that these labels are complete and accurate. It means pressing for more environment-friendly farming methods, striving for greater energy efficiency.

The point has been made, since the dawn of time, by many eloquent folk. (Here translate "liberty" as, environmentally, "survival.")

Demosthenes (circa 350 B.C.):
*"There is one safeguard known generally to the wise, which is an advantage
and security to all…What is it? Distrust."*

John Philpot Curran (1790):
*"The condition upon which God hath given liberty to man is eternal vigilance; which condition if he break,
servitude is at once the consequence of his crime and the punishment of his guilt."*

**An American novelist, essayist, journalist, and war correspondent,
Elmer Holmes Davis, said it, too, in 1954:**
"'Freedom can only be retained by the eternal vigilance which has always been its price."

There is a relatively simple first step open to us. We think all manufactured chemicals and synthetics should be judged guilty 'til proven innocent. The notion of "onus" legislation is not new to the traditions of British common law. Anywhere in the world, if asked by a police officer, you must prove your possession of a valid driver's licence by producing it; you are not assumed innocent of driving without a licence until proven guilty. That's an "onus" law – the onus or responsibility to demonstrate innocence is yours.

We have, for a long time, required drug companies to prove their new medications safe before licensing them for sale. The same strictures apply to food additives (though one can – and should – question the efficiency of regulation, labelling, and, most of all, inspection). It's clearly past time to insist on equally rigid standards for any of the myriad of environmental toxins and pollutants.

Progress of all kinds demands many forms of evolution. So the processes that saw the demise of the buggy whip and the button hook may well combine to end the production of harmful CFCs, dioxins, and PCBs. The descendants of the buggy whip factory employees, or their neighbours, are probably doing okay servicing carburetors. The development of the zipper during the First World War did not cause mass unemployment, though it may have discommoded the executive officers and shareholders of factories churning out trouser-fly buttons. In blunt fact, no "net" jobs have ever been directly destroyed through environmental clean-ups. Industry has often used the excuse to close geriatric plants that had long since "paid themselves down," as the economists say. But net employment always gains in the face of action to save our planet – and our lives. Indeed, as we'll see, ambitious young people can ignore the sirens of the past.

In our grandfathers' time the formula for success was "Go west." A generation later the advice was "Go into aeronautics or automobiles." For the next decade or two the magic formula was "Go into plastics," and, in the 1970s and 1980s, the call became "Go into computers." No more. Today – and for as many tomorrows as we preserve – the biggest growth industry is and will be that of environmental protection.

FOREWORD

I n 1971, I researched and produced a documentary film on a vexing modern problem: bystander apathy. Early in the research I learned bystanders and passers-by stop being apathetic – stop ignoring danger to their fellows in the street – when, simply, they are told such a phenomenon exists. People who know about bystander apathy – that is, who aren't apathetic bystanders any more – intervene to help a victim of rape, robbery, traffic accident, or epileptic seizure. Awareness of the problem is, literally, the first step towards its cure. We think and hope the same may be true of our shared environmental difficulties.

Beginning most dramatically with Rachel Carson's *Silent Spring*, in 1962, we've become at least generally informed – and, respectably, frightened of the grave, immediate threats to our ecosystems. First as individuals, now as societies, and ultimately as a global community, we've learned problems exist. So, by definition, we want to help.

With the publication, in late April 1987, of the report of the World Commission on Environment and Development (the Brundtland report, after its chairman), we learned apathy is not an appropriate response to ozone depletion, acid rain, or the greenhouse effect. Our cause is not hopeless: we can help. It's not too late to save our planet, our environment, our futures. Moreover, said Norway's prime minister, Gro Harlem Brundtland, and her colleagues, it's okay to develop, all right to have aspirations, respectable to grow, if our development is "sustainable." Development (call it lifestyle, if you wish – Gro Brundtland said, wisely, "'Development' is what we all do") – will work only if it does not diminish, deplete, or destroy elements of our shared environment.

Perhaps some definitions are in order here.

Environment:

"The sum of all external conditions and influences affecting the development and life of organisms… The aggregate of all the conditions and influences that determine the behaviour of a physical system." (*The McGraw Hill Dictionary of Scientific and Technical Terms*)

"External conditions or surrounding… The external surrounding in which a plant or animal lives, which tend to influence its development or behaviour." (*The Collins English Dictionary*)

"The conditions under which any person or thing lives or is developed; the sum total of influences which modify and determine the development of life or character." (*The Oxford English Dictionary*)

All okay definitions, especially, perhaps, that from the *Oxford Dictionary*. But we still like the simpler and more elegant description provided by Madame Brundtland. "The environment," she said, "is where we all live."

Ecology:

"The study of relationships between living organisms and their environment." (*Collins*)
"Ecology," is, in brief, a branch of biology – a science, not a word to describe our physical surroundings.

Ecosphere:

"The parts of the universe, especially on earth, in which life can exist." (*Collins*)

Consider this. *Eco* – as in *ecology, ecosphere, ecosystem,* and, interestingly, *economics* – is from the Greek, meaning "a household," or, closer to home, "the stewardship/management of a household." As we'll see, the links between economics and ecological health and survival are very clear and real. "Good housekeeping," in short, is what it's all about. We don't walk by orange peel dropped on the kitchen floor, or scrap paper on the living room carpet. Nor (if we're paying attention) do we throw trash out the car window, dump toxic solvents down the sink, leave that same car's motor running for 15 minutes while we chat with the butcher or baker, or buy products in non-returnable bottles or tins.

The point is that very few if any of our environmental concerns can be treated or understood in isolation. Running our cars, for instance, when we needn't contributes to acid rain, which washes metals, including aluminum, from the soil. The aluminum, leached from the soil into the surface water, can flow into our lakes, triggering a fish kill. That same metal, scientists now believe, clogs the root system of trees, prevents them from taking up nutrients from the soil, and so starves them until they die.

"The earth is one," Gro Brundtland has observed, "but the world is not." Of course, it *must* be. As surely as a mathematical abstraction, the world is indivisible. What's done here, wherever we are, has consequences – everywhere. The destruction of a Canadian stream, the poisoning of a water table beneath a pesticide-soaked Quebec farm or a Manitoba landfill site can have both national and global consequences, as surely as a snake bite on one's finger can still the heart.

Left unchecked, our carelessness today, our profligacy, our greed, our pollutants, our waste products will, like Jacob Marley's chains, drag us down and return to haunt us. We shall indeed hang separately if we do not "hang together."

When someone is struck by an auto, or collapses on the street, it may be a bit late for us to go learn "the kiss of life," or study how to make a leg splint. Early, "preventive" preparation for environmental first aid is easier, more effective. Let's make a start:

- Become an informed consumer of the products you buy and services you use.
- Tell your local shopkeeper to stock the things you want to buy because they're good for the environment. You have a vote for a healthy world, every time you go through a checkout counter.
- Join an environmental organization, and help lobby our governments to do more to preserve this planet for all of our children.
- Encourage your family, friends, neighbours, and co-workers to do the same.

Pass it on.

Warner Troyer
Smoke Lake, Ontario
July 1989

INTRODUCTION

"FROM SPACE, WE SEE A SMALL AND FRAGILE BALL *dominated not by human activity and edifice but by a pattern of clouds, oceans, greenery, and soils. Humanity's inability to fit its doings into that pattern is changing planetary systems, fundamentally. Many such changes are accompanied by life-threatening hazards. This new reality, from which there is no escape, must be recognized – and managed."*

The World Commission on Environment and Development, 1987

The natural systems that have sustained the planet for more than two million years are showing signs of stress. The delicate balance between land, water, and atmosphere, between plants, animals, and minerals, is being disturbed in ways we don't even fully understand, although the results are all too evident.

Human beings have always exploited the earth's rich resources, of course. Since civilization began we have cut down forests, planted crops, built fences, and waged wars. Damage was being done, but the global impact was much less while the population was smaller. And until the Industrial Revolution, we did not make major use of fossil fuels like coal and oil, we did not know how to make synthetic toxic chemicals that would pose a health risk both to ourselves and to other species, and our waste products were relatively biodegradable.

The Industrial Revolution marked the beginning of our access to knowledge and technology that could destroy the planet. We started by damming rivers and harnessing water power, without regard to the fish and wildlife that lived in and around those rivers. We started burning coal, without regard for the consequences of the smoke that came from our factory chimneys. We started dumping chemical waste into the ground, without regard to the impact of that waste on underground water supplies. In short, we took advantage of the resources of the planet and the creativity of humankind without regard for the consequences of our actions.

People who fail to consider the consequences of their actions often find that this failure leads to their downfall. So it is with the planet today. We have acted for so long without regard to the future that the planet is close to major environmental change, change so significant that the earth may soon become inhospitable to human beings.

No one knows how close we are to that kind of change. Some have estimated that it may come within 50 years, within the lifetime of our grandchildren if not of our children. Nor do we know which is our most serious problem. Within 25 years the ocean might flood most of the coastal cities around the world. Within 25 years we could have another Chernobyl nuclear accident, one that would contaminate food supplies not just in northern and central Europe but over a much greater area of the world. Within 25 years temperatures could have risen so much that our temperate cities become tropical and our prairies become desert.

Or perhaps it won't be that serious. Maybe we'll just have to treat our water to remove toxic chemicals with such sophisticated equipment that drinking water costs us a dollar a litre, or $725 per person per year. Within 25 years perhaps we'll just have to put on suntan oil every time we venture out of doors, because the ultraviolet light will be capable of causing cancer after only a few hours' exposure. Within 25 years perhaps our agriculture will have suffered so badly from soil erosion that the only meat we can afford to produce is cockroaches.

In 1983 the United Nations General Assembly instructed a commission to examine these urgent questions and formulate "a global agenda for change." The World Commission on Environment and Development, chaired by Gro Harlem Brundtland, prime minister of Norway, issued its report in 1987. It called for a joint effort: from business as well as government, in national and multilateral forums, by scientists, educators, and environmentalists. Most of all, it called for individual citizens to become involved rather than relying on governments to resolve the environmental mess to which we have all contributed.

Four of the key messages from the Brundtland Commission report can help us understand why we can't leave it all to government.

The Brundtland Messages
Environmental pollution is expensive
– for our grandchildren!

Until now it has seemed cheaper to pollute – to treat the planet like a big garbage dump, assuming that it can absorb unlimited quantities of garbage, toxic waste, PCBs, CFCs, acids, carbon dioxide, and more. But we must recognize the long-term costs of environmental pollution in everything we do. Our grandchildren expect to inherit a clean planet, brimming with natural resources. If we have ruined the place, they won't just be mad – they might not be able to survive.

We must move forward, not back.

Solving our environmental problems does not mean abolishing industry or returning to cave dwellings with a tallow candle for heat and light. In fact, solving our environmental problems requires healthy industry and a healthy economy, simply because it is when the economy is growing that we can most easily afford to make the choices that are essential if we are all to live within the planet's ecological means. When productive agricultural land in Africa or tropical rainforest in South America is turned to desert, it's not necessarily because the people there are ignorant, or greedy, or insensitive to environmental concerns. It's most often because they are so poor that they must choose between destroying the land today and surviving through tomorrow, or dying from malnutrition today.

We can't afford <u>not</u> to clean up.

The third Brundtland message is that a healthy economy requires a healthy environment. If the environment is collapsing, if our drinking water is being contaminated, our farmland turning to desert, our coastal cities inundated by rising oceans, then our economy will be in deep trouble too and we will probably all be out of work.

Problems must be stopped before they happen.

Finally, the Brundtland report tells us that we must abandon our react-and-cure approach, our emphasis on cleaning up environmental problems after they have occurred. We must replace it with a strategy of anticipate-and-prevent, predicting potential environmental problems before we undertake a new venture and modifying it to ensure that those problems will not happen. Solving problems after they have arisen is always more expensive than preventing them.

The good news from the Brundtland Commission was that we shouldn't even think of solving our environmental problems by moving backwards. The commission said not only that a healthy economy and a clean environment are compatible objectives, not only that we can have jobs and environmental protection, but that we *must* have both, because if we do not adopt a strategy of what it called "sustainable development," the polluted environment will destroy our economy, our society, and our planet.

And the commission pointed out that government and industry will need all the help they can get from citizens. It will still be government's duty to regulate, to prosecute, and to manage crises. Citizens can do what government is not very good at: long-range planning, setting priorities, and changing society's attitudes. And as consumers, we can use buying power to shift industry away from producing wasteful and polluting products towards goods that do the least possible harm to the environment.

Buying power is the idea behind Green Consumerism. It is the consumer's ability to change from Brand X to Brand Y – or, even more worryingly for manufacturers and retailers, to stop buying a particular product altogether – that makes producers sit up and take notice. The purpose of this book is to provide the information that will allow Green Consumers to use this power most effectively for the benefit of the environment.

It isn't always easy to point to the "best" choices. Environmental science is a relatively new area, and we just don't know yet how to tackle some of the problems we've created. The repeated cutbacks in government research programs haven't helped.

With other environmental problems we know what to do, but the lack of labelling makes it impossible for consumers to tell which products have the right characteristics. Take chlorofluorocarbons (CFCs), for example, which threaten the earth's ozone layer. Many aerosols and other products now on the market no longer use these chemicals, but in Canada manufacturers are not required to label their products one way or the other. Nor will the federal government release a complete list of products that contain or are made with CFCs, because some companies consider this information "proprietary"– a trade secret. Most of our non-food products, in fact, have no ingredient labelling.

And finally, the Green Consumer often faces those frustrating choices where all options are imperfect. Is cotton clothing better than polyester, because artificial fibres use up non-renewable resources and go through a lot of processing, which creates pollution? Or is polyester better after all, because cotton growers use massive amounts of chemical fertilizers and pesticides, which run off into local water supplies? There is no definitive answer here. The best available environmentalist rule of thumb is: When in doubt, prefer the natural to the synthetic.

Another guideline for choices is known as the "three Rs" rule, which you will see many times in this book: *Reduce, Reuse, Recycle.* Reduce consumption and waste; reuse, by getting more out of the items you already own; and recycle, to conserve resources. These are not new ideas; in many ways they represent simple old-fashioned thrift. But in our throwaway society they add up to a revolution.

Green Consumers need to make their voices heard directly, too. Joining environmental groups and writing letters can be effective ways of spreading the word. Write to politicians to demand better labelling, stricter regulation and enforcement, and stronger commitment to cutting pollution. Write to manufacturers and retailers to ask for more green products. When you decide to stop buying one brand and switch to another, tell both makers why. If businesses weren't interested in your behaviour, after all, they wouldn't spend thousands trying to decipher it through surveys and studies.

Does buying green mean paying more? Not necessarily. Some environment-friendly products cost more than their conventional counterparts; that's partly because retailers charge what the market will bear, and consumers have generally been willing to pay more for green items.

Another factor is that manufacturers often need to make large capital investments to get a new product line going. But one of the key goals of being a Green Consumer is to reduce overall consumption, so Green Consumers could end up paying less simply because they buy less.

Readers may wonder whether they can really make a difference, given the overwhelming scope and complexity of the dangers our planet faces. The answer is yes, because the interconnectedness of our ecosystem means that every action you take starts a chain reaction – for good or for ill.

For instance, when you make a point of turning off the lights in your home more often, you're reducing the amount of electricity you use, so your local power plant needs to generate less. If the plant burns coal or oil, reduced demand means it will emit less of the pollutants that cause acid rain and global warming. If it's a nuclear plant, switching your light off has a more long-term effect. The plant continues to generate hazardous radioactive waste whether you use the power or not, but reducing demand will discourage the utility company from building more nuclear plants.

If your electricity comes from hydroelectric sources, your energy conservation efforts could benefit wildlife. Development of more massive hydro dams in northern Quebec, under consideration by the Quebec government, could lead to more floods like the one caused by water released from a James Bay dam a few years ago, which killed thousands of caribou. New dams would probably cause more disruption to native communities and contaminate fish with mercury; it is even possible that they would bring about a change in the climate of northern Quebec and Labrador. Lowering our energy demands makes these developments less likely.

Another example of the wide impact we can make is our use of paper. When Green Consumers reduce their consumption of disposable papers, they put fewer polluting chemicals into the water near pulp mills, and fewer emissions into the air above paper factories. With a reduction in garbage at the curb, garbage trucks need to make fewer trips to the landfill sites, so they use less fuel and reduce their exhaust emissions. And farmland is preserved that might have been used for more landfill sites.

So don't underestimate your power and influence. With this first edition of *The Canadian Green Consumer Guide* in your hands, you can make a difference at the supermarket, at the hardware store, at your workplace, when you pay your bills and your taxes – in fact, whenever and wherever you spend your money.

Responsible shopping need not cost the earth.

About Pollution Probe

The Pollution Probe Foundation, established in 1969, is an independent, non-profit, research-based charitable organization. Through memberships or donations, more than 45,000 Canadians are Pollution Probe Partners. The foundation's mission for the year 2000 is to have all Canadians – as individuals, and as participants in governments, businesses, organizations, unions, schools, communities, and families – thinking about the environmental impact of everything they do and taking action to support a clean environment. The foundation also publishes a quarterly magazine, *Probe Post*, which deals with topical environmental issues.

We welcome your suggestions for products or services that could be included in future editions of *The Canadian Green Consumer Guide*. Write to:

The Pollution Probe Foundation
12 Madison Avenue,
Toronto, ON M5R 2S1

KEY ISSUES for the Green Consumer

In general, the Green Consumer avoids products that are likely to:

- endanger the health of the consumer or of others
- cause significant damage to the environment during manufacture, use, or disposal
- cause unnecessary waste, either because of overpackaging or because of an unduly short useful life
- use materials derived from threatened species or from threatened environments
- involve the unnecessary use of – or cruelty to – animals, whether for toxicity testing or for other purposes
- adversely affect other countries, particularly in the Third World

To the best of our knowledge, the information in this book was correct at press time. But with the rapid pace of developments in the Green Consumer's world, events may have overtaken us in some areas by the time you read this. The omission of any particular brand, company, or organization implies neither censure nor recommendation.

1. COSTING THE EARTH

"We now know that spring is not automatic. We now know that the responsibility is ours to restore and maintain the health of the biosphere."

Pierre Elliott Trudeau (1970)

PUTTING TOGETHER A SIMPLE PICTURE *of the many different types of damage we are inflicting on the world is not easy. But we must attempt it before looking at what the individual consumer can do to help prevent such damage. Let's approach the task from the outside in.*

▲▲▲▲▲▲▲▲▲▲▲▲▲▲▲

The sun burns 5 million tonnes of hydrogen a second and its core reaches temperatures of some 15 million °C. It radiates a phenomenal amount of energy into space: more than would be produced by 200,000 trillion of our largest existing commercial nuclear reactors.

Earth intercepts only a billionth of the sun's total output, but this is enough to do everything from driving the climate, including the winds and water cycle, and fuelling the growth of the world's crops, right through to burning

▲▲▲▲▲▲▲▲▲▲▲▲▲▲▲

incautious sunbathers. Indeed, the solar energy entering our atmosphere every year is roughly equivalent to 500,000 billion barrels of oil or 800,000 billion tonnes of coal. This is about a million times more oil than we think there may be left in the planet's proven oil reserves.

Only a small proportion of this energy ever reaches the ground where we jog, walk, and sunbathe, which is just as well. If the sun's raw energy were ever to break through to ground level, life as we know it would be sizzled off the face of the earth. Luckily, much of it is reflected back into space by cloud cover. And the sunshine that does reach the ground is made much less hazardous by something that happens in the upper reaches of the atmosphere.

OZONE

THE DEPLETION OF THE OZONE LAYER

Located between 20 and 50 km above the earth's surface, the ozone layer screens out around 99% of the potentially deadly ultraviolet radiation in the incoming sunshine. Yet the ozone layer is so rarefied that if you could compress it to the density of air at sea level, it would be little thicker than the sole of your shoe. Any thinning of this fragile shield inevitably increases the amount of UV radiation reaching the ground.

UV radiation increases the number of skin cancers – it has been estimated that even a 1% reduction in atmospheric ozone could cause 15,000 new cases of skin cancer each year in the United States alone. It increases the number of people suffering from cataracts and other eye diseases and causes extensive damage to crops and other vegetation. It also threatens ocean food chains, because many plankton are highly sensitive to UV radiation. Plankton are the essential food source for many fish and are also important in oxygen production.

The first real evidence that the ozone layer might be threatened was produced by two American scientists in 1974. They warned that synthetic chemicals known as chlorofluorocarbons (CFCs) could thin the ozone layer. CFCs have been used as propellants in aerosols, in fridges and air-conditioning plants (where they serve as coolants), in dry-cleaning solvents, in the plastic foam used to make hamburger and other fast-food cartons, in materials used for furniture stuffing, and in insulation products.

When they were discovered in 1928, CFCs seemed to be perfect chemicals. They were odourless, non-toxic, non-flammable, and chemically inert. Unfortunately, however, they are so stable that they can hang around in the atmosphere for more than 100 years,

slowly drifting up into the stratosphere. Ironically, too, the most useful types of CFC (particularly CFCs 11 and 12) turn out to be the most damaging. Once in the stratosphere, their chemical structure means that they begin to destroy the ozone molecules that protect the earth from UV radiation.

The scientific debate about the extent to which such chemicals destroy ozone raged for years, but eventually a new scientific consensus began to emerge. CFCs, it was concluded by the late 1970s, certainly could damage the ozone layer, but the effects were likely to be less serious than had originally been thought and would be a long time coming. But the chemical industry, which produced nearly 800,000 tonnes of CFCs in 1985 alone, was sitting on a time bomb. That year, British scientists discovered an "ozone hole" opening up over Antarctica.

The evidence had been in American hands for ten years, in the form of data collected by orbiting space satellites, but the computers that process the data ignored the ozone hole because they had been programmed to treat such things as impossible. Once these data were processed into images, it became clear that the computers had been turning a blind eye to an extraordinary phenomenon. The size of the hole varies through the year but can cover an area as large as the United States. Soon Canadian scientists were finding evidence of at least one more ozone hole, this time over the Arctic.

Scientists agreed that the peculiar conditions found at the Poles, particularly the extreme cold and low sunlight for months on end, may have been aggravating the situation. However, the implication was that CFCs could well lead to a global thinning of the ozone layer.

A mass of new research results and growing public concern led to the signing of the Montreal Protocol by

ONE YEAR'S ATMOSPHERIC SOLAR ENERGY

THE SAME AS

500,000 BILLION BARRELS OF OIL

THE SAME AS

800,000 BILLION TONNES OF COAL

Canada, the United States, the European Community, and 23 other countries late in 1987. The aim was to cut world CFC consumption 20% by 1993 and another 30% by 1998. (The Canadian government is considering increasing its commitment from the 50% level to a full 100% reduction in 1998; Green Consumers may wish to let their MPs know there is public support for this commendable proposal.) But, for the foreseeable future, this agreement will simply slow down the rate of ozone depletion because of the longevity of CFCs. Consequently, the destruction of the ozone layer is likely to be in the headlines for many years to come.

✳ ✳

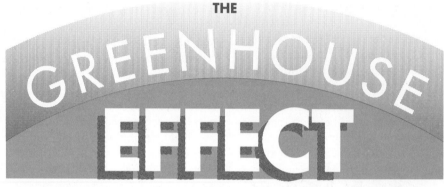

THE GREENHOUSE EFFECT

CFCs are also a minor contributor to another environmental problem whose longer-term impact could be even greater: the greenhouse effect, also known as global warming.

Although between a third and a half of the earth's incoming solar energy is immediately reflected back into space by clouds, the atmosphere as a whole works very much like a greenhouse, trapping heat. When too much heat is retained, we have not just a greenhouse but a hothouse, and the entire global climate system is affected.

The average global surface air temperature has increased by around 1°C over the last 150 years. Within the next few decades, the greenhouse effect could raise the average temperature by another degree, with a rise of several more degrees possible by the second half of the 21st century. Such temperature rises would cause dramatic changes in the earth's climate and weather patterns. The increasingly severe droughts in the River Nile's water catchment area may be just an early symptom.

A warmer atmosphere would also cause melting of glaciers and ice-caps, with the result that sea levels could rise by a metre or more. In the longer term, low-lying cities like Charlottetown, London, Bangkok, New York, and Tokyo could be swamped by the ever-rising tides. Rainfall and monsoon patterns would shift, possibly turning areas like the rice-growing regions of Asia and the North American prairies into dust bowls. Kansas could become the Ethiopia of the 21st century.

These changes in global temperature may not sound enormous, but the earth has not been 1°C warmer than it is today since before the dawn of civilization. In short, we are conducting an unprecedented experiment with our planet.

A warmer atmosphere would also cause melting of glaciers and ice-caps, with the result that sea levels could rise by a metre or more.

What causes the greenhouse effect?

Carbon dioxide is the most important "greenhouse gas." It acts rather like a blanket around the planet, holding in much of the solar radiation that would otherwise escape into space.

The level of carbon dioxide in the atmosphere has been growing inexorably since the Industrial Revolution. Between the 1850s and the 1970s, carbon dioxide levels grew by as much as 25%. The main reason for this worrying trend is the ever-growing quantity of fossil fuels (coal, oil, and gas) burned for heat or power.

According to the Worldwatch Institute, humanity added 5.5 billion tonnes of carbon to the atmosphere in 1988 through burning of coal, oil, and gas. If growth in worldwide consumption continues at its recent rate of about 3% per year, fossil fuels could contribute 10 billion tonnes of new carbon annually by the year 2010.

Consumption of fossil fuel is not a transgression committed by industry alone; every consumer must share the blame. Even a relatively conservation-minded household in Canada, without electric heat, uses about 30 kilowatt-hours of electricity per day, about 1.25kWyear/year. If that electricity is all produced by power plants burning fossil fuels, that household would be contributing almost 5 tonnes of carbon dioxide to the atmosphere each year, just through its electricity use.

Of that household also uses fossil fuel for heating, it's adding more carbon. A household in southern Ontario can use 1,000 L of heating fuel each season, which would produce 11 or 12 tonnes of carbon dioxide each year. Added to the 5 tonnes produced by electricity generation, that's a total of at least 16 tonnes per household per year: there's no question our domestic energy use accounts for a substantial share of the 50 million tonnes of carbon that Canada adds to the atmosphere each year.

Some politicians and industrialists have suggested that depletion of tropical rainforests is the biggest contributor to global climate change. Perhaps governments find it easier to shift the blame half a continent away. The burning of firewood – and of forests – does aggravate the problem, but the scientific data show that it is our energy use that is the biggest factor. Deforestation contributes much less carbon to the atmosphere than burning of fossil fuel: estimates vary from 0.4 billion tonnes to 2.5 billion tonnes.

So the notion that we can just plant trees to absorb the excess carbon dioxide is misguided, if well-meaning. Proposals to exchange massive tree-planting for the right to burn more coal and oil are based on a scientific misunderstanding. Trees do have the capacity to absorb carbon dioxide and turn it into healthy oxygen, but that capacity is limited. To grow enough trees to absorb all the carbon from fossil fuels, we would have to grow forests at triple or quadruple their natural density or even more, a feat we have not come close to achieving.

ACID
R · A · I · N

Acid rain is distinctly a phenomenon of the industrial age. Throughout North America literally thousands of tonnes of sulphur and nitrogen oxides, the raw ingredients of acid rain, spew forth daily from a variety of sources – the furnaces of coal-fired generating stations, the smokestacks of ore smelters, steel mills, and chemical factories, and the exhaust pipes of buses, cars, and trucks. These industrial activities are all taking place to produce things that will ultimately become consumer items: generating stations produce electricity that we use in our homes and that is used to make other consumer goods; steel mills produce steel for cans, cars, buildings, and bridges; chemical factories produce plastics, pesticides, and more; and the buses, cars, and trucks are used to move goods and people around the continent.

The acids that come from industry and fossil-fuel-powered transportation often rise high into the atmosphere where they can travel with the winds and clouds for thousands of kilometres. Eventually, however, they will come back to earth, either after being washed out of the sky by rain or simply falling out of the sky as dry particles. Even as air pollution, sulphur and nitrogen oxides can have a serious effect on our health. As acids on the ground they have a devastating effect on our environment.

Acid rain was first brought to the attention of most Canadians when Pollution Probe wrote about the damage to our lakes in 1970. Today we know that acid rain kills lakes but also does far more damage.

■■■■ The Ontario Ministry of the Environment estimates that as many as 4,000 lakes in that province alone are already unable to support life because of acid rain. Thousands more in other parts of eastern Canada are dead or dying, and European lakes are also suffering the same fate. Within the next 20 years, the $620-million sport and commercial fishery of the pre-Cambrian Shield will suffer a loss of 20% to 50%.

■■■■ Trees covering about 4 million hectares of Europe are now showing injury and dying from acid rain. Signs of injury are already appearing in Canada; the maple syrup industry of central Canada, for instance, is seriously threatened. The value of Canada's forests is estimated at $4 billion a year; even a 10% reduction in forest productivity over the next 25 years would be expensive, in resources and in jobs.

■■■■ Acid rain literally dissolves the surface of stone buildings and monuments and corrodes metal, including cars. In Greece, six marble maidens that have been holding up a temple on the Acropolis for 25 centuries have had to be removed, their faces almost completely washed away. In Canada, historic marble and limestone tombstones are being erased. The Parliament Buildings in Ottawa are crumbling under the assault of acid rain.

■■■■ Respiratory ailments related to sulphur and nitrogen oxides in the air are estimated to be costing Canada $160 million a year.

Acid rain literally dissolves the surface of stone buildings and monuments and corrodes metal, including cars.

STOP ACID RAIN

More than 50 million tonnes of sulphur and nitrogen oxides drift up from sources in Canada and the United States each year. Since 1980 the Canadian government has made reducing acid rain its most high-profile environmental cause, but it was not until 1985 that the government actually started to impose restrictions on Canadian sources of sulphur dioxide. Canada's program calls for a 50% reduction in sulphur dioxide emissions by 1994, and nitrogen oxide levels are being tackled through tougher automobile emission standards. The U.S. government did not even acknowledge the acid rain problem until 1989, and legislation is still making its way through Congress at the time of writing.

About half of Canada's acid rain comes from the U.S., and many environmentalists are concerned that the American program may turn out to be too little, too late. Even if the American program matches the Canadian acid rain reduction program, no one knows whether a 50% reduction is enough to save our lakes, forests, buildings, and health. Some experts have suggested that we may need to reduce sulphur and nitrogen oxide emissions by at least 80% if we want to reverse the terrible damage that has already been done by acid rain.

Recycling, saving electricity, and reducing automobile use are good ways to help reduce acid rain. It has been estimated that the average household can reduce its contribution to acid rain by 5 tonnes each year simply by recycling its cans, bottles, and papers. Making new products out of old produces less than one-tenth the acid rain created by making the same products from raw materials.

> **Recycling, saving electricity, and reducing automobile use are good ways to help reduce acid rain.**

* *

Deforestation
and Land Loss

The rapid destruction of forests in many parts of the world is one of the contributors to the greenhouse effect and to loss of animal and plant species. Together with bad land use planning and poor agricultural practices, deforestation also contributes to soil erosion. From the tropics to the prairies, we are literally losing ground.

Of an estimated total area of 2 billion hectares of tropical forests worldwide, some 11 to 15 million hectares are lost each year – an area the size of India in 30 years. An area equal to 20 soccer fields is lost every minute.

In 1982, in what was described as the worst ecological disaster of the century, some 3.24 million hectares of forest were destroyed in a fire which swept across Kalimantan, Indonesia. The risk of such catastrophic fires increases as deforestation reduces rainfall in nearby areas.

We tend to think of tropical forests when we think of disappearing forests, forgetting that Canada is also losing forests at an alarming rate. In Canada, we cut an area of forest equal in size to Vancouver Island every four years, just to meet North America's insatiable and environmentally destructive demand for pulp and paper products. Much of the forest cut by the pulp and forest products industries is not properly replanted, some of it is not replanted at all, and some of the areas most recently cut, especially on steep mountain slopes in western Canada, cannot be replanted and will not regrow before the rain washes away most of the topsoil.

In Canada, we cut an area of forest equal in size to Vancouver Island every four years.

As the forests disappear, the pace of soil erosion accelerates. In Guatemala, an average of around 1,200 tonnes of soil are lost every year from each square kilometre of land. As a result, it becomes harder to feed the population, and in countries like India and Bangladesh, the silt shortens the life of dams and can cause widespread flooding in lowland areas.

In 1988 at least 300 people died and over 60,000 were left homeless during "freak" floods in Rio de Janeiro. Brazilian geologists say the floods were no freak. They were caused by the relentless felling of the country's forests - and there is worse to come.

While the global population increases by 84 million people a year, we endanger our ability to feed those people. Each year, for various reasons, we lose 25 billion tonnes of topsoil, enough to cover the wheatlands of Australia. In mid-1989, world grain reserves were at their lowest level since World War II, largely because of the loss of agricultural land.

Although Canada's land mass is huge, only 9% of it is arable, and only half of that amount has climate suitable for agricultural production. Yet we continue to take our farmland out of production: nearly 19% of it was converted to other uses or abandoned between 1961 and 1981.

More than half of Canada's best farmland is within 200 km of Toronto, but we've already built on or paved over 10% of it, and non-agricultural development shows no signs of slowing down. Nor are we taking proper care of the farmland that remains: as much as half of the organic matter in the soil of Ontario, Quebec, and the prairies has been stripped because of monocropping, and we are not putting it back through mulch and manure.

Of concern too is the loss of our wetlands. These marshes, bogs, swamps, and low-lying coastal regions have a crucial environmental role. They protect shorelines, hold back floodwaters, control sedimentation, prevent eutrophication, filter water, and serve as breeding grounds and habitat for fish and waterfowl.

In addition to these natural functions, wetlands are an important economic asset, providing $9.32 billion in uses such as recreation, fishing, peat and wild rice harvesting, and peatland forestry. Yet many are succumbing to urban and agricultural pressures.

In mid-1989, world grain reserves were at their lowest level since World War II, largely because of the loss of agricultural land.

POWER
POLLUTION

Our future contribution to such pollution problems as smog, the greenhouse effect, and acid rain will very much depend on what mix of energy supply technologies we end up using. The options include:

■ **fossil fuels**, such as oil, gas, and coal;

■ **nuclear power**, using today's fission reactors or (possibly) tomorrow's fast breeder or fusion reactors;

■ **renewable energy,** harnessing the sun, winds, waves, tides, geothermal heat, or plants and animals; and

■ **energy efficiency**, which cuts across all of these – and is the key to *The Canadian Green Consumer Guide*'s recommendations on energy.

In addition to our own energy needs here in Canada, we must consider the increasing demands for energy of the developing world. Even if per-capita energy consumption were to remain at its current level worldwide, total consumption would still increase by 40% by 2025; but if people in the developing nations increase their consumption to match Western rates, the increase in total consumption by 2025 would reach 550%, according to the World Commission on Environment and Development.

Even a 40% increase – a scenario that ignores the very real needs and aspirations of the Third World – will strain our collective environment. Clearly we must find effective and equitable means of reining in the ill effects of galloping energy consumption and, ultimately, of reducing its growth.

S upertanker disasters like the spill from the Exxon Valdez may ensure that tanker operations are better managed and policed in the future, but the industry's history of repeated spills around the world does not give us great confidence.

* *

Fossil Fuels

O il is the most popular fuel at present, but it is a finite resource. World supplies are likely to be severely depleted within 35 years. Pollution from oil – during manufacture and transport, and in the form of emissions when it is burned – also remains a considerable problem. Supertanker disasters like the spill from the Exxon Valdez may ensure that tanker operations are better managed and policed in the future, but the industry's history of repeated spills around the world does not give us great confidence. Pipelines may appear to be a safer means of transporting crude oil and petroleum products, but pipelines, especially in Canada's north, disrupt wildlife, disturb the fragile vegetation, and are not immune from accident.

Natural gas is often touted as Canada's "clean and plentiful" alternative to oil. But it too is non-renewable and a source of greenhouse gases. Sour gas, natural gas with a high sulphur content, can also worsen local air quality and contribute to acid rain.

A hundred years from now, we will still be using liquid fuels, although they will be very much more expensive. Some of them may well be made from coal, the old fossil fuel standby. There may be enough coal in the world for 200 or 300 years, but its extraction causes considerable environmental damage, and when

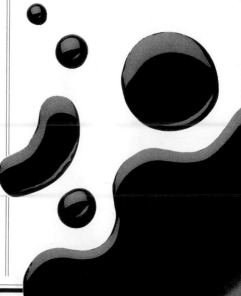

burned, it is often a serious contributor to acid rain (via the production of sulphur dioxide and nitrogen oxides) and to the greenhouse effect (via carbon dioxide).

✳ ✳

Nuclear Power

However much damage the burning of fossil fuels may cause, nuclear power remains the least popular energy technology with environmentalists – and with the public. The major problems with nuclear power are reactor safety and waste disposal.

The shadows of the Chernobyl nuclear disaster in the Soviet Union and of the Three Mile Island accident in the United States remind us that even complex machinery with all kinds of failsafe systems can still go wrong through system failure or operator error.

A study by the European Consumer Bureau concluded that the radioactive cloud that spread out from the damaged reactor at Chernobyl carried radiation equivalent to that which would be produced by 2,000 atomic bombs of the size that obliterated Hiroshima in 1945. Some 135,000 people had to be evacuated, and the immediate death toll of over 30 lives is likely to grow considerably as radiation-related diseases surface. The relevant Soviet ministries have been instructed to ensure "the 100% safety of nuclear power plants." Given the experiences of Chernobyl, of Three Mile Island, and of Sellafield in Britain, it would take an ultra-optimist to believe that this is a reasonable target for any country possessing nuclear power.

Nuclear power is often described as the "clean" alternative to fossil fuel. But it too yields undesired by-products – and even ardent supporters of nuclear power tend to draw the line at having those wastes dumped in their own back yards. We have not found a "safe" place for the disposal of nuclear waste.

Large water-filled holding tanks provide temporary storage locations for spent fuel at the power station, but we are a long way from knowing whether permanent safe storage exists for larger quantities of spent fuel and for the decommissioned power plants at the end of their useful lives. Toxic chemicals like PCBs are now a political and environmental nightmare because we allowed them onto the market *before* we knew what damage they could cause and before we knew how to destroy the waste material safely. Nuclear power shows that we still have not learned the lesson.

✳ ✳

Renewable Energy

Renewable energy sources are less polluting and won't blow up or melt down, but because they produce energy less intensively than fossil fuel or nuclear power, the facilities needed to capture that energy may be more extensive. A solar energy installation able to produce as much energy as a nuclear reactor might take up to 2,000 hectares, compared with about 60 hectares needed for the reactor plant. It would take perhaps 200 or 300 large windmills to produce the same amount of power as a nuclear reactor, with each group of 25 machines needing an area of around 1,600 hectares. (Also, large windmills, as their neighbours know, can be noisy and may interfere with TV reception.) And if you decide to grow crops to convert into oil, fuel alcohol, or gas, you would need to plant up to 50,000 hectares to achieve the same energy output as a nuclear reactor.

In itself this is no argument against renewable energy, whose role is bound to grow in the future. But it helps to demonstrate that, as you will find throughout

Nuclear power is often described as the "clean" alternative to fossil fuel. But it too yields undesired by-products

this book, many choices that face the Green Consumer involve trade-offs. There is no such thing as a totally "green" means of energy production. But *reducing* consumption – energy efficiency – provides a promising option.

* *

Energy Efficiency

Many Canadian energy experts now regard energy efficiency, or energy conservation, as a "source" of energy. Some estimates suggest that we could easily trim our energy use by as much as 25%, by eliminating energy waste and buying more efficient energy-consuming devices. A 25% reduction in Ontario demand would eliminate the need to complete Darlington, the world's largest nuclear power plant; moreover, we could shut down another two Darlingtons' worth of smaller nuclear plants, coal-fired or oil-fired power stations, or hydro dams. A study by the World Resources Institute suggests that conservation and efficiency measures could cut the industrialized world's carbon emissions in half; presumably, similarly happy reductions in other pollutants would follow, too.

* *

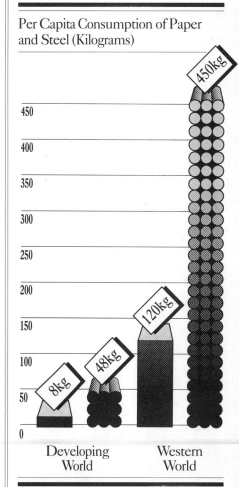

Per Capita Consumption of Paper and Steel (Kilograms)

Garbage is a by-product of a consumer society, and one that we used to regard as unavoidable – until its mountainous quantities began to overwhelm us. Now the problems of what to do with garbage are becoming ever more pressing, and ways to reduce it simply *must* be found. Wastes in the wrong place cause pollution. Finding enough holes in which to dump our garbage is becoming increasingly difficult and less satisfactory as a solution.

Whether we are punching round washers from rectangular sheets of metal, unwrapping a chocolate bar, or removing the packaging from a new washing machine, each of us produces an ever-increasing volume of waste every year. If there were only a few million of us that might be acceptable, but with over 26 million Canadians and around 200 times as many people now living on the planet as a whole, it simply cannot go on.

The galloping increase in consumption has been a largely Western phenomenon until recent years. An average person in the developed world consumes, directly and indirectly, more than 120 kg of paper and more than 450 kg of steel each year; in the developing nations, the figures are 8 kg of paper, 43 kg of steel. Promotion of Western patterns of consumption and waste to the developing world could multiply the environmental damage of the garbage crisis.

The galloping increase in consumption has been a largely Western phenomenon until recent years.

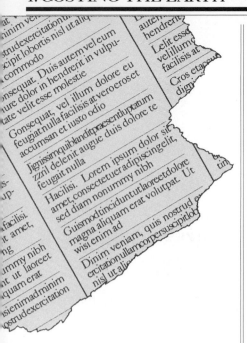

Lorem ipsum placeholder text

We've spent an estimated $10 billion trying to clean up the Great Lakes but the menace of toxic chemicals remains.

Throwaway Lines

■ The average Canadian household throws away one tonne of garbage each year. Canada produces a total of 27 million tonnes of garbage each year, from household, industrial, and other sources.

■ More than 40,000 trees each day are cut down to make the paper for Canada's daily newspapers alone.

■ We discard 1,500 tonnes of steel every day just in food and drink cans. Over a year, that's enough steel to make 350,000 cars − a lineup stretching from Toronto to Winnipeg.

■ Every week Canadians take home 55 million plastic bags from grocery stores. Many of those bags are reused, but eventually they will all be piled into landfill sites.

Garbage is a waste of our natural resources: land, trees, iron ore, and much more. And the manufacture of all the materials we put into the dump has consumed energy and produced pollution. Every tree that is pulped in Canada's mills adds to the dioxin that is polluting the global environment; manufacture of cans and bottles contributes to acid rain and adds greenhouse gases to the atmosphere. The waste that goes into landfill is simply the last remnant of a planet-destroying system that consumes our resources, discharges pollutants, and ultimately threatens human survival.

Chapter 7 of this book focusses on the three Rs of waste management: Reduce, Reuse, and Recycle. Other chapters will show you how to avoid overpackaging and how to dispose of the waste you can't avoid in the most environment-friendly ways possible.

WATER POLLUTION

We need no better barometer for the state of our rivers, lakes, and oceans than the health of the creatures that live in them.

In the high Arctic, polychlorinated biphenyls (PCBs) and other persistent toxins are detectable in the fat tissue of sea mammals. In the St. Lawrence River, the outlet to the ocean for the Great Lakes, the survival of the beluga whale population is at stake because of massive pollution. Nine of the deadliest chemicals found in the Great Lakes have been identified in tissue samples of dead beluga from the St. Lawrence.

The Great Lakes, our sweetwater inland seas containing 20% of the world's fresh water, are the most compelling example of how we have polluted our waters. Cancerous tumours are found on fish in Lake Ontario. Women of child-bearing age and children under the age of 15 are routinely warned against eating salmon from the lake.

Over 1,000 chemicals used by industry on both sides of the border have been detected in the lakes. Some are highly toxic; others have not been adequately tested to determine their toxicity. Most of the clearly identified hazardous chemicals are not removed by existing water treatment plants, which use 19th-century technology.

Remarkably, there has been little public protest from the 37 million Canadian and American users of Great Lakes water about its quality. We've spent an estimated $10 billion trying to clean up the lakes, and although we've made some headway – saving Lake Erie from "dying" – the menace of toxic chemicals remains.

So, too, on the eve of the 21st century, do problems caused by inadequate treatment of our sewage. For years, residents of Toronto have been unable to swim at its beaches in the summertime because the level of fecal bacteria is so high.

This disgrace is not limited to the Great Lakes, however. On the east coast, Halifax harbour has been a convenient receptacle for the metropolitan area's raw sewage and now enjoys the notoriety of being one of the most polluted bodies of water in Canada. On the west coast, the Fraser River has been no less abused.

Even Canada's northern waters, so vast that one would think pollution would simply dissolve away in them, are vulnerable to environmental attack. The fragility of our northern coasts was clearly demonstrated by the massive oil spill from the Exxon Valdez in Alaska. In northern Quebec, where the James Bay project has wrought massive environmental change, mercury, a sadly familiar pollutant in Canada, is poisoning native fishing grounds.

Not all water pollution is caused by the discharge of substances directly into water bodies. The most salient example of water damage from airborne sources is, of course, acid rain; across the Canadian Shield, lakes are succumbing to it and no longer bear life. It is now recognized that industrial and urban air pollution swept out to sea is also a major contributor to some forms of ocean pollution.

For too long, our approach has been one of "out of sight, out of mind." But change is now very much in the wind.

ENDANGERED SPECIES

Extinction is a natural process. Well over 90% of species that have ever lived on Earth have disappeared. Many were replaced by others that were better adapted to changing environments, although some disappeared as the result of massive natural disasters.

The appearance of the human species began a significant acceleration in the average extinction rate, however, as we hunted for food, commerce, and sport and converted entire landscapes into increasingly controlled farm and city scapes.

By the early years of the 20th century, roughly one species a year was being lost to extinction, but the pace of environmental degradation and species destruction has since taken off at an alarming rate. In the 1980s, we are losing perhaps one species a day from the 5 to 10 million species thought to exist. We may lose another million species by the end of the century. In 50 years more than half of all species will be gone if present rates of extinction continue.

Without our realizing it, our consumer choices can sometimes tighten the screw on endangered animals and plants.

Each species we push into extinction is like a thread pulled from the tapestry of life. You can pull a fair number of threads out of a tapestry without appearing to affect it, but then whole sections fall to pieces.

As consumers, we may be encouraged to buy a range of products made from animal or plant products derived from endangered species. Without our realizing it, our consumer choices can sometimes tighten the screw on endangered animals and plants.

While most of us may now be aware of the threat to species like the tiger, gorilla, elephant, or rhinoceros, the threat to many other species is not yet widely recognized. Following consumer boycotts during the 1970s, whale products are no longer used in cosmetics, although oil from the endangered basking shark is. Endangered reptiles may turn up in the form of handbags, wallets, purses, belts, or suitcases. Sea turtles are turned into stuffed specimens, shells, soup, oil, combs, or jewellery.

Many of us know of the threat to cacti and orchids, but few of us realize that even plants like the cyclamen, widely sold in garden centres, are now endangered in the wild. As long as it is cheaper to uproot wild plants than to artificially propagate the species, some people will continue to raid the threatened wild resources of countries like Portugal, Spain, or Turkey. Guidance on some products to avoid is given in later chapters.

* *

Animal Welfare

Animal welfare is an issue that the Green Consumer can hardly overlook, emotionally charged though it may be. The debate about the acceptable limits to the use or abuse of animals encompasses moral, legal, and economic issues too complex for this book to set out in detail. But we can point out instances where the consumer can make choices that have implications for animal welfare.

According to government figures, 440 million animals are raised in Canada each year for consumption. Each year, too, over 2 million animals die in Canadian laboratories, says the Canadian Federation of Humane Societies (CFHS). Founded in 1957, the CFHS acknowledges that the Canadian Council on Animal Care has brought about "major improvements for lab animals" but "we need to go much further." In 1989 the federation formed a legislative working group to develop and press for national legislation for the protection of lab animals. Animal welfare advocates argue alternatives to the use of animals in experiments exist; these include mathematical and computer models, and the use of eggs and discarded human placenta.

There are signs of changing public attitudes towards animals. In late 1988, three young grey whales trapped in the

Arctic ice were rescued by international effort, to the approbation of a world watching it on television. Only a few decades ago, the grey whales were being slaughtered by North Americans and Europeans; public pressure brought that hunt to a close.

Leisure activities whose aim is to observe animals rather than capturing or killing them are growing in popularity. Birdwatching is one of the fastest-growing pastimes of North Americans. Increasing numbers of travellers are going on safari to the Amazon and Africa's Rift Valley. They carry cameras and identification books rather than guns.

The methods of the more radical animal rights groups are disturbing to many Canadians. Slogans such as "Meat is murder" have been painted on the walls of fast-food outlets; activists have raided laboratories and released animals intended for research. These are the tactics of groups that see no distinction between violence against animals and violence against humans, and their methods are keyed to the strength of their convictions. It is not necessary for Green Consumers to join the paint brigades in order to make a contribution to the welfare of the other species of our planet.

✻✻

WITH SUCH A MASS *of serious environmental dangers surrounding us, it is tempting to throw up our hands in despair. But despair can only make things worse. We can save the planet if we all take responsibility for it in every aspect of our daily lives, starting now.*

GREEN CONSUMER POWER CAN MAKE A DIFFERENCE.

2. FOOD and DRINK

FAR MORE THAN BREAD IS THE STAFF OF LIFE.

Food and drink in general are as close to home as we can get. Yet as with much else in our world, things have gone very wrong in the supply of these vital ingredients that we and our children consume every day of our lives. Indeed, Canadian studies have shown that between 85% and 95% of all our exposure to poisonous chemicals in the environment comes through our food.

▲▲▲▲▲▲▲▲▲▲▲▲▲▲▲

Governments haven't been much help here. Less than 1% of all imported food is tested by Canada's Health and Welfare department, and that for only a percentage of the possible pesticides it might contain. Even Auditor General Kenneth Dye has criticized what he has called "our very limited testing" for pesticide residues in domestic and imported produce.

These facts are far from comforting, but you know that already. Many Green Consumers already seek out foods considered wholesome – fresh fruits and vegetables, and the pack-

▲▲▲▲▲▲▲▲▲▲▲▲▲▲▲

aged foods with labels that say "additive-free" or "natural" or "pure." Too often, however, those labels and that fresh produce are not enough to protect you and your family from the consequences of harmful foods. And although life expectancy is increasing, cancer and other ailments may take decades to show up.

But this is not a book about personal health; it's a book about the health of our planet. Even so, the two are inextricably entwined. As we work to improve our world's flagging health, so too is our own health likely to be less endangered.

You don't have to feel helpless about contributing to the solutions. Anyone who buys food is a consumer, and consumers have a great deal of clout. Take, for one example, the growth agent Alar, a synthetic chemical sprayed primarily on apples. It cannot be removed by either washing or peeling the fruit. After a U.S. report in early 1989 showed that preschoolers were consuming dangerously high amounts of Alar, particularly if they drank a great deal of apple juice, con-

"Our fathers and ourselves sowed dragon's teeth Our children know and suffer."
Stephen Vincent Benet

ALAR
IT CANNOT BE REMOVED BY EITHER WASHING OR PEELING THE FRUIT

sumers began pressing retailers for Alar-free apples and juice, refusing to buy if they couldn't be found. Eventually the manufacturer voluntarily withdrew Alar from the U.S. market, although it would still be sold overseas. A week later, it was withdrawn in Canada as well – at the request not of government but of the organization that represents apple growers, who were concerned about falling sales.

Similarly, H.J. Heinz in the U.S. ordered farmers supplying the products for its baby foods to stop using 12 still-legal chemicals on their crops. The company's concern was that babies are at especially high risk when exposed to pesticide residues because of their low body weight and high consumption of fruits and vegetables.

Personal health considerations aside, the synthetic chemicals used to produce our food have enormous potential to damage our entire environment, including the air we breathe and the water we drink. Much damage has already been done. And although ever more food companies are realizing just how valuable a good environmental image can be, simply removing all additives from a product, proclaiming by inference that it is now "good" for us, is not the answer. To be truly environment-friendly, the company must find a source of food that isn't contaminated by pesticides and similar chemical residues – which are *not* additives in the legal sense and do not have to be listed on labels.

THE WAY WE FARM

N·O·W

Most of the food we eat today is produced with the aid of vast amounts of synthetically produced chemicals. Where once farms were "mixed" and all-round farmers worked with nature to produce a variety of crops and animals, there is now "monoculture." Enormous agribusinesses produce only one or two types of crop, year after year, and most managers of this industrial farming are single-minded specialists to whom the use of chemicals to extract everything possible from the land is now the natural order of things. However, less than 0.1% of most of those chemicals actually reaches their intended targets. The remaining 99.9% contaminates our air, water, and soil and, of course, other food.

These "modern" methods have been very successful in increasing crop yields around the world, but that success is becoming tarnished. Insects, finding single crops a paradise of reliable food, increase, multiply, and eventually become resistant to the chemicals used to get rid of them. Yet another new chemical then has to be devised to combat the new problem.

Those who work to grow the food we eat are in most immediate danger. The world's use of pesticides has gone from almost nothing in the mid-1940s to about

Most of the food we eat today is produced with the aid of vast amounts of synthetically produced chemicals

2 million tonnes a year. It's estimated that three people are now poisoned by pesticides every minute. Improper handling and application of fertilizers result in an estimated 10,000 deaths per year in the Third World.

Here in Canada, a 1983 Alberta Department of Agriculture study reported that 10% of the province's grain farmers showed symptoms of pesticide poisoning – and that 90% were concerned about such poisonings in general. In June 1989, preliminary results of a federal study of 70,000 Saskatchewan farmers were announced: those who sprayed the most 2,4-D and other herbicides died of several cancers of the lymphatic system (non-Hodgkin's lymphoma) more often than those who used fewer such weedkillers.

There are problems far beyond pesticides, as well. Rather than being treated and recycled into the soil, farm manure is either discarded or improperly applied as fertilizer, seeping into waterways where its nitrogen content poisons fish and, possibly, people. The soil in the fields erodes and disappears with the wind and the rain because of its low humus content and today's planting practices. A centimetre of topsoil takes about 150 years to form naturally; we're losing it at the rate of about a centimetre every four to eight years.

We can no longer assume that the world's supply of food will continue to increase. Not even our grain crops and stockpiles, a prime indicator of global food security, are growing. Washington's Worldwatch Institute reports that the growth of global grain production was rapid from 1950 to 1984, a period that included a ninefold increase in fertilizer use and a threefold increase in irrigation area. But total grain production declined slightly in 1985 and 1986, then sharply in 1987 and 1988, putting us right back where we were in the mid-1970s. In the late 1960s, every additional tonne of fertilizer used in the U.S. corn belt could add 15 to 20 tonnes of grain to the world's harvest; now it may add only 5 to 10 tonnes.

Despite this, about 450 million tonnes of a world harvest of 1.5 billion tonnes of grain are fed only to livestock, primarily beef cattle. There are few more inefficient ways of producing food: the grain needed to provide a family of four with just one serving of hamburgers wolfed down in minutes could feed someone in a developing country for more than a week.

Today's type of farming gobbles up huge amounts of energy, too. For each square kilometre of land, U.S. farmers use about 5 tonnes of fuel a year; European farmers about 12 tonnes. In food production, Canada is among the most energy-intensive countries in the world: nine units of petrochemical energy go to produce just one unit of food energy.

In addition, the burning of these fossil fuels and of wood releases large amounts of nitrous oxide into the atmosphere, contributing to the greenhouse effect. And so, for that matter, does the chemical nitrogen in artificial fertilizers. Less than 50% of these fertilizers are taken up by a crop; some of the nitrogen is also converted to nitrous oxide in the soil and escapes into the atmosphere, where it contributes to acid rain.

Those fertilizers, along with pesticides, contaminate more than our air. From the soil they seep into groundwater, the source of water that lies underground. In rural areas, groundwater may be the only source of well water fed to people, livestock, and crops. Contaminants from groundwater also seep into lakes and rivers and occasionally even bubble back to the surface of the ground. In a sense, we are recycling our own poisons.

We're growing food from oil not soil

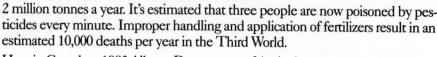

THE ECOLOGICAL ALTERNATIVE

Our great hope for a food supply that is safer for both ourselves and our planet is the alternative type of farming called "sustainable agriculture." It includes the farming systems referred to as organic or biological agriculture, bio-dynamic agriculture, the French intensive method, and ecological agriculture. All share the common goals of stressing the quality of food and of growing it in sympathy with natural processes. We'll use organic farming as an example.

There are six basic standards drawn up by the International Federation of Organic Agriculture Movements. Briefly, they call for the following:

▪ that an organic farm draw upon local resources instead of using outside material;

▪ that the organic farmer maintain and improve the fertility of the soil instead of depleting it;

▪ that the organic farmer avoid any form of pollution when raising and harvesting crops;

▪ that a high nutritional quality in food be emphasized, as well as quantity of food;

▪ that the use of fossil fuels like oil be kept to a minimum; and

▪ that the organic farmer offer satisfying and financially rewarding employment for farmworkers.

You will find, then, no synthetic fertilizers or pesticides, no growth hormones or livestock feed additives, on an organic farm. Instead there is self-sustaining soil that has a high humus content and suffers minimal erosion, producing plants less susceptible to attacks from diseases and pests. Plant residues and compost also help to build a more fertile soil full of earthworms and bacteria; the aim of an organic farmer is soil that gets a little richer every year.

Crop variety and rotation are important on an organic farm because growing just one crop year after year is an open-house invitation to insects and to the quick spread of fungi. This type of farming is a closed, regenerative system where nature's cycles and recycling take precedence. The extractive type of system, on the other hand, uses up soil and doesn't replace what was taken away.

Animals benefit from organic farming as well. They're not penned in, and they're not routinely given antibiotics or other drugs to stop the spread of disease. There is usually so little disease, indeed, that vet bills may be non-existent. Livestock help to recycle nutrients too: fed the organically grown vegetables and grains, they in turn provide manure that will eventually enrich the soil.

Not surprisingly, organic farms tend to use more labour than other types. It's time-consuming just to observe changing conditions in the fields, to feel the soil and see "how many earthworms are in a handful," to compost and to hand-weed. "We suffer badly from the weeds," says a Manitoba farmer quoted in a Canadian Organic Growers study. "But so do the people who spray."

The Directory of Canadian Organic Agriculture, published by **Canadian Organic Growers** and **Les Editions Humus**, provides a national listing of organic producers, retailers, wholesalers, and suppliers of everything from food to gardening supplies, water analysis services to bed-and-breakfast accommodations serving organic meals. You can order it for $8 from COG, Box 6408, Station J, Ottawa, Ont. K2A 3Y6.

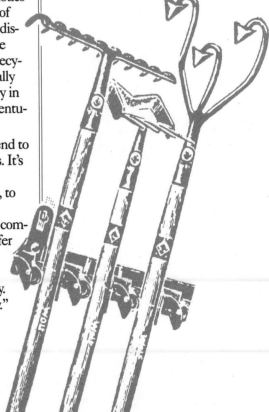

Shopping for a Food Store

One of the best things you can do for yourself and your family is to talk to the manager of your grocery store or supermarket about the types of food you'd like to be able to buy and the practices you'd like to see followed. Take a few minutes too to write a postcard or letter to the president or head office of each supermarket chain in your area (ask the local manager for the address). Often it takes only a few comments from concerned consumers to make retailers start thinking about changing their strategies, especially if they must do so to remain competitive. And see how many "yes" answers your store rates on the following aspects:

Bags
❑ Does it offer a choice of different kinds?
❑ Does it charge for bags?
❑ Does it provide rebates for bringing your own bags?
❑ Can bags be returned for recycling into new bags or other products?

Packaging
❑ Does it have a meat counter where you can get products not wrapped in plastic?
❑ Does it avoid plastic-wrapped vegetables?
❑ Does it have a bulk section and, if so, can you bring your own containers?

Waste
❑ Does it recycle its cardboard containers?
❑ Does it have a recycling program in its offices?
❑ Does it put unsold food to good use, by giving it to charities or by sending it to be composted?

Products
❑ Does it offer certified organic food?
❑ Does it offer alternative cleaning products (see Chapter 3) in the cleaning products section?
❑ Does it label country of origin on its produce?
❑ Does it boycott California grapes?

Cleaning
❑ Does it refuse to use chemical extermination techniques?
❑ Does it use non-toxic cleaning products on its floors and fixtures?

Promotion
❑ Does it advertise any of the above with the reason why it's important?
❑ Does it have in-store promotional material and announcements about environmentally beneficial consumer products?

In recent years some Canadian supermarket chains have introduced, or announced plans to introduce, products they deem "environment-friendly," "natural," or "green." Consumers should be aware that such products can be more a matter of marketing and packaging than of substantial benefit to the environment. Of Canada's large grocery retailers, Toronto-based Loblaws has been in the forefront of producing and promoting so-called "green" items such as the Pollution Probe-endorsed **President's Choice** Green Baking Soda. Consumer response has been favourable, indicating there is a sizeable market for such goods. Again, environment-conscious consumers should make sure that their purchases are truly a matter of substance over style.

The Demand for Organic Food

More and more Canadian farmers are switching to organic methods. (Some, of course, have always used them.) The Quebec Ministry of Agriculture, for example, estimates that the province has 2,000 farmers who've converted to organic practices or are planning to do so.

Since we buy a great deal of our food from the U.S., it's interesting to note that American organic farmers already share an estimated $5-billion portion of that country's $36-billion annual fruit and vegetable market. Consumer demand is growing rapidly in North America; in Canada it is so heavy that many organic producers sell everything they can grow at the farm gate or their front door. Quebec's estimated demand is ten times the available supply of most products.

And consumers are also prepared to pay more for organic food. A mid-1988 consumer survey found that even 70% of those who don't buy organic food at present would be interested in doing so if the products were easily available. Not only that, 53% of all those polled said they were willing to pay up to 25% more for organic foods.

Most of the extra cost of organic products is due not to production costs but to the lack of economies of scale in processing, transportation, and retailing; larger farm operations can get their products to buyers for less money per item. And even if our environmental problems were solved, organic farming is never likely to be done on the scale achieved by large corporate farms.

That being the case, many farmers are considering using at least some of the techniques of organic farming, including Integrated Pest Management (IPM). It relies on ecological control of pests, resorting to chemical treatments only if that defence fails. Among IPM's goals are the use of tactics that are most in harmony with human and environmental health and most conserving of non-renewable energy fuels.

✳✳✳

Organic Certification

Not a few Canadians produce organic foods in their own gardens (see Chapter 6). But if any chemicals have been used on your garden or adjacent lawns – including your neighbours' – in the past three years, your produce won't qualify as organic in Canada. California farmers must meet far less rigid standards; they can qualify for a "certified organic" label when their fields have been free of chemicals for only a year.

Commercial foods that are trumpeted as being "fresh," "natural," "green," or "pure" aren't organic either. Food that is should fall within the Canadian definition accepted by Consumer and Corporate Affairs Canada, although you may be prepared to accept the one-year-organic rules allowed by the California Certified Organic Farmers (CCOF). Look for those letters on labels or, even better, buy the Canadian Organic Crop Improvement Association (OCIA), British Columbia's SOOPA, or Ontario's "Demeter" label. And make sure you do see the label if a grocer is offering you "organic" food. If you don't see it and you get vague answers to your questions, contact OFPANA, the **Organic Foods Production Association of North America** (c/o Ecological Agriculture Project, Macdonald College, Ste-Anne-de-Bellevue, PQ H9X 1C0).

Any Canadian farmer wanting certification must undergo stringent inspection and accept rigid production standards. There are at least 39 different organic certifications worldwide, but OCIA International (it also operates in the U.S., Mexico, Argentina, Peru, Belize, and Turkey) has been successful in developing generally agreed standards in North and South America, and hopes to have them accepted around the world.

* *

Living with Blemishes

Anti-pesticide consumers say "Beware of perfect-looking produce," because it is likely to contain high chemical residues. And indeed organic food may be less symmetrical, a bit uneven in colour, with the occasional bruise, spot, or other blemish. But any cosmetic defects are just that – cosmetic. Don't confuse good looks with character.

* *

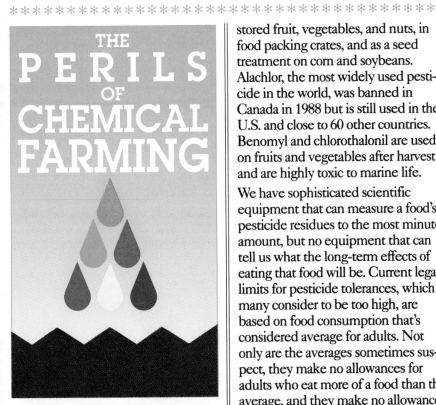

THE PERILS OF CHEMICAL FARMING

In one recent year, Canadian farmers used 88,000 tonnes of pesticides to kill insects, weeds, and plant diseases, on which they spent a total of $869 million. That amount, added to our food bills, bought 5,000 different chemicals. Many of them were systemic toxins that penetrate the skins of fruits and such vegetables as lettuce and can't be washed off. In addition, some pesticides degrade slowly and can appear in foods years after the chemicals were last used in the fields.

One of the most questionable of those 5,000 chemicals was Captan, a fungicide known to be lethal to fish, birds, and bees and commonly used on stored fruit, vegetables, and nuts, in food packing crates, and as a seed treatment on corn and soybeans. Alachlor, the most widely used pesticide in the world, was banned in Canada in 1988 but is still used in the U.S. and close to 60 other countries. Benomyl and chlorothalonil are used on fruits and vegetables after harvest and are highly toxic to marine life.

We have sophisticated scientific equipment that can measure a food's pesticide residues to the most minute amount, but no equipment that can tell us what the long-term effects of eating that food will be. Current legal limits for pesticide tolerances, which many consider to be too high, are based on food consumption that's considered average for adults. Not only are the averages sometimes suspect, they make no allowances for adults who eat more of a food than the average, and they make no allowances for children. Where fruit might be considered 20% of an adult's diet, it can be 34% of a preschooler's.

Nor can any scientific test yet tell us the results of eating a combination of pesticide residues. A Nova Scotia study on Canadian produce found that 60% of the strawberries and 50% of the celery tested showed traces of up to 39 pesticides. It's more than likely that imported produce would have shown even higher residues – including residues of pesticides that have been banned in Canada.

Sick and Vanishing Land

There is no question that we are threatening our food supply by debasing our environment. Soil degradation is an enormous problem everywhere in the world: an estimated 25 billion tonnes of topsoil is lost every year through erosion.

In Canada B.C.'s Fraser River valley was losing up to 30 tonnes a year per hectare in the mid-1980s; Nova Scotia's cultivated land, 2 to 26 tonnes. Prince Edward Island has already lost half its topsoil since the turn of the century.

Soil degradation includes erosion by wind and water, soil salinization, and oxidation. It costs Canadian farmers more than $1 billion annually, with up to $400 million of the damage due to water erosion, $300 million due to wind. The economic impact from prairie erosion is $380 million a year and growing 5% a year. To complete the cycle, soil degradation contributes to the deterioration of surface water and groundwater, passing along residues of chemicals that may have increased crop yields but did not prevent the land from eroding.

An equally alarming problem is the rate at which Canadian farmland is disappearing under concrete. Only about 10% of Canada's land can support food production; only 0.5% is rated Class 1 farmland (suitable for most crops). More than 50% of the latter is in southern Ontario, and the Region of Peel alone lost 15,700 hectares of primarily Class 1 farmland between 1971 and 1986, about 3 hectares a day. Yet Ontario is a net importer of food, relying increasingly on foreign foods that could be grown in the province but aren't.

In Canada as a whole, a quarter of a million hectares of rural land was converted to urban use between 1966 and 1981, 57% of it "prime" (Classes 1 to 3) agricultural land. And about two-thirds of Canada's considerable food imports are now of products that are grown here already.

* *

THE IRRADIATION OF FOOD

There is a continuing and passionate debate over both the safety and the wisdom of irradiating food.

The next thing we're going to have to come to terms with in our food is irradiation. Briefly, this is a process of bombarding food with radiation to preserve it. Given crop losses of up to 50% from spoilage in tropical countries, and the lack of refrigeration facilities, it sounds like a good idea. It has some drawbacks, however, as you might expect.

First, though, it must be said that irradiation does *not* leave food radioactive; the food never touches radioactive material. The process developed in Canada uses gamma rays from cobalt-60 in much the same way as they are used in radiation therapy for cancer. As in that therapy, the dose of radiation is designed to suspend the growth of living cells or destroy them. It can preserve or disinfect foods, as well as prevent sprouting and kill pests like flour weevils.

Irradiation has been used in our health care industry for more than 20 years; by the mid-1980s, almost half of all disposable medical supplies were being sterilized by the process. Irradiation of potatoes, onions, wheat, and flour has been permitted here for about 25 years, although it has never been done commercially, and no irradiated food has ever been sold here. In May 1987, a parliamentary committee said there were still too many troubling and unanswered questions about the potential hazards. Yet in early 1989 the federal government decided to make irradiation more commercially attractive to the food industry. Health and Welfare Canada declared irradiation a food process under the Food and Drugs Act, rather than a food additive, meaning it is subject to less stringent control. Critics suggest that the main reason for the decision was to keep our faltering nuclear industry in business – few countries are buying nuclear power stations these days.

The international unit of measure for an absorbed dose of radiation is the kilo-gray (kGy), and 1 kGy equals 100 kilorads. The range of irradiation normally used with food now ranges from 15 kilorads for potatoes to as much as 10 kGy to completely sterilize meat and poultry. Up to 1 kGy is a "low dose" that inhibits sprouting, delays ripening, and helps destroy insects; 5 kGy, a "medium dose," kills some bacteria and so extends shelf life; 10 kGy, a "high dose," will destroy viruses and totally sterilize meat and poultry so that they will keep with no refrigeration.

Health and Welfare sets no maximum permissible dosage for human consumption. Under Canada's new regulations, "efficacy tests" will be required to determine the level of irradiation for which an applicant wants approval. Because of this, it's unlikely that any new foods would be added to the approved list before mid-1990. The most likely early candidates will be fresh poultry, fish and other seafood, fruit, and vegetables.

Treated food will carry a green label (see illustration) with the RADURA, the internationally recognized symbol for use on irradiated foods. The word "radiation" will not appear on the label. Non-packaged food like loose produce should have an adjacent sign displaying the symbol. There's a catch with packaged products, however. If they contain an irradiated food that makes up less than 10% of the total ingredients (say, the chicken or mushrooms in soup), no label is required. In theory, then, a processed food could have 11 irradiated ingredients, each making up less than 10% of the product, be 100% irradiated in other words, and not need a label. Even so, that's better than in the U.S., where labelling is required only when an entire food item is irradiated.

✳✳

The Safety Question

There is a continuing and passionate debate over both the safety and the wisdom of irradiating food. A growing body of scientific opinion states that irradiation destroys some vitamins and other nutrients. Many scientists believe it creates entirely new chemicals and that these "radiolytic" products could be toxic or carcinogenic or both.

Although the health effects are still in doubt, there is no question that the use of the technology has great environmental implications. Critics don't like the idea of putting potentially dangerous nuclear technology into Third World countries that often suffer power cuts and where highly trained technicians and reliable maintenance are in acutely short supply. This, they say, increases the possibility of accidents causing deaths and widespread environmental contamination.

Food distributors and retailers use a lot of refrigeration equipment in their warehouses, trucks, and stores.

Miracle Foodmart and **Steinberg** are gradually replacing the air conditioners, coolers, and freezers in their stores with units that use more ozone-safe freon. The companies' Quebec division has begun filtering and reusing the freon in its refrigerated vans rather than allowing used freon to escape into the atmosphere.

Opponents make these arguments against irradiation:

■ It's unnecessary; present food preservation processes are perfectly adequate.

■ It will increase the cost of food, and that will be of no benefit to those in developing countries who can barely afford food now.

■ It could turn the food on our plates into poisons and cancer triggers, although we won't learn about these effects for many years.

■ It will create nuclear wastes and the hazards of transporting those wastes without accidents, and it will create both health and safety risks for those working and living with the technology.

■ It doesn't do many of the jobs its proponents say it does – long-term preservation, for example. If a food is re-exposed to bacteria after irradiation, it can become re-contaminated.

■ The technology is easily open to abuse. Irradiation should be used only on fresh food, but it can disguise non-freshness. There have been several instances in Europe in which seafood badly contaminated with bacteria was irradiated to make it saleable.

■ It encourages the nuclear industry and chemical-based agribusiness, both of which have already damaged the environment in too many other ways.

For consumers of food, the bottom line is that there is no readily available scientific test by which we or any government inspector can definitely know whether a food product has been irradiated – or at what dose. Until there is such a test, a ban on irradiated food in this country would help, even though it would be no guarantee. Yet more than 75% of Canadians are opposed to food irradiation, and both U.S. and Canadian food processors who've announced they were about to irradiate food have backed off when faced with consumer backlashes.

Those who advocate the use of irradiation say there is no conclusive case against it. Those with grave concerns say there's enough doubt and scientific evidence to more than justify delaying its implementation until we're sure the process is safe. West Germany, New Zealand, and several American states have all banned the sale of irradiated food.

* *

Beyond the food there is the package, a problem unto itself.

The production, use, and disposal of the materials we use to wrap our foods contribute to many environmental problems, from litter though waste disposal to acid rain.

The more expensive the item, the more layers of wrapping. Witness that expensive box of chocolates or the pricey mushrooms in a plastic box wrapped in plastic. There are few food products that need more than one layer of packaging, almost none that need more than two layers. Yet a common sight in supermarkets is two or four tomatoes sitting in a cardboard box and surrounded by plastic wrap.

Traditional packing materials have given way to foamed plastics and aluminum; plastic wrappers and the plastic rings on six-packs (banned in 12 U.S. states) strangle and suffocate birds and fish. Although paper and cardboard are excellent packaging materials that break down as waste, they're rarely made from recycled material. In a year each of us might use two trees' worth of packaging material.

Even juice drinking boxes, valued because they're light and store neatly without wasting space (hence saving fuel used in transportation), are environment-unfriendly because they're not recyclable. But instead of buying one large recyclable glass container of juice, we opt for boxes made from plastic wrap, cardboard, and foil, then packaged in sixes wrapped in more plastic. And, as Chapter 7 makes clear, biodegradable and photodegradable plastics aren't a solution either; many environmentalists feel they will only leave us with plastic dust, the environmental impact of which isn't known.

Consumers do have a say in packaging. Their reaction, for example, removed a new plastic soft-drink can from the market in the U.S. Some U.S. states are imposing waste taxes on packaging materials that can't be recycled, which are added to the price of products like toothpaste. There's also a shopping bag tax: bring your own bag to the store (and get a rebate, in some places) or pay for a new one.

A British borough council has a campaign called Don't Choose What You Can't Reuse. This won't do the whole job; reuse must be combined with recycling and – most important – reduced consumption. But every bit counts. Here are some measures you can take that will help considerably.

- Use your municipality's Blue Box recycling campaign, if it has one, for cans, bottles, and acceptable plastics.
- Buy only returnable bottles whenever possible.
- Don't litter anywhere with anything.
- Cut down on the amount of plastic and foam packaging you bring home.
- Buy products made from recycled materials whenever possible; if they're not available, ask why.
- Reuse plastic bags when you can't avoid buying foods in them. For example, plastic milk bags are excellent for storing foods.

The following sections will show you some of the other ways in which you can vote environmentally with your food dollars. For example, buying as many Brazil nuts as you can will support the farmers whose range has been halved in a decade by the destruction of Brazil's tropical forests, and give their dying business a commercial return from the trees left standing.

* *

Fruits and Vegetables

For years we've been urged to increase our consumption of fruits and vegetables for health reasons. And we certainly have. The average Canadian goes through 185 kg of fruits and vegetables a year, twice as much as Americans and an increase of about 75 kg since 1973.

Although the U.S. supplies most of the 2.3 million tonnes of fresh and processed produce we import, in all we buy from 80 other countries. Yet imported produce can be considered truly fresh only if you can afford to fly it in, preferably by Concorde. Most of ours is trucked in, and it can be weeks old by the time it appears in a store. If it has also been stockpiled by a seller because there was too much on the market at once, it may be many weeks old. (It still looks good, of course; synthetic chemicals have made sure it does.) Vitamin C is lost rapidly from many foods once they're picked, and so are other valuable nutrients.

And then there's the wax. Not the sort of wax we're used to on cucumbers and turnips, but the application of products that may bear a close resemblance to something you'd wax a floor or car with. It's not enough to be suspicious of shiny

STORING FOODS

To avoid the possibility of toxic metals leaching into your food, especially acidic or fatty foods, don't cook or store anything in pots or pans that are scratched, chipped, pitted, or made of unlined copper. Use enamelled roasting pans, and don't make sherbet or fruit juice popsicles in metal ice-cube trays or store unused food in its opened can.

Never use glazed pottery dishes or containers unless you know the glaze doesn't contain lead or cadmium. Federal regulations deem lead and cadmium glazes illegal for food or beverage containers and are now labelled as such for potters. Food container glazes must have a glossy, smooth finish to seal in potential toxins from underlying paint and/or clay. Federal officials say testing and enforcement of these regulations have increased and the problem now is minimal. It never hurts to ask, though.

Reserve glasses with coloured decals, logos, or slogans for display only. At the very least, don't put them in a dishwasher or let children drink from them; chances are the decals are loaded with lead. If you want souvenir glasses, stick to those with silver or gold embossing. Drinking from inexpensive plastic glasses isn't always a good idea, either.

The seal of aluminum foil can be broken by salty or acidic foods. In any case, tin foil, like waxed paper, plastic wrap, and plastic sandwich and freezer bags, isn't reusable. Use washable, reusable storage containers like old glass jars or heavy plastic containers like Tupperware. Yogurt and margarine tubs are fine, too, but be careful when storing foods with strong flavours – once a plastic container has held chili sauce, everything you put in it afterwards will have a soupçon of chili sauce to it, too.

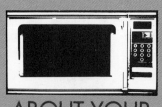

ABOUT YOUR MICROWAVE OVEN

Unlike the radiation used to irradiate food, the radiation used by microwaves is non-ionizing, the type found in light from the sun or a light-bulb, radio frequency waves, infra-red heaters, and lasers. Microwave ovens are said to be about 40% energy-efficient; that is, only 40% of the energy they use actually helps cook the food. The remainder is simply frittered away. But by comparison, electric ovens are only about 14% efficient and gas ovens 7%. So you'll save some energy costs but use a lot more electricity, if only for a much shorter time. One study found that a microwave oven saves a grand total of about $10 a year in electricity costs for the average family.

Some simple rules for your microwave:

▬▬ Keep in mind that cooking vegetables in a microwave may cut down on nutrients. It depends on how many you're cooking – a small amount won't cause any great loss in nutrients because the cooking time is short and little water is used. If you're cooking large amounts, however, consider another method, such as steaming.

▬▬ Use only dishes specifically made and sold for use in microwave ovens. Cover them with the glass lid from a casserole instead of any sort of food wrap. If the food should be vented, put the glass lid on crooked.

▬▬ Make sure the seals around the door are kept clean. If they're cracked or broken, have them replaced immediately – and don't use the oven until they are. The radiation that can leak from microwave ovens isn't nuclear, but it isn't good for you either. Pay attention to loose hinges as well, or an oven that is bent, bashed, or skewed in any way.

▬▬ Stay at least a metre away from your microwave oven when it's on, for the same reason you wouldn't put your hand against a hot lightbulb or sleep under a sun lamp. Make sure children observe this rule, too. And if you have a pacemaker, stay many metres away.

apples, peppers, eggplants, avocadoes, and tomatoes; waxes to prevent loss of moisture are routinely used on citrus fruits, melons, peaches, squashes, parsnips, and other produce as well.

The best way around these problems is to buy, whenever possible, small, locally produced, irregular fruits and vegetables, organic if possible, that have a minimum of packaging. Why should they be small? Well, the larger and more lush-looking the vegetable, the more chemicals probably were used to get it that way.

Buying local produce encourages preservation of agricultural land in your area. In addition, produce grown locally is far more likely to have most of its nutrients left, and a minimum of energy resources have been used (with fewer pollutants emitted) to transport it to you. Irregular-looking produce is produce that has almost certainly been in contact with few chemicals. It may or may not be organic, and in any case even organic products may have very slight traces of chemical residues because of spray drift and environmental contamination that farmers can do nothing about.

When you are ready to eat your produce, scrub it well in a basin of water. (Some use a mild detergent or vinegar solution before a thorough rinse, which is probably better at removing residues.) Peel the item if you're concerned about or don't know its source; blanching beforehand helps with tomatoes and peppers.

Remove outer layers of leafy vegetables like cabbage or lettuce, and flush a strong flow of water over the remaining layers. These measures won't remove residues of systemic pesticides that have been absorbed by the produce, however, and they will undoubtedly cost you the nutrients that concentrate under the skin. Like much in life, it's a trade-off.

The less you cut up vegetables, the more nutrients will be retained in cooking; for the same reason, don't soak them beforehand or add baking soda. And try not to overcook; just-tender is fine. Cook them in a covered pot with a minimum of water, preferably by steaming them. Stir-frying (which can be done with broth, consommé, or a minimum of fat) and pressure-cooking also help preserve nutrients. If you have a microwave oven, see our box on that subject. Finally, never use citrus peels in cooking unless you know the fruit was grown organically; they may contain dye as well as pesticide residues.

✳✳

Meat and Poultry

T hese foods cause concern as well. In addition to the chemical residues that farm animals pick up in their feed and water, many poultry, swine, beef cattle, and dairy cows are given antibiotics. If we eat enough of this food, the next antibiotic our doctors give us may not work effectively. Livestock may also be given drugs that were never meant for human use. And Canadians allergic to some drugs, such as penicillin, have suffered dangerous reactions after eating meat.

Hormones are also administered to some of these animals to make them grow faster. Disturbingly, this practice has caused premature sexual development in children who eat a lot of meat or chicken. Use of hormones in this way is regulated in both Canada and the U.S. but enforced only by occasional spot checks. Although producers are supposed to allow for a suitable withdrawal period before milking or slaughter, during which no new doses are given, it's clear the rules are not always followed. Britain and the other countries of the European Economic Community banned this use of hormones in 1986 and, as of 1989, allow no imports of hormone-fed meat. Trade considerations may now move

Canada and the U.S. to a hormone-free point of view.

Humane concerns about the manner in which the animals we eat are raised can't be separated from these health issues. The larger the commercial operation that produces them, the more likely they are to be confined for life under conditions that we wouldn't – literally – inflict upon a dog. Disease spreads quickly in such factory-farming conditions, hence the need for antibiotics.

We may be choosing to eat more poultry for health reasons, but the practice is also helping to stretch the world's food supply. Beef cattle produced in feed lots need about 2.6 kg of grain to produce a single pound of meat; broilers require only 0.7 kg. We still love beef though, which has created another problem. North America's appetite for hamburgers and steaks is so great that vast tracts of rainforest are levelled to make grazing land for cattle raised for export.

Buying less beef, for home cooking and in restaurants, is one measure you can take. When you buy poultry, look for suppliers of free-range birds, but bear in mind that free-range does not necessarily mean organic. At least one supermarket chain, **Loblaws**, sells Alberta beef (under the name *Natural Choice*) that has never been fed antibiotics or hormones, and many other sources sell organic meat.

If you can't find what you want, at least buy only lean cuts of meat and trim all visible fat, and remove the skin from poultry. Many pesticides and other unwelcome chemical visitors in our ecosystems tend to concentrate in fatty tissue.

****

Fish and Shellfish

Fish convert feed into protein more efficiently than farm animals and are growing increasingly valuable from the health point of view. But on fish farms too (see below), antibiotics and hormones may find a home. Once biotechnologists had injected growth hormones from chicken and cattle into young salmon and found the fish grew up to 50% faster, they began planning to isolate and mass-produce the salmon's own hormones for injection. Already here is the possibility that colouring methods have been used on farmed salmon since it isn't as rosy a pink as the wild varieties.

Sources say that Canadian fish farmers do not use growth hormones. Antibiotics are administered only when disease breaks out, and tranquillizers when big fish have to be handled to milk their sperm or extract eggs. A 1988 report by the Ontario Ministry of Natural Resources says that chemicals and drugs like antibiotics are gone from fish flesh before it reaches our tables. But under new regulations in B.C., farmers will have to keep logs detailing which antibiotics are used and when; none may be used within 120 days of marketing.

At present, the federal government allows no antibiotic residues in any fish sold – although the technology for testing fish for such residues won't be available for several years. The Consumers Association of Canada has warned that even sub-clinical doses could lead to the development of resistant strains of bacteria in human beings, and cited the possibility of allergic reactions in those sensitive to antibiotics.

The association also asked for research to learn if farmed fish have the same quality and quantity of Omega-3 as wild fish. (This fatty acid helps prevent heart attacks and is one of the reasons for the increased popularity of fish in Canadian diets; testing for its presence in farmed fish has begun at the University of Victoria.) And it wanted fish identified as "farmed" or "wild" in the marketplace. Until that happens, you'll have to follow your own guide: from September

Fish convert feed into protein more efficiently than farm animals.

to May, any fresh Canadian salmon or trout you buy is almost certainly from a farm. Shellfish is usually identified because producers believe consumers prefer "cultivated" oysters and mussels.

Finally, the association raised the question of dyes. Although many B.C. salmon farmers do use dyes, the amount is unlikely to pose a serious health hazard. However, only strong consumer demand is likely to bring clear data from our federal and provincial governments, as well as a tough and well-organized code of environmental safeguards at every Canadian fish farm.

What about the non-farmed fish and seafood you buy? With ocean fish, over-fishing puts so much stress on many species that their average weights fall. Big, technologically advanced factory trawlers vacuum up the small with the large. Our lakes, streams, and coastal waters are affected by fertilizer and pesticide runoff; industries still dump their wastes, legally and illegally. The sale of trout from Lake Ontario is banned, yet fish from any waters may now contain residues and industrial toxins. PCBs, banned for years, still show up in significant concentrations; so do dioxin and chlordane.

Shellfish frequently have low levels of arsenic, cadmium, chromium, and lead; high levels of methyl mercury have been found in large fish such as swordfish, shark, marlin, albacore tuna, and halibut. Fish and shellfish with cancerous tumours have been found in many lakes and coastal waters; bottom-feeding fish are contaminated by sediment laden with toxins.

This depressing litany does not mean you can't eat fish. Fatty fish such as carp, catfish, white perch, and mackerel tend to have the highest concentrations of contaminants; offshore species the least. Cod, haddock, flounder, pollock, fish sticks made from these fish, salmon, and shrimp are likely to have little.

If you like fish and want to continue eating it, follow these suggestions for minimal exposure to possible contaminants:

- Learn what species are likely to have high residues and eat them only once a month.
- Buy small young fish that have had less time to accumulate residues.
- Ask where the fish you buy comes from; choose something else if it originated in waters close to a major city or industrial area.
- Cook your fish only by broiling, baking, or poaching it, and don't make sauces from the drippings or poaching water.
- Trim away the fattiest tissue (the skin, belly flap, and dark meat) after cooking.
- If you're a fish lover, make sure you eat a variety of types instead of only one or two favourites.
- Eat little fish that comes in undercooked or raw form (ceviche, sashimi, sushi) and don't eat raw shellfish.
- Buy fish canned in water rather than oil, and rinse it off before serving.

Finally, consider the dolphins. Greenpeace has started a grass-roots campaign to boycott certain varieties of tuna because fleets fishing for them in the southeastern Pacific have put dolphins in great danger. Swept up in the nets with the tuna, they're dying at the rate of up to 100,000 a year. The harvesting of tongol and albacore tuna, however, does not threaten dolphins.

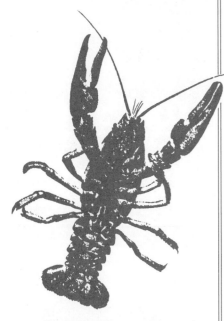

Fleets fishing for tuna in the southeastern Pacific have put dolphins in great danger. Swept up in the nets with the tuna, they are dying at the rate of up to 100,000 a year.

Fish Farming

Aquaculture now produces 12% of the world's total fish harvest. The family-run "farms" previously typical of the business have become an industry that is the equivalent of agribusiness. In Canada, that industry is expected to double in just three years, from $50 million in 1987 to $100 million in 1990.

All 10 provinces have some form of aquaculture, but the British Columbia salmon farming business has increased dramatically in the last five years with the influx of offshore capital. Most of this capital is from Norway, where the government now limits the number and size of fish farms for social and environmental reasons. Greenpeace reports that in a search for new areas in which to expand, the Norwegian industry focussed on B.C., "which had an abundant supply of good farm sites, proximity to the U.S. and Japanese markets, and an 'open' development policy." Money has also been raised by promotion on the Vancouver Stock Exchange.

On the face of it fish farming sounds terrific. Basically, it involves raising fish in enclosed ponds or pens, most often pens built in natural waterways. Salmon, mostly from B.C., accounts for almost 52% of our national total; trout, chiefly from Ontario and Quebec, 30%; oysters and mussels, which are simply put in a specific location to grow just as wild mollusks do, 13% and more than 5% respectively.

The major environmental problem with fish farms is all the waste that goes into the water. Fecal manure and uneaten feeds form a blanket under the fish pens that smothers the habitat of wild fish and uses up oxygen and other nutrients as they decompose, which in turn stimulates the growth of weeds and algae. Also in the waste matter are cleaning chemicals, herbicides used to control aquatic weeds, and drugs used to treat diseases and parasites, as well as soluble products like the ammonia that fish produce through metabolism and any parasites and bacteria the hatchery may harbour.

Farm fish are vaccinated against disease but single-species fish farming causes the same problems as monocrop agriculture: the fish develop diseases more easily, pass them on more quickly, and must then be treated with antibiotics. The excess antibiotics move into the surrounding waters and affect wild fish, likely reducing their own immunity to disease. Sometimes, however, even drugs can't save farmed fish. In Washington State just south of the B.C. border, liver lesions spread quickly among penned Atlantic salmon in 1987 and killed 30,000. There was great concern that the disease might be passed on to free-swimming fish colonies. Two years later, Washington State officials had to destroy 3 million young salmon and a million eggs to stop a disease from spreading to wild stocks – a disease never before seen in North America.

There is also serious concern that Atlantic salmon imported into B.C. may spread new diseases to wild stocks if they escape from their farm pens, and concern that they will reduce the variety in gene pools. The genetically engineered salmon from farms may, like some other over-bred species, be easy victims of infection and have poor survivability in general. This could well threaten the survival of ocean salmon through interbreeding. On B.C.'s Sechelt Peninsula, at least 100,000 fish from seven farms recently escaped into the wild after a storm damaged their pens.

From September to May, any fresh Canadian salmon or trout you buy is almost certainly from a farm.

Dioxins in Paper Products

Dioxins, a chemical family with 75 members, are some of the most lethal poisons ever created. Even small amounts can trigger a wide range of health effects, including suppression of the immune system and birth defects. The growing dioxin contamination of the environment has concerned North American scientists and researchers since 1980. Found in the effluents from papermaking processes, they contaminate rivers and lakes; garbage incinerators also release dioxins and the closely related furans into the air, to fall on water and soil.

Many paper companies are changing their processes, but dioxins are still pervasive. They are in all bleached paper products, such as paper towels, writing paper, and paper napkins. Although Canadian law bans any dioxin residues in food at all, they recently showed up in cardboard milk cartons – and in the milk inside them. Residues are also commonly found at low levels in fruit, meat, eggs, and vegetables, and have even appeared in breast milk. Buy unbleached paper products whenever you have the opportunity; demand created by Green Consumers could make a difference to the paper industry.

The environmental hazards caused by pollution from fish farms – and the risks to the wild fish population – flourish in the confusing and overlapping areas of fishing regulations between Ottawa and the provinces, although Ontario has introduced Canada's toughest legislation for inland aquaculture. But experience in every environmental field has demonstrated too clearly the sometimes horrendous costs of taking a chance with nature.

✳ ✳ ✳ ✳ ✳ ✳ ✳ ✳ ✳ ✳ ✳ ✳ ✳ ✳ ✳ ✳ ✳ ✳

Grains

It's possible to find packaged bread free of preservatives or other additives, but these would have been added during processing, not growing: the grains in the field may still have been sprayed with pesticides. For breads made from organically grown grains, check a health-food store.

And don't assume that the darker the bread, the better it is for you. Questionable colourings may have been added to make it look more "whole grain." As Linda Pim says in *Additive Alert*, "You can be sure that any rye bread that looks like chocolate cake has added colour!"

The tidbits and treats of life – cakes, cookies, muffins, biscuits, and breakfast cereals – can be a double-barrelled threat. As well as containing residues and additives, they're likely to be made with the heavily saturated tropical vegetable oils (coconut, palm, or palm kernel), butter, or even beef fat. If you want to check the fat content of a biscuit or cookie, rub it on a paper napkin; if it leaves a grease spot, you can believe it has at least 50% fat.

As with everything else, check the labels. Look for the type of fat used ("vegetable oil" isn't enough information if you're trying to avoid saturated fats) and how high it comes on the list of ingredients. If you're watching cavities as well as calories, also note how high sugar or any word ending in -ose

(sucrose, glucose, fructose, and such) appears in the list. Even organic breads, cereals, and goodies may contain unhealthy fats or sweeteners.

✳ ✳ ✳ ✳ ✳ ✳ ✳ ✳ ✳ ✳ ✳ ✳ ✳ ✳ ✳ ✳ ✳ ✳ ✳

Eggs and Dairy Products

Many of the cautions that apply to other foods from animals should be considered when you go down the dairy aisle. With these products too you can meet the problem of antibiotics and hormones because, of course, eggs, butter, milk, cheese, yogurt, and such come from animals that may have been given drugs. And a study conducted for the Toronto Department of Public Health found the heaviest concentration of pesticides and dioxins in dairy products.

Organic dairy products and free-range eggs are available as substitutes in many areas. But it is next to impossible to buy organic fluid milk. And free-range eggs are not regulated and are not always organically produced. If non-organic products have to be your choice, you'd be wiser to reach for skim milk, sour creams, and cottage cheeses, since the higher-fat products have higher levels of chemical residues. Teach yourself to love partly skimmed mozzarella and skim milk cheeses instead of high-fat cheddar, brie, and camembert.

When buying eggs, choose cardboard containers over spongey foam plastic. Buy milk in returnable glass bottles in the few communities where they are available. If your local dairies still use plastic or cardboard containers, encourage them to switch.

The plastic containers that yogurt, margarine, and other dairy products come in are not environment-friendly when you discard them, but at least you can reuse them many times before you throw them out.

Fats and Oils

You'll be glad to know that any pesticide residues that may be in the vegetable sources used to make oils for cooking and salads are reduced during commercial processing to undetectable limits. And there are organic cooking oils to be found, as well.

No vegetable oils contain cholesterol, which comes only from animal sources, but some oils are far more saturated than others, a point that should be taken into account if you're one of the many Canadians trying to lower their consumption of fat in general and saturated fat in particular. As you've learned, there is now an additional but vital reason for doing so: toxic residues moving up the food chain are retained in the fat we get from meat, animal products, fowl, and fish. In short, these fats can give us much more than cholesterol.

Note, however, that the fat restrictions adults may place on themselves should not be extended to children without consultation with a doctor or nutritionist. The young need fats for growth and development; without a sufficient amount, they can become malnourished.

* * * * * * * * * * * * * * * * * * * *

Hot and Cold Beverages

To the environmentalist, the first question about beverages is: what sort of container do they come in? Buy cold ones in returnable or recyclable containers whenever possible. With hot beverages, try to avoid the foam plastic containers into which they are forever poured; ask your take-out sources to change to another type of cup or get the office a set of washable mugs.

Coffee and Tea

Cultivation of land for coffee, our favourite hot drink, has led to the wholesale clearance of forest in many parts of the world, and to the exhaustion of fragile soils. Coffee crops, being prime examples of the monoculture system of growing, are sprayed with large quantities of pesticides, some of which may be illegal in North America. As well, coffee-washing plants pollute many rivers with very strong effluents, and enormous amounts of energy are used to roast, grind, and process coffee.

There are at least two brands of organic coffee sold in Canada: *Café Altura*, an American brand; and *Reingold Santa Catarina*, distributed by **Linquist** in Vancouver. Organic tea – or tea bags – may be hard to come by, but *l'espérance* organic herbal teas are produced in Quebec. *Bridgehead* coffee and teas, sold in many health-food stores, are the non-organic products of workers' co-ops in developing countries, a system that ensures that more of the profits go to those workers.

If you drink decaffeinated coffee, look for a brand that is produced by a water process rather than a chemical one. And remember that bleached coffee filters contain dioxins, produced during the heavily polluting paper-bleaching process. Unbleached filters (and other papers) are beginning to appear in stores now.

* * * * * * * * * * * * * * * * * * * *

Fruit Juices

First make sure it's really fruit juice, and not just a fruit drink. Then try to buy it in large bottles or cans instead of in non-recyclable drink boxes. There are few organic juices, but it should be fairly easy to find apple cider that's organically produced. Keep in mind that although Alar has been withdrawn from the Canadian market, it stays in the fruit of apple trees for three years after their last spraying.

ORGANIC Wines

These wines are additive-free and made from grapes grown by organic viticulture.

FRANCE
Champagne and Méthode Champenoise:
Carte d'Or Champagne José Ardinat
Saumur Méthode Champenoise Brut Gérard Leroux
(Red Wines:)
(Midi, Provence, and South)
Domaine de Clairac Jougla Vin de Table
Domaine de l'Ile, Vin de Pays de l'Aude
(Bordeaux)
Château du Moulin de Peyronin
Château Renaissance
Château de Prade Bordeaux Supérieur
Château Méric Graves
Château Barrail des Graves St Emilion
Domaine St Anne Entre-deux-mers
(Rhône)
Cave la Vigneronne Villedieu
Vignoble de la Jasse
(Burgundy)
Mâcon Alain Guillot
Bourgogne Alain Guillot
(Beaujolais)
Château de Boisfranc Beaujolais Supérieur
(White Wines)
(Loire)
Blancs de Blancs Guy Bossard
Gros Plant du Pays Nantais sur Lie Guy Bossard
Muscadet de Sèvre et Maine sur Lie Guy Bossard
Sancerre Christian et Nicole Dauny
(South of France)
Mauzac Vin de Pays de l'Aude
Limoux, Domaine de Clairac
Chardonnay Vin de Pays de l'Aude
Pétillant de Raisin
Coteaux des Baux-de-Provence Terres Blanches
(Bordeaux)
Château Ballue Mondon Sec
Château Ballue Mondon Moelleux
Château Meric Graves Supérieur
Château le Barradis Monbazillac
(Burgundy)
Bourgogne Rouge Alain Guillot
(Alsace)
Sylvaner Pierre Frick
Klevner Cuvée Spéciale Pierre Frick
Gewurztraminer Pierre Frick
(Rosé Wines)
Rosé d'Anjou Gérard Leroux
Domaine de Clairac Jubio Rose

SPAIN
(Red Wines)
Biovîn Valdepenas

ITALY
(Red Wines)
Chianti Roberto Drighi
Valpolicella Classico Superiore
(White Wines)
San Vito Verdiglio Roberto Drighi
San Vito Bianco Toscano Roberto Drighi
Soave Classico Guerrieri-Rizzardi

ENGLAND
Organic Apple Wine – Avalon Vineyard

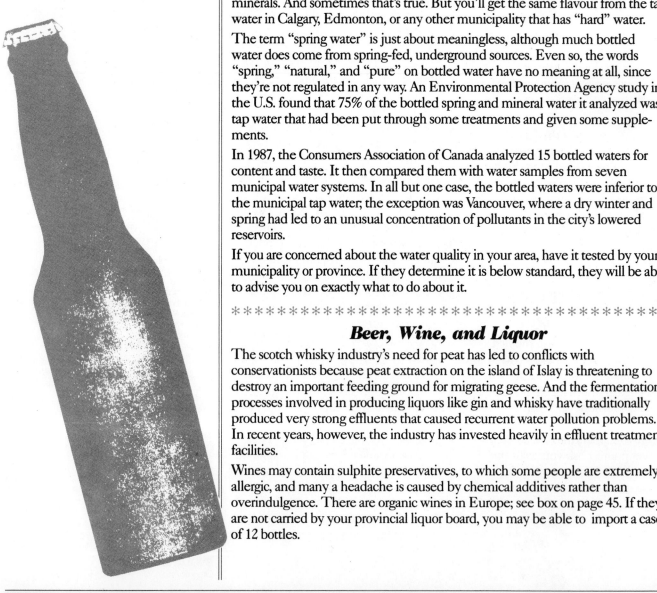

For a laboratory fee of $235, the Consumers Association of Canada will test your tap water for 92 different substances, including PCBs, pesticides, and sundry carcinogens. For information, send a stamped, self-addressed, business-sized envelope to: Water Quality Analysis, Consumers Association of Canada, Box 9300, Ottawa ON, K1G 3T9.

Bottled Waters

The state of our drinking water is a pressing problem that Green Consumers should tackle at the political level. Buying bottled water, after all, does nothing to remedy the pollution of the water that continues to flow from our taps. Moreover, most bottled waters are no better than the tap water their buyers are trying to avoid.

Now a major industry in Canada, bottled water has doubled in sales every five years or so since the mid-1970s. (Consumption is highest in Quebec, which goes through well over 50 million litres each year.) Given that bottled water is a commercial food product, you might expect that it is carefully regulated and regularly monitored. It is neither; the regulation and inspection of municipal tap water supplies are much more rigid.

For a start, then, club soda is merely carbon-filtered tap water with a heavy dose of carbonation added by the manufacturer. Mineral waters (which may sparkle only because of the manufacturer's carbonation) are meant to have more flavour because they come from underground sources where rock formations supply minerals. And sometimes that's true. But you'll get the same flavour from the tap water in Calgary, Edmonton, or any other municipality that has "hard" water.

The term "spring water" is just about meaningless, although much bottled water does come from spring-fed, underground sources. Even so, the words "spring," "natural," and "pure" on bottled water have no meaning at all, since they're not regulated in any way. An Environmental Protection Agency study in the U.S. found that 75% of the bottled spring and mineral water it analyzed was tap water that had been put through some treatments and given some supplements.

In 1987, the Consumers Association of Canada analyzed 15 bottled waters for content and taste. It then compared them with water samples from seven municipal water systems. In all but one case, the bottled waters were inferior to the municipal tap water; the exception was Vancouver, where a dry winter and spring had led to an unusual concentration of pollutants in the city's lowered reservoirs.

If you are concerned about the water quality in your area, have it tested by your municipality or province. If they determine it is below standard, they will be able to advise you on exactly what to do about it.

✳✳✳✳✳✳✳✳✳✳✳✳✳✳✳✳✳✳✳✳✳✳✳✳✳✳✳✳✳✳✳✳✳✳✳✳✳

Beer, Wine, and Liquor

The scotch whisky industry's need for peat has led to conflicts with conservationists because peat extraction on the island of Islay is threatening to destroy an important feeding ground for migrating geese. And the fermentation processes involved in producing liquors like gin and whisky have traditionally produced very strong effluents that caused recurrent water pollution problems. In recent years, however, the industry has invested heavily in effluent treatment facilities.

Wines may contain sulphite preservatives, to which some people are extremely allergic, and many a headache is caused by chemical additives rather than overindulgence. There are organic wines in Europe; see box on page 45. If they are not carried by your provincial liquor board, you may be able to import a case of 12 bottles.

West German beers contain only hops, malt, and water; no additives are allowed. Canada now has many micro-breweries that produce additive-free beer and ale. Most are affiliated with Britain's **Campaign for Real Ale** (CAMRA), and all use only malt, barley, hops, yeast, water, and, in some cases, brown sugar colouring in their beers. These are not organic beers, however. For more information, contact CAMRA at P.O. Box 2036, Station D, Ottawa, ON, K1P 5W3.

****

10 WAYS TO A GREENER DIET

1. Eat organic foods whenever possible, preferably Canadian ones, and don't expect perfection in appearance.
2. Where you can't find organic, try to keep your imported food choices to a minimum; off-shore pesticide controls and inspections may be less rigid than Canada's.
3. Concentrate on in-season food grown locally; out-of-season produce is shipped a long way for a long time and is often treated with chemicals to keep it from spoiling.
4. With non-organic foods, follow our preparation and cooking instructions in each section; even with organic meat and poultry you'd be wise to remove all visible fat for dietary reasons.
5. Keep yourself informed about the pesticides used on foods and the additives used in them (see separate box on books), and ask your grocer to stock foods without them.
6. Read the labels of all processed foods, on which the ingredients must be listed in order of quantity; buy the products with the fewest ingredients listed after the food itself.
7. If you're concerned about possible chemical residues or want to complain about additives in a packaged food, write to the manufacturer listed on the label; usually only the company name, city, and postal code are listed, but that should be enough for a letter to reach "The President."
8. Consider sending a photocopy of your letter to the president of your grocery chain; the store manager can give you the name and address.
9. Consider, too, sending photocopies of your letter to your municipal, provincial, and federal political representatives, and to the departments of health at all three levels of government.
10. Take a few minutes to write a thank-you note when you are pleased about finding an additive-free, certified organic, or otherwise environment-friendly product in a store.

To Learn More

If you'd like further information about chemical residues in American fruits and vegetables, read *Pesticide Alert*, by Lawrie Mott and Karen Snyder ($9.95, Sierra Club Books, 1987). For information on the environmental contaminants in Canadian food, read *The Invisible Additives*, by Linda Pim ($9.95, Doubleday, 1981). And if you're concerned about the additives that manufacturers and processors contribute to your food, read *Additive Alert*, also by Linda Pim (3rd edition, $4.95, Dell Books, 1986). Should you not be able to find these in bookstores, write Sierra Club, 730 Polk Street, San Francisco, CA 94109, or for the two Pim books, Pollution Probe, 12 Madison Avenue, Toronto, ON, M5R 2S1.

Large Canadian grocery chains often sell products through affiliated or associated companies. Besides its **Loblaws** stores, **Loblaw Companies Ltd.** trades under the names Supercentre, Zehrs, Real Canadian Superstore, Super-Valu, Save Easy and Real Atlantic Superstores. **Provigo** trades under the names Provigo, Axep, Proprio, Maxi, Héritage, Jovi, Intermarché, Octofruit, IGA, LOEB IGA, LOEB, M/M, Orange Store, Food Giant, Mayfair, Garden Market, Triple S, Reddi Mart, Petrini's, Quality Plus, Cost Less, Better Buy, Provi-Soir, Winks, Winks Express, Pinto, Red Rooster, and Top Valu. **Steinberg:** Miracle Mart, Valdi, Price Clubs. **Safeway:** Woodwards, Food for Less. **A&P/Dominion:** Super Fresh, Sav-A-Centre, Farmer Jack.

3. CLEANERS

HE AVERAGE CANADIAN HOME *plays host every year to about 45 aerosol sprays and another 24 non-aerosol cleansers, solvents, spot removers, deodorants, and polishes. Some experts say as much as 30% of the average family's weekly shopping bill goes to pay for cleaners.*

▲▲▲▲▲▲▲▲▲▲▲▲▲▲▲

Most of these products contain, in varying amounts, substances toxic to health or to the environment. There are cancer-causing agents, compounds that affect the central nervous system (the brain), chemicals that can cause birth defects, and others dangerous to those with heart disease or respiratory disorders. Once they've passed through our kitchens and bathrooms, and through our sewer systems or garbage dumps, these same chemicals can disrupt the delicate ecology of our waterways and marine life, despoil our soil and groundwater, and find their way, all too quickly, back into our kitchen taps.

We buy these complex chemical concoctions largely because manufacturers have convinced us that our bodies and our homes need to be shielded from an onslaught of germs and bacteria that plain old soap and water are too weak to hold back. In fact, everyday "house-

▲▲▲▲▲▲▲▲▲▲▲▲▲▲▲

hold germs" do little or no harm to us and indeed have their own helpful roles to play in the domestic ecosystem. The basic cleaning agents that have served us for generations provide all the sanitation we need, at much lower risk to the environment and to ourselves. Bleach and other chemicals that kill germs continue their disinfecting action once they're in the sewer system, thereby inhibiting the work of the bacteria that water treatment systems depend on.

Homemade cleaners can be substituted for almost all commercial products; they are always safer and usually much cheaper. Do-it-yourself cleaners for most purposes can be made from just six major ingredients (see box) plus a few other items, all easily found in supermarkets, paint stores, or hardware stores. Many books and guides are now available with non-polluting home recipes for almost every conceivable cleaning chore; the recipes in this chapter come from *The Natural Formula Book for Home and Yard* (Rodale Press).

Probably the most important ingredient for environment-friendly cleaning

"I've been to day-school, too," said Alice; "You needn't be so proud as all that."

"With extras?" asked the Mock Turtle a little anxiously.

"Yes," said Alice, "we learned French and music."

"And washing?" said the Mock Turtle.

"Certainly not!" said Alice indignantly.

"Ah! Then yours wasn't a really good school," said the Mock Turtle in a tone of great relief.

"Now at ours they had at the end of the bill, 'French, music, and washing – extra.'"

"You couldn't have wanted it much," said Alice; "living at the bottom of the sea."

Lewis Carroll, *Alice's Adventures in Wonderland*

wrap some cloves and a cinnamon stick in cheesecloth, put it in a pot of boiling water, and let it simmer on the stove for a while. A lighted beeswax candle can burn gaseous odours away.

✳ ✳

All-Purpose Cleaners

Commercial liquids used for floors and general household cleaning contain varying combinations of toxins. The "heavy-duty" versions have higher concentrations of these substances, which include toluene, acetone, and xylene; some include zinc stearate, a known carcinogen.

These two recipes will provide safe, lower-cost cleaners for bathroom fixtures, floors, tiles, and painted walls. They will also deodorize drains. After washing, rinse surfaces with clear water.

ALL-PURPOSE CLEANER NO.1	ALL-PURPOSE CLEANER NO. 2
125 mL ammonia	50 mL baking soda
75 mL washing soda	250 mL ammonia
4 L warm water	125 mL white vinegar
	4 L warm water

Two brands available chiefly in health-food stores are *Nature Clean* (from **Frank T. Ross & Sons**) and *Infinity* (**Jedmon Products**). *Murphy's Oil Soap* makes a good, biodegradable cleaner for wood. Most of the manufacturers listed on page 56 have all-purpose cleaners, too.

✳ ✳

Bathroom Disinfectants

The sprays on your supermarket shelves are unnecessary and harmful; they contain phenols, cresol, and formaldehyde. Regular cleaning with the all-purpose cleaners listed above will keep your bathroom fixtures "disinfected."

✳ ✳

Bleach

Bleach is corrosive and must be kept out of the reach of children. Use commercial bleaches sparingly; although the contents of various brands differ, most contain some ingredients that contribute to water pollution.

For delicate fabrics that cannot be exposed to chlorine bleach, try:

HYDROGEN PEROXIDE BLEACH
1 part hydrogen peroxide
8 parts water
Soak garments in this solution, then rinse.

✳ ✳

Descalers

Removing the scale that accumulates in your kettle or iron will increase its energy efficiency by helping it to work faster. There are commercial products for descaling appliances, but vinegar and water will do the trick more cheaply.

Use a solution of one part white vinegar, two parts water. Pour some into your electric kettle and let it boil; rinse the kettle thoroughly. For your iron, pour in some of the solution and let it stand for 30 minutes; rinse several times.

Probably the most important ingredient for environment-friendly cleaning is the one manufacturers want us to avoid: elbow grease.

> **" Everyday 'household germs' do little or no harm to us and indeed have their own helpful roles to play in the domestic ecosystem "**

is the one manufacturers want us to avoid: elbow grease. The physical component of cleaning – the sweeping, the wiping, the mopping, the churning action in your washing machine– is often more effective than the chemical component. When you make your own cleaners, you contribute, too, to an overall savings in resources: lower use of industrial power, fewer raw materials con-

sumed, less packaging to throw away.

Also worth considering are the more environmentally acceptable household products that have been available for years in health-food stores and that are now beginning to appear in supermarkets, as consumer pressure grows. See page 56 as well as the item-by-item listings for alternatives to the big-name commercial brands.

ALONG THE SHELVES

Aerosols

Many commercial cleaning products are packaged in aerosol cans. Although only one aerosol can in ten still contains CFC propellants, the government does not require manufacturers to indicate CFCs on the labels – so you won't always be able to tell which cleaners have CFCs and which don't. Avoid buying *any* aerosols if you want to be safe.

Non-CFC aerosols can be hazardous, too. Many contain nitrous oxide, organic solvents, ketone, or acetone – all substances that present a variety of serious health hazards, including the risk of carcinogenesis and brain damage. Furthermore, the aerosol format delivers the contents of the can in a fine mist, which you will inhale; that means that whatever toxins lurk inside the product can penetrate your bloodstream with great speed, via your lungs.

A final reason not to buy aerosols is the difficulty of disposing of them. Full or empty, with or without CFCs, all aerosol cans are explosive. They can blow up in an incinerator, in a garbage truck (injuring sanitation workers), or even in the depths of a landfill site. For proper disposal of aerosols and other household hazardous waste, see Chapter 7.

Air Fresheners

Air fresheners," both sprays and solids, are frivolous at best and dangerous at worst. They coat your nasal passages with an oily film that prevents you from smelling things you don't like, or they simply mask the unwanted odour with a much stronger one. Some use chemicals that actually numb the nerves you use to smell. They also contain a wide variety of toxic substances that you would inhale along with the fragrance.

There are simpler and safer alternatives. Start with good ventilation in your bathroom, kitchen, and bedrooms. A dish of potpourri is harmless, attractive, and chic, and can be bought in bulk rather than in wasteful plastic packaging. Or

6
1 2 3 4 5 6

S·A·F·E·R SUBSTANCES

These are the Big Six of environment-friendly cleaning. All are safer than their manufactured chemical counterparts, but some still need to be handled with care.

VINEGAR
removes mildew, stains, and wax buildup. Use it to clean coffeepots, glass, paintbrushes, grout, windows, and fireplaces.

PURE SOAP
cleans everything from dishes to cars.

BAKING SODA
the all-round champion. Baking soda cleans, deodorizes, scours, polishes, removes stains, and softens fabrics. Use it on plastic, vinyl, carpeting, and upholstery; on silver and stainless steel; inside refrigerators; down drains…

BORAX
cleans wallpaper, painted walls, and floors. It deodorizes, removes stains, and boosts the cleaning power of your detergents.

WASHING SODA
cleans clothing and softens water. But it is moderately toxic. Wear gloves and use it in well-ventilated areas to avoid irritation of mucous membranes.

AMMONIA
a hardworking liquid, it cleans carpets and linoleum, copper and enamel, and most appliances. Ammonia can irritate the skin and the eyes, so wear gloves and use it in a well-ventilated area. **Never mix it with chlorine bleach; the mixture creates a poisonous gas.**

These ingredients, on their own or in the recipes in this chapter, can become your household staples. You can make up economy-size batches of various cleaners in the strengths you need, and store them in reusable containers. One factor to consider when mixing your formulas is what sewage treatment is like in your area: at the cottage or in municipalities with no sewage treatment, go easy on the ammonia and the bleach.

DETERGENTS

In the 1960s and 1970s, countless television documentaries alerted consumers and governments to the dangers of phosphates in laundry, dish, and automatic dishwasher detergents. Phosphates are not harmful in themselves; they are basic fertilizing agents that generally benefit plant life. But the amounts of phosphates we have been adding to the ecosystem are too much of a good thing.

In places where there are no sewage treatment plants, phosphate-based detergents help create a proliferation of nutrients. This excess of nutrients causes "algae bloom" in our waterways. As the algae grow and spread, they use up oxygen in the water, and the marine life dies.

Once the public outcry reached the manufacturers' ears, many of us assumed that phosphates would be removed from commercial detergents. In fact, only a few restrictions were imposed, and most detergents continue to pose a threat to the environment.

Phosphates, in any case, are only part of the problem. Unless the package says otherwise, your commercial detergent probably contains a variety of other chemical agents that may improve the brightness of your laundry but will contribute to the pollution of your water. NTA (nitro-tri-acetic acid) and EDTA (ethylene diamino-tetra-acetate), for instance, join with heavy metals in the water to form compounds that do not biodegrade well and are difficult for purification systems to remove.

Laundry Detergents

In Canada, laundry detergents have been restricted to no more than 5% phosphate content since 1972. Pure soaps, such as *Ivory*, have always been phosphate-free. *Ivory Snow* is also enzyme-free.

Some well-known brands are phosphate-free in the United States but not in Canada: stock up on *All-Temperature Cheer*, *Tide Liquid*, *Wisk*, and *All* if you have access to American goods. (*Tide Powder* with the code "O" on the label has less than 0.5% phosphates; the formulations with codes "L" and "P," however, have higher phosphate levels than the Canadian Tide Powder.)

Loblaws and **Miracle Foodmart** both carry 100% phosphate-free detergents under their house labels. **Amway**'s *Kool Wash* is a biodegradable, no-phosphate detergent for fine fabrics. The standard Amway laundry detergent has 1.8% phosphates. See also page 56.

To switch from commercial detergents to a more responsible solution, you will first have to get rid of the detergent residues now in your clothes. Use hot water and 50 mL washing soda for each load; do this once for all your laundry, then switch to:

LAUNDRY POWDER

250 mL pure soap flakes or powder
25 to 50 mL washing soda

If you have really hard water in your area, increase the amount of washing soda – it's a very efficient water softener.

Almost all household cleaning products – pure soap is the exception – are poisonous to some degree. Many are lethal, and very few have child-resistant or child-proof packaging. What's worse, studies have shown that most cleaning products have inadequate or even *incorrect* information on their labels about first aid and antidotes to counter their effects. So if you have even the slightest suspicion that your child has swallowed or inhaled a cleaning product, or gotten some on his or her skin, don't rely on the label: call for medical help *immediately*. Take the product package or container with you to the phone, and to the hospital. Take a few minutes today – *before* the need arises – to find the phone number of the poison control centre in your community. If it's not in the phone book, your family doctor or the nearest hospital will be able to help you find it. Keep the number next to the phone and make sure everyone in your family knows what to do in a poison emergency.

Enzymes

Some manufacturers have replaced some or all of the phosphate in their detergents with a variety of "enzymes." Enzymes are biodegradable in our water systems and harmless to the environment. They are not normally harmful to health but can cause allergic reactions in a small fraction of the population.

Powders with enzymes have a fine dust that may affect asthma sufferers. Since manufacturers are not required to show enzyme content on labels, households with asthmatic or hyper-allergic members should avoid powder detergents altogether in favour of liquids.

The Canadian government has placed no restrictions on phosphate content in dish detergents.

Dish Detergents

Dish detergents do not have phosphates in their formulations. As a result, the government of Canada has placed no restrictions on phosphate content in liquid dish detergents.

The Canadian Green Consumer, however, may wish to make his or her own liquid dish detergent which contains no phosphates and is biodegradable. There also are environment-friendly detergents that can be bought. **Amway**'s *Dishdrops*, for instance, is biodegradable and contains no phosphates or solvents. You can also make your own easily.

DISH DETERGENT

500 mL grated hard bar soap or soap flakes

4 L water

Rub salad oil on the grater before grating bar soap; it will be easier to clean.

Place soap in a pot; add water and stir. Heat over medium heat until the mixture boils, stirring occasionally until the soap dissolves. Lower heat and simmer 10 minutes, stirring occasionally. Remove from heat and let cool. Store in a tightly covered container. (**Not for use in automatic dishwashers.**)

* * * * * * * * * * * * * * * * * * *

Automatic Dishwasher Detergents

Automatic dishwasher detergents are not restricted as to phosphate content, nor is labelling required.

The consumer magazine *Protect Yourself* studied some Canadian powder brands in 1985, with these results.

Brand	Phosphate Content
Electrasol	18%
Calgonite	19%
Steinberg	27%
Provigo	27%
Cascade	28%
Metro	28%
Pharmaprix	28%
All	30%
Sunlight	31%

Even the best of these products contains many times the phosphate level permitted in laundry detergent. Many brands have lower phosphate content in their American formulations, but the levels are still well above 5%.

Dish-a-matic, from **The Soap Factory**, has no phosphates or enzymes. **President's Choice** *Green Automatic Dishwashing Detergent* is phosphate-free. *Bio-Dish*, from **Prime Pacific** of Vancouver, is phosphate-free, chlorine-free, and biodegradable. Check pages 56 for other suppliers of environment-friendly detergents.

* * * * * * * * * * * * * * * * * * *

Drain Openers

Powders and liquids for clearing plugged drains usually contain corrosive sodium hydroxide. Along with oven cleaner, they are the most dangerous products in your cleaning cupboard – dangerous to both people and environment.

Try using a plunger first. If that doesn't suffice, this safe substitute should.

NON-CAUSTIC DRAIN OPENER

250 mL baking soda

250 mL salt

125 mL white vinegar

1 kettle boiling water

Pour baking soda, salt, and vinegar down drain and leave for 15 minutes. Pour on boiling water.

To keep your drains clear, pour about 50 mL salt down the drain, followed by a kettle of boiling water, once or twice a week. Instead of the salt, you could use 50 mL washing soda, or 50 mL baking soda plus 50 mL vinegar.

* * * * * * * * * * * * * * * * * * * *

Fabric Softeners

Adding 50 mL baking soda to the wash cycle, or 50 mL vinegar to the rinse cycle, will soften your laundry just as well as the costly commercial liquids.

As for fabric softener sheets, they are plastics – usually rayon – soaked with chemicals not identified on the label. You can eliminate static cling without them by tossing a small wet towel into the dryer a few minutes before the end of the cycle. Remove the garments and hang them up as soon as the dryer stops, and they'll be wrinkle-free, too

* * * * * * * * * * * * * * * * * * * *

Floor and Furniture Polishes

The hazards of these products lie in the naphtha and other chemicals you can inhale while using them. Pure beeswax is a suitable substitute when you want a glossy finish. Other polishes can be made easily.

FURNITURE POLISH NO. 1

This is for furniture that's been varnished, lacquered, or shellacked.

25 mL olive oil

15 mL white vinegar

1 L warm water

Mix ingredients and put into a spray bottle. The polish works best when warm; heat by letting the bottle sit in a pan of hot water. After applying, rub dry with a soft cloth.

FURNITURE POLISH NO. 2

Use this on furniture that doesn't have a protective hard coating.

15 mL lemon oil

1 L mineral oil

Put into a spray bottle. Spray on, rub in, then wipe clean.

HEAVY-DUTY POLISH FOR FLOORS AND FURNITURE

15 mL carnauba wax

500 mL mineral oil

Stir over low heat in a double boiler, cool, then apply with a soft rag. Carnauba wax can be bought at auto-supply stores or hobby shops.

* * * * * * * * * * * * * * * * * * * *

Moth Repellents

Instead of smelly (and toxic) moth balls and flakes, sprinkle cedar chips or dried lavender in your closets.

WIPE IT CLEAN

Don't use paper towels: they're wasteful and often bleached, using processes that contribute to water pollution.

Better
reusable sheets such as J-Cloths.

Best
real cloths that are even more reusable, such as dishcloths or rags from old clothing. Sponges are good, too.

NEVER MIX CHLORINE BLEACH WITH AMMONIA

Deadly fumes will result. The same applies to any acid mixed with bleach, such as vinegar.

Oven cleaners are caustic to your skin, irritating to your lungs, and damaging to the environment.

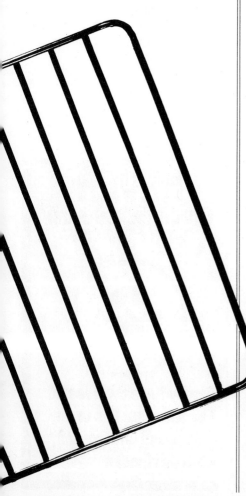

Oven Cleaners

Oven cleaners are among the very worst of cleaning products, especially in aerosol containers: they're caustic to your skin, irritating to your lungs, and damaging to the environment. After you've disposed safely of any commercial sprays you've accumulated (see Chapter 7), try this safer alternative.

OVEN CLEANER
250 mL ammonia
750 mL boiling water

Ammonia fumes are dangerous – although not as toxic as the gases given off by aerosol oven cleaners. The kitchen doors and windows should be open while you're using ammonia.

Warm the oven to 100° C. Place boiling water in the broiler pan on the bottom shelf. Put the ammonia in a small dish on the top shelf. Shut the oven door and leave overnight. Before you open the oven again, open all doors and windows, and leave the room while the vapours clear. Wash the oven with liquid detergent and water.

To clean the oven racks, put them in a large garbage bag with 250 to 500 mL of ammonia. Seal the bag with a twist tie and leave it outside for a couple of hours. Remove the racks and rinse them clean with a garden hose. In apartments with well-ventilated bathrooms, put the bag in the bathtub, then fill the tub with water when you untie the bag.

* * * * * * * * * * * * * * * * * *

Rug Cleaners

Dozens of toxic ingredients, many of them suspected or proven carcinogens or mutagens, are found in these convenience products (upholstery cleaners and spot removers are similar in composition).

Greasy soil and odours can be removed from carpets by sprinkling them generously with a mixture of two parts cornmeal and one part borax. Leave for an hour, then vacuum thoroughly. For spills, sponge the rug promptly with a mixture of vinegar and water. Then sponge with clean water, and pat dry.

* * * * * * * * * * * * * * * * * *

Silver Polish

A clean, low-cost alternative is to soak silver items in this solution until they are clean.

SILVER CLEANER
1 L warm water
5 mL baking soda
5 mL salt
small piece of aluminum foil
Put in a new piece of foil whenever the old one turns black.

* * * * * * * * * * * * * * * * * *

Spot Removers

These convenience products contain numerous toxins, carcinogens, and suspected carcinogens. It's wiser to get that shirt with the gravy stain into the wash as soon as possible. Here are just a few of the many home-style remedies.

For Grease

Rub the stain with a damp cloth dipped in borax. Or apply a paste of cornstarch and water; let it dry and brush it off.

For Ink

For an ink stain on white fabric, wet the fabric with cold water and apply a paste of lemon juice and cream of tartar. Let it sit for an hour, then wash as usual.

For Red Wine

Clean immediately with club soda.

Starch

Cornstarch provides a cheap, non-aerosol alternative to spray starch.

STARCH

15 mL cornstarch

250 mL water

Combine ingredients in a pump spray bottle and shake vigorously. You can adjust the proportions to get the degree of stiffness you prefer.

* * * * * * * * * * * * * * * * *

Toilet Bowl Cleaners

Liquid cleaners for toilet bowls often contain toxins such as quartenary ammonium compounds. The solid drop-in tablets and over-the-rim devices contain sodium bisulphide and disinfectant, as well as useless dyes in many cases. A safe all-purpose cleaner (see page 50) will keep the toilet clean if used regularly.

To remove stains, mix borax and lemon juice to a paste. Wet the sides of the toilet bowl, rub on the paste, and let it stand for about two hours before scrubbing off.

For regular cleaning, use:

AMMONIA/PEROXIDE TOILET BOWL CLEANER

5 mL household ammonia

250 mL hydrogen peroxide

2 L water

Mix ingredients in a bucket and pour mixture into toilet. Let stand for 30 minutes, then scrub toilet bowl with long-handled brush and flush. The cleaner can be left in the bowl for several hours if needed to remove hard stains.

Tub & Tile Cleaners

Foams and liquids for bathroom cleaning can be replaced by an all-purpose cleaner (see page 50).

Baking soda and a damp cloth will clean a tub as efficiently as commercial scouring powders, which may contain bleach, phosphate builders, or corrosive ingredients. Use an old toothbrush to get at the grout.

For a general-purpose scouring powder, try this recipe.

SCOURING POWDER

50 mL pure soap flakes or powder

10 mL borax

375 mL boiling water

50 mL whiting (a chalk powder)

Dissolve the borax and soap in the boiling water. Cool to room temperature, add whiting, and pour into a sealed plastic or glass container. Shake well before using. If you want it to be more abrasive, add more whiting, 15 mL at a time until it's right for you.

* * * * * * * * * * * * * * * * * *

Window & Glass Cleaners

Ammonia is the most common active ingredient in commercial brands. It's poisonous. Vinegar is one tried-and-true substitute; old newspapers are another.

For heavy-duty use – greasy kitchen windows, stove tops, and the like – here's an alternative.

WINDOW AND GLASS CLEANER

28.5 mL cornstarch

250 mL household ammonia

250 mL white vinegar

4.5 L water

MOST LIQUID CLEANING PRODUCTS are 95% water – but they cost a lot more! Included in the 5% "active ingredients" are costly but useless substances such as perfumes and dyes.

If your clothes develop STATIC CLING while you're wearing them, flip up the hem and shake a few drops of water on the inside surface. Use the plants' spray-mister if it's handy. Static cling is much more common with artificial fibres, like rayon, nylon, and polyester. Wear more natural fibres – cotton, wool, silk – and your clothes will hang more naturally.

Better CHOICES

Talk to your local retailers if you don't see the products you want – let them know there's a demand for cleaner, healthier cleaners.

A wide range of more environment-friendly cleaning products can be found in health-food stores, in some supermarkets, and through direct-sales agents. Talk to your local retailers if you don't see the products you want – let them know there's a demand for cleaner, healthier cleaners.

Amway

Local Amway representatives are listed in the phone book; the products are not sold in retail outlets. Amway's liquid organic cleaner is biodegradable and can be used for everything from floors to clothes. Other products include dish and laundry detergents.

Ecover Ecologically Safe Bio-Degradable Cleaners

These products, made in Belgium, are very popular with environmentalists in Western Europe and Britain. For the most part, they are vegetable-based cleaners, which are readily biodegradable in the environment. They are carried by many health-food stores, and Loblaws is test-marketing them.

Shaklee

This is another firm using sales agents only. If you can't find a representative listed in your phone book, you can get a catalogue by writing to Shaklee Canada Inc., 952 Century Drive, Burlington, ON L7L 5P2.

Shaklee's Basic L line of cleaning products contain no phosphates, no borates, and no enzymes.

The Soap Factory

The Soap Factory has a full line of environment-friendly products, such as laundry soaps, dish detergents, automatic dishwasher powder, bathroom cleaners, and all-purpose cleaner. They do not use phosphates or enzymes. Soap Factory products are distributed across the country in health-food stores and some IGA stores.

Also available are *Double Team* products (from the U.S.), *Auro* products (from West Germany), and *Cooperative La Balance* products (made in Montreal).

THINK GREEN WHEN YOU CLEAN

DRY CLEANING

The solvents used by dry cleaners are hazardous to the environment, especially if they find their way into groundwater. About 80% of operators use perchlorethylene, known as "perc," which is a hazardous and potentially carcinogenic chemical. Most of the others use varsol, a petroleum distillate. Some cleaners use a fluorocarbon called F-113, which harms the earth's ozone layer.

Cleaning solvents are regularly filtered and distilled to be re-used, but the process is not always efficient and a lot of perc gets into sewers or into the air without recycling. Moreover, even careful distillation produces sludge and used filters that are loaded with perc, and these are often discarded in landfills. There the perc rinses toxins out of the other garbage and moves them into the soil.

The technology is available for dry cleaners to retrieve and reuse up to 99% of their perc; operators who do so find their costs reduced dramatically. Whatever remains in the sludge can be incinerated by hazardous waste specialists – but only if the operator doesn't dump it in the garbage first.

Regulations and practices vary from province to province. Dry cleaners in the Atlantic provinces are farthest ahead, after a serious problem of groundwater contamination was discovered a few years ago. Operators are forbidden to dump waste in landfills and must show proof of safe, legal disposal. British Columbia cleaners also seem to be practising safe disposal. Green Consumers in these provinces can rest easy when their clothes are at the cleaners.

Most other provinces have good regulations, but enforcement is generally lax. Many operators still use landfill disposal. The best way for you to find out what your local cleaner does with contaminated waste is to ask – and you may be pleasantly surprised. Some cleaners have certificates on their walls, showing that their waste is carted away by a licensed shipper such as **Safety-Kleen.**

These dry cleaners practise responsible disposal of hazardous waste.

Bellingham
Montreal

Miss Brown's
Montreal

Langley Parisienne
Ontario

Perth Services
Northern Ontario, Manitoba, Saskatchewan

Queen City
Saskatchewan

Page
Alberta

Fabricare
Alberta

Todd's
Alberta

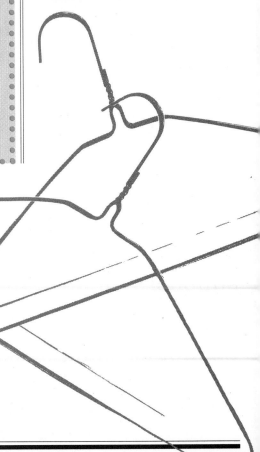

4. CLOTHING and TOILETRIES

s.quinlan

CLOTHING PRESENTS ESPECIALLY DIFFICULT PROBLEMS

for the Green Consumer who wishes to make informed choices. Once a garment arrives on the rack of your local boutique or department store, it probably has several labels: the brand label, a label indicating the fibre content and care instructions, and maybe a union label.

▲▲▲▲▲▲▲▲▲▲▲▲▲▲

But only in the rarest instances will you be able to find out by inspecting the item how the fibre was grown or spun and where the fabric was woven or knitted. These are the processes that do potential damage to the environment; some textile mills are notorious polluters.

As a rule of thumb, natural fibres – linen, silk, cotton, and wool – can be said to be preferable to artificial ones, such as acrylics. The cellulostic fibres, such as rayon, are derived from wood and other natural sources, but are heavily processed. Most artificial fibres are made from petroleum, a non-renewable resource and one that must undergo complex – and often polluting – processing before it can be used in textiles.

▲▲▲▲▲▲▲▲▲▲▲▲▲▲▲▲

Natural fibres, on the other hand, are often grown with the assistance of harmful pesticides and herbicides. Wool takes the smallest amount of chemicals to grow; the cotton industry, on the other hand, is the third-largest user of pesticides in the world. Some cotton farmers are switching to organic farming techniques, and consumers can encourage this trend by buying clothes made of organically grown cotton as soon as they become available through Canadian retailers. The **Roots Canada** chain is seeking suppliers of organic cotton and hoping to have a clothing line available in the near future.

There are other ways in which the environment-conscious consumer can be a better clothing buyer and user.

▬ Consider whether you are getting enough wear out of the clothes you already have. Could you repair it or remodel it rather than throwing it away?

"Good sense is as much marked by …a person's dress as by their conversation."

Catherine Parr Traill

The Roots Canada chain is seeking suppliers of organic cotton and is hoping to have a clothing line available in the near future.

> **"Wool takes the smallest amount of chemicals to grow. Cotton, on the other hand, is the third-largest user of pesticides in the world"**

■ If it's too far gone, could you use it for cleaning rags and polishing cloths? That's a better practice than buying wasteful paper towels.

■ If it's still wearable, but not by you, give it to a friend or relative, or to a charity rather than adding it to your garbage.

* *

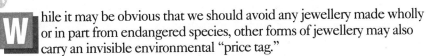

J·E·W·E·L·L·E·R·Y

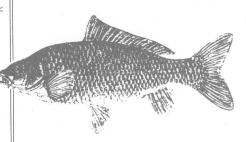

While it may be obvious that we should avoid any jewellery made wholly or in part from endangered species, other forms of jewellery may also carry an invisible environmental "price tag."

A great deal of cyanide is used in gold processing, and cyanide is particularly toxic to fish.

Pearls, whether harvested from the wild or cultured, are unlikely to have caused major environmental problems, but precious metals are another matter entirely. Take gold, which presents a number of major pollution problems. A great deal of cyanide is used in gold processing, for example, and this can cause widespread water pollution. Cyanide is particularly toxic to fish. Later in the process, when the sulphides are burned off, sulphur dioxide is produced, which can cause acid rain.

The production of diamonds and other gemstones has often been associated with such environmental problems as deforestation (whether to clear the land for the mine and associated buildings, or to provide pit props and fuel), soil erosion, silt accumulation in rivers, water pollution, air pollution, and excessive water use. In some areas, like the Okavango Delta in Botswana, a planned diamond mine is threatening to disrupt the sensitive water regime of a wildlife-rich region completely.

* *

Toiletries and Cosmetics

Walk into an outlet of one of the major drugstore chains anywhere in Canada and it is clear that the environmentalist pressures of the 1970s and 1980s *have* had an impact. For one thing, although you can still find glaring examples of over-packaging, there is less of it – for good economic reasons. But there still remain many environmental problems to be faced and positive choices to be made by the Green Consumer.

There has been growing concern about the use of animals in the safety testing of all types of products, but cosmetics have been particularly controversial because they are seen as non-essential. It is worth noting that just about every ingredient that goes into a perfume or cosmetic has had to be tested on animals. Three main types of tests are carried out:

4. CLOTHING and TOILETRIES

CRUELTY-FREE SHOPPER'S G·U·I·D·E

The Canadian Federation of Humane Societies and the Toronto Humane Society list the following brands of cruelty-free toiletries.

- Abracadabra • Aditi-Nutri-Sentials
- Aloegen • Aloette • Annemarie Borlind • Aubrey Organics
- Bare Escentuals • Beauty Without Cruelty • Biokosma • Body Shop
- Canada's All Natural Soap
- Carme • Chello Herbal Cosmetics
- Chenti • Country Comfort
- Clientele • Derma • Desert Essence • Dr. Grandel
- Dr. Hauschka • Faces
- Faunus Herbal Products
- General Nutrition Care Products
- Germination/Bushwacky
- Goldwell • Gruene Kosmetik Hain Pure Food Co. • I+M Natural Skincare • Infinity
- Innoxa • Isis • Jamieson's
- Jason Natural Products
- John Paul Mitchell Systems
- Jojoba Farms • Jurlique • Kappus
- Kiss My Face • KMS Inc.
- La Coupe • Leichner Stage Makeup • L'Occitane • Marks & Spencer • Mavala Nail Care
- Micro Balanced • Mill Creek
- Mira Linder • Naturade
- Natural Care   Nature Clean
- Nature Cosmetics • Nature de France • Nexxus • Ombra
- O'Naturel • Oriflame • Orjene Natural Products • Paul Penders
- Peelu Dentifrice • Phytoderm
- Rachel Perry • Schiff
- Schwarzkopf • Shikai • Sleepy Hollow Naturals • Soapberry
- Soap Works • Sombra
- Substance International
- Sunshine Fragrance Therapy
- Swiss Herbal • Tiki Cosmetics
- Tom's of Maine • Vita-Wave Products • Weleda
- Wolf Herbal Products

For Toxicity: the most common test is the "LD50" procedure, which aims to find the lethal dose– LD – of any given substance. A group of animals, normally small mammals like mice or rats, are force-fed with the substance, be it a bleach or a lipstick, until 50% die.

For Eye Irritation: the Draize eye test is the most notorious test among animal rights campaigners. Products such as shampoos or hair sprays are dripped or sprayed into the eyes of conscious rabbits. Their tear ducts are structured in such a way that they cannot flush such substances away. This procedure can continue for some days while scientists watch to see whether the eye is damaged.

For Skin Irritation: substances such as deodorants and face cream are applied to the shaved skin of animals, usually guinea pigs or rabbits. They are held in place for some time with adhesive tape to see whether there will be any irritation, inflammation, or swelling.

As pressure grows from lobbying groups and consumers to abandon animal testing, industries become more interested in alternative testing methods. In fact, many large North American cosmetic companies contribute to the work of the Johns Hopkins Center for Alternatives to Animal Testing in Baltimore, Maryland.

Avon, the world's largest cosmetics company, is a major donor and stopped all animal testing on its products in June 1989. Says Christina Gold, president of Avon Canada Inc., "I'm glad it's over. Animal testing is not something I ever wanted us to do, but I respected the reasons why we did it – you have to be certain in your heart that the product is safe for the consumer." At the same time, although Avon no longer tests it products on animals, it does not guarantee or require that its suppliers of raw ingredients refrain from animal testing.

Marks & Spencer has not used laboratory animals in the testing of cosmetics and toiletries for more than ten years; they are the only department store in Canada with a full line of cruelty-free products. The 73 Marks & Spencer stores across Canada carry 300 toiletries and cosmetics items. They choose only ingredients that have a proven safety record so that testing is no longer required; of course, some of those records might have been established by the use of animals in the past. Unlike most companies that follow a similar practice, Marks & Spencer guarantees that its suppliers refrain from animal testing.

Going cruelty-free is not an easy step for companies – product innovation may be severely stunted, production costs can be higher, reformulation can be more difficult if an ingredient becomes unavailable, and it is much harder to develop a new, exclusive substance. A company's claim that a product or ingredient has "never been tested on animals" is rarely true: usually the most that can be confirmed is that they themselves have not tested it on animals within the past, say, five years.

A growing number of suppliers try to avoid products that contain any animal ingredients, whether or not they come from endangered species. Animal products used in cosmetics include tallow, made from animal fat and used in some soaps and lipsticks; stearic acid, a solid fat found in soaps, shaving creams, and some foundation creams; and collagen and gelatin, produced by boiling down bones, skin, tendons, and connective tissue.

A fair number of cosmetic manufacturers still use products derived from rare species. Now that whale products like spermaceti (a white waxy substance from the head of the sperm whale, traditionally used in cosmetics) are banned in Canada, the attention of lobbying organizations has turned to creatures like the harmless, filter-feeding basking shark.

The livers of harpooned basking sharks are used to produce a refined oil called squalene, which has a low freezing point. A single six-tonne basking shark can produce 1,000 litres of oil. It is used for a range of consumer products, including cosmetic face creams. Companies using basking shark oil, including **Estée Lauder**, admit that other oils from fish and seeds could be used. But Estée Lauder, based in New York, has claimed that such oils do not have the proven safety or efficacy of squalene.

The elaborate packaging of cosmetics and toiletries is part of the costly marketing of these products; the layers of paper and plastic wrap ensure that the products arrive "fresh" and "sanitary" as well as advertising their carefully cultivated images. Manufacturers often spend as much as ten times the actual cost of the product on promotion.

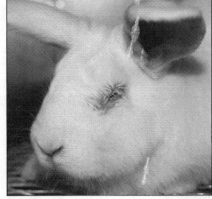

The Draize eye test is the most notorious among animal rights campaigners.

Antiperspirants and Deodorants

The use of CFCs as propellants in antiperspirants and deodorants has been banned in Canada since 1980. However, they can still be used as a slurrying agent (which keeps powders in suspension in gases) in powder antiperspirant sprays. Avoid all the spray products in favour of less wasteful forms of packaging, such as creams and sticks.

Baby Care

The most salient environmental issue in baby care products is the question of diapers: cloth or disposable?

Disposable diapers may be a great leap forward in convenience. But for the environment they're more like one baby step forward, ten giant steps back. On this score, mums and dads of Canada, your guilty conscience is right.

Disposables waste resources.

Making the 1.7 billion diapers that Canadian babies go through each year requires chopping down 2.4 million trees and converting 77,000 cubic metres of non-renewable natural gas into non-degradable polypropylene plastic. It costs the public $50 million a year to operate the landfill sites, monitor pollution, and replant forests to keep up with the surging tide of disposables.

Disposables clog landfills.

Between 2% and 5% (by weight) of the garbage sent to Canadian landfills is disposable diapers: about 240,000 tonnes a year. They constitute the single largest non-recyclable component of household garbage.

Disposables create health risks.

Human waste does not belong in landfill sites; that's why we have sewers. It's actually against the law to dump human waste anywhere but in sewers. Workers at landfill sites are exposed daily to these mounds of contamination. Community health may be at risk near older landfill sites where contamination is seeping into soil and groundwater.

There are risks for babies, too. Because babies wear each disposable longer than they would wear a cloth diaper, they are more prone to diaper rash with disposables. And if you buy disposables that contain chlorine-bleached pulp, there's a good chance that toxic dioxins and furans will be absorbed into your baby's skin.

Making the 1.7 billion diapers that Canadian babies go through each year requires chopping down 2.4 million trees.

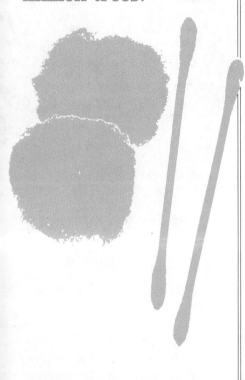

■ Disposables cost more than cloth.

Alternatives in Diapering, an information clearinghouse, has these estimates of the costs of diapering a baby for two and a half years.

① Cloth Diapers,
home laundering (including diaper covers, laundry soap, night liners, diaper pail, hydro costs for laundering):
$870

② Cloth Diapers,
diaper service (including diaper covers):
$1,200

③ Disposables
(including diaper liners):
$2,300

Diaper services are making a comeback as the number of parents using cloth diapers climbs a solid 11% each year. Check the Yellow Pages or write to Alternatives in Diapering (5015 - 46 Street, Camrose, AB, T4V 3G3) for the services in your area.

Do-it-yourself cloth diaperers will find a variety of brands available, from plain old-fashioned flat ones to fancier fitted ones with built-in fasteners. Cloth diaper covers such as *Nikky Pants* can replace pins and plastic pants, increasing convenience for parents and eliminating uncomfortable elastic for babies.

* * * * * * * * * * * * * * * * * * *

Bath Products

Foams, gels, and oils are often tested on animals; see page 60 for cruelty-free brand names. Some foaming products contain formaldehyde, which can irritate the skin.

Contraceptives

It is often forgotten that the first oral contraceptives were derived from substances found in wild yams, many of which are now locally extinct. Central American Indians knew of their contraceptive effect long before Western scientists recognized that they might become a mainstay of family planning, the number one priority worldwide for population control.

Some forms of contraception bring their own problems, however. The London *Sunday Times* reported that the increased use of condoms brought on by the spread of AIDS was causing problems in the countryside. Farmers are apparently worried about grazing animals choking on discarded condoms. If you engage in such rural pursuits, at least remember not to litter!

* * * * * * * * * * * * * * * * * * *

Cotton Balls & Swabs

The "cotton" in these items is actually rayon, which does not readily biodegrade. Carbon disulphide is discharged into the air during the production of rayon. Rather than these disposable products, use a washcloth.

* * * * * * * * * * * * * * * * * * *

Depilatories

Watch out for products in aerosols, which may contain CFCs.

* * * * * * * * * * * * * * * * * * *

Facials

Many pleasant facial masks and other cosmetics can be made from natural ingredients. Oatmeal and ground almonds both make good scrubs, for instance; they help degrease oily skin.

For homemade natural cosmetics recipes, look for *Kitty Little's Book of Herbal Beauty* (Penguin, 1987, $12.95) or *Cosmetics from the Earth: A Guide to Natural Beauty* by Roy Genders (Alfred Van Der Merck Editions, 1986, $24.99).

* * * * * * * * * * * * * * * * *

Hair Spray

Aerosol hair spray sold in Canada no longer contains CFCs. Gels are packaged less wastefully; consider switching.

* * * * * * * * * * * * * * * * *

Makeup

See the list on page 60 for cruelty-free makeup brands.

Some forms of makeup contain ingredients from rare plants and animals, but the lack of labelling requirements in Canada makes it difficult to know which products are better in this respect.

* * * * * * * * * * * * * * * * *

Moisturizers

When buying creams, lotions, and oils, look for the cruelty-free brands listed on page 60.

* * * * * * * * * * * * * * * * *

Nail Care

Nail polish and nail polish remover contain a host of synthetic chemicals, including acetone and toluene; remover, in particular, is very toxic. If you must use these products, be sure not to let them spill into water sources, where they could cause contamination.

Perfumes & Scents

Perfume production depends on animals in at least two main ways: for fixatives used to retain the scent, and, secondly, for safety testing.

Among the animal products used as fixatives are musk (taken from the musk deer), castoreum or civet (extracted from the anal sex gland of beavers or civet cats, respectively), and ambergris (from the intestines of the sperm whale). Both the musk deer and the sperm whale are endangered species. Unfortunately, because full product labelling is not required in Canada, it is generally impossible to find out what is in perfumes and other forms of scent.

The French perfume houses, which depend on many long-established recipes, are most likely to use rare, high-priced animal ingredients. Many other parfumiers have replaced such animal products, usually because of their scarcity and price rather than for humanitarian reasons. Many parfumiers have not used musk for more than 20 years, having switched to synthetics or vegetable materials.

Perfumes made by **The Body Shop** and **Beauty Without Cruelty** have not been tested on animals; also cruelty-free are *Passion by Elizabeth Taylor* and *Uninhibited by Cher.*

* * * * * * * * * * * * * * * * *

Shampoos and Conditioners

Look for cruelty-free brands: see page 60.

One of the great business *and* environment success stories of recent years is **The Body Shop,** an international franchise chain founded by Anita Roddick in 1976. Canada has 72 Body Shop stores selling the company's own environmentally acceptable personal care products.

Among the Body Shop's attractions for Green Consumers are:
* its formulation of products from natural ingredients, many of which are from Third World countries.
* its refusal to sell products whose ingredients have been tested on animals during the last five years
* its use of minimum packaging.
* its support for educational programs and projects around the world that focus on Third World and environmental issues

Each store has a book listing the ingredients in all Body Shop products. If a particular ingredient is a genuine "trade secret," it won't be listed in the book, but the Body Shop will release the information if requested by a doctor on behalf of a client who might be sensitive.

Shaving Aids

If you want to take things to extremes, the greenest approach to facial hair is probably to grow a beard. For those who shave, however – more than 90% of men – here are the options.

If you wet-shave, beware of CFC-propelled shaving cream, disposable razors, and excessive packaging. (Particularly undesirable products are the packs of use-'em-once disposables.) Also avoid shaving brushes with badger bristles or ivory handles. On the other hand, electric razors run on electric power, with all its attendant pollution problems. On balance, however, the electric shaver seems to come out on top.

* * * * * * * * * * * * * * *

Soaps

Many cruelty-free soaps and soaps made with natural ingredients are available.

A noteworthy Canadian product called *Canada's All Natural Soap* is available in health-food stores. It contains only lye, water, vegetable oil, and natural essences such as chamomile and marigold –no dyes, bleaches, or synthetic perfumes. Its manufacturing process is non-polluting.

Tampons and Sanitary Pads

Contrary to manufacturers' claims, it is *not* safe to flush tampons down the toilet. Sewage systems cannot deal adequately with either the fibres in the tampons or the menstrual fluids they are used to absorb. Both tampons and sanitary pads should be disposed of with your garbage.

Some sanitary pads made with unbleached fibre are now available. **President's Choice** *Green Maxi Pads* (unscented), for example, are made with non-chlorine bleached fluff pulp. Look for pads and tampons with the least packaging; avoid tampons with plastic applicators and pads in individual plastic pouches.

* * * * * * * * * * * * * * * * *

Tissues

Washable cloth handkerchiefs are a better choice than throwaway paper tissues. For removing makeup, use a facecloth or sponge.

* * * * * * * * * * * * * * * * *

Toilet Paper

Look for toilet paper made from recycled paper.

The greenest approach to shaving is probably to grow a beard.

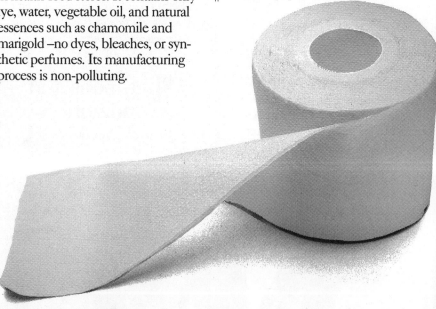

TOOTHPASTE

Toothpaste may be the last product to come to mind when you are thinking of environmental pollution, but the acid effluents produced during the manufacture of the titanium dioxide pigments used to make white toothpastes white are worth thinking about. These effluents have helped to make waterways near the manufacturing plants more acidic.

This is not a simple story of good and evil, however. Used in a wide range of paints, paper, plastics, inks, and man-made fibres, titanium dioxide has revolutionized some parts of the paint industry, where it has replaced materials like zinc oxide and lead. Unlike lead, it is completely non-toxic, and therefore a distinct improvement in terms of both health and environment. Furthermore, the two companies making titanium dioxide in Canada, N.L. Chem Canada and Tioxide Canada, are installing facilities to neutralize their acidic waste water. By 1991, white toothpaste and other products containing titanium dioxide should be back in the good books.

In the meantime, consider gel toothpastes, which contain less titanium dioxide, or natural-formula toothpastes made from ingredients such as oil of fennel, glycerine, chalk, and sodium laurel sulphate (from coconuts). *Weleda* and *Peelu* are two natural brands found in health-food stores.

* *

By 1991, white toothpaste and other products containing titanium dioxide should be back in the good books.

FOR MORE INFORMATION

Canadian Cosmetic, Toiletry and Fragrance Association
24 Merton St.
Toronto, ON
M4S 1A1

Canadian Animal Rights Network
P.O. Box 66,
Station O,
Toronto, ON
M4S 2M8

Canadian Federation of Humane Societies
102 - 30 Concourse Gate,
Nepean, ON
K2E 7V7

5. THE HOME

CANADIANS USE MORE ENERGY *per capita than any other people in the world, and they use a lot of it at home. In fact, Home Sweet Home is the third-biggest energy hog in the country (after industry and transportation), accounting for 18% of all energy consumed. And because most of this energy comes from the burning of fossil fuels, our homes are*

▲▲▲▲▲▲▲▲▲▲▲▲▲▲▲▲

major contributors to the tonnes of carbon dioxide that get spewed into the environment every day.

▲▲▲▲▲▲▲▲▲▲▲▲▲▲

"What use is a house if you haven't got a tolerable planet to put it on?"

Henry David Thoreau

The breakdown of residential energy use looks like this:

Space heating	67%
Water heating	17%
Appliances	14%
Lighting	2%

The average Canadian home gobbles about 40,000 kWh (kilowatt-hours) of energy a year. Most of it is simply wasted, primarily because of inefficient house design and construction practices, and inefficient furnaces, water heaters, and appliances.

And this isn't where the story ends. Everything inside your home, from construction materials to cake tins, accounts for more energy use in its manufacture. Many products are potential polluters, too. It all adds to the environmental load.

But the irony is that, besides being a giant energy-gobbler, Canada is also a

world leader in the design of energy-efficient houses. There's the R-2000 house, for example, developed under a federal program. Annual energy consumption runs at about 25,000 kWh, just over half the figure for a conventional home. Most of the savings comes from airtight design and construction to prevent heat loss.

And then there are high-performance homes like the Ontario Advanced House, a demonstration project in Brampton, Ontario, jointly sponsored by the provincial and federal energy ministries, the Fram Building Group,

Ontario Hydro, and the Canadian Home Builders Association. It's a normal-looking 250-square-metre house, but its annual energy consumption is just above 10,500 kWh, about a quarter what a conventional house uses. What makes the difference is state-of-the-art energy-efficient technology.

Both these projects show that Canadians can drastically reduce the energy their homes consume. That doesn't mean you need to run out tomorrow and buy an R-2000 house or undertake a complete home makeover. Simple retrofit measures – like sealing leaky windows, insulating a hot-water tank, having a furnace tuned up – can reduce energy consumption by 20% to 30%. And Green Consumers can save more energy by choosing wisely when they're shopping for wallboard or wall hangings.

Individual energy-saving efforts should focus first on where it hurts most – space heating.

* *

SPACE
HEATING

An investment of about $150 in sealing products and a do-it-yourself weekend can cut as much as 25% from the space-heating bill of a leaky house.

Two-thirds of the energy consumed in Canadian homes goes to space heating. This means that, during the winter, Canadian furnaces burning fossil fuels discharge into the environment enormous quantities of carbon dioxide and sulphur dioxide, two of the major culprits behind global warming and acid rain.

It's astonishing how much of the heat these furnaces produce simply goes to waste. It slips through cracks under doors, escapes through walls and attics, and flows up the chimney. Contrary to what many Canadians think, chilly draughts and cold feet are not inevitable features of winter in this country. The real villain here is house-construction practices developed in the heyday of cheap fuel and environmental ignorance.

There is a lot that individual energy consumers can do to spare the environment, and at the same time cut their energy bills and increase their wintertime comfort. Retrofit measures such as sealing air leaks, adding insulation, and upgrading or replacing windows can reduce by as much as 40% the energy a typical Canadian family uses to keep warm in the winter. The first step – and also the cheapest – involves caulking and weatherstripping all the spots where warm air escapes.

* *

Keeping the Heat In

I f you were to add up all the draughty leaks and cracks in a typical Canadian home, you would probably end up with the equivalent of a window-sized hole in the wall. Warm air escaping through cracks and crevices around windows and doors, basement walls, and other sites can account for 25% to 30% of your home's heat loss.

Sealing the air leaks in your home does involve an environmental trade-off: significant energy conservation versus small amounts of harmful by-products.

Sealants are based on synthetic chemicals; most contain solvents, and all of them produce environmentally detrimental effects during manufacture and disposal. And then there's the health issue. At least three days of good ventilation is required after the sealing job is finished to get rid of toxic vapours.

Weatherstripping involves less odious ingredients, but its use is restricted to only a few heat-loss sites – primarily the movable parts of windows and doors. Rubber weatherstripping products provide an effective and durable pressure seal; felt and foam products, on the other hand, have a poor performance record. There are two site-specific products that are well worth the few dollars they cost – electrical outlet gaskets, and door sweeps or thresholds that are attached to the bottom of exterior doors.

> Rubber weatherstripping products provide an effective and durable pressure seal; felt and foam products, on the other hand, have a poor performance record.

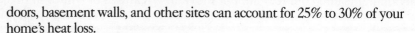

SEALING THE LEAKS		
Air Leakage Sites	**Heat Loss**	**Sealing Products**
Basement sill plate	25%	acrylic latex, butyl rubber, polyurethane foam
Exterior electrical outlets	20%	butyl rubber, acrylic latex
Windows	13%	silicone, polyurethane foam
Pipe and wire entrances	13%	polyurethane foam
Vents (bath, dryer, kitchen)	10%	butyl rubber
Baseboards, light fixtures, electrical outlets, attic hatches	7%	silicone, acrylic latex
Exterior doors	6%	silicone, weatherstripping
Fireplaces	6%	insulated fireplace covers

If your energy-saving plans include adding insulation, you should consider installing an air-vapour barrier at the same time. It's a big job but will cut draughts and energy waste throughout the house to a bare minimum. The barrier, usually a plastic sheet, stops air leakage and keeps water vapour from penetrating into walls and ceilings. About 20 L of moist air gets deposited in a typical home every day just from routine bathing, cooking, and breathing, and it can cause structural rot as well as compact insulation materials to the point where they lose much of their effectiveness.

Insulation

After caulking and weatherstripping to control the flow of warm and cold air in and out of your leaky house, the next step on your energy-conserving agenda is adding insulation to stop the direct flow of heat to the outside. The major escape routes are the walls, the roof and ceilings, and the foundation.

Before the oil crisis of the 1970s, few people worried about insulation, let alone how much they needed. Every five years or so since then, energy-efficiency experts have increased their recommended minimum levels. The following chart gives 1989 levels for new home construction.

RECOMMENDED MINIMUM RSI (R) LEVELS*				
Site	Zone A	Zone B	Zone C	Zone D
Walls	RSI4.9 (R28)	RSI6.3 (R36)	RSI7.0 (R40)	RSI7.0 (R40)
Basement walls	RSI2.1 (R12)	RSI2.8 (R16)	RSI3.5 (R20)	RSI4.2 (R24)
Roof/ceiling	RSI7.0 (R40)	RSI7.0 (R40)	RSI9.2 (R52)	RSI10.6 (R60)
Floor (over crawl spaces)	RSI5.6 (R32)	RSI7.0 (R40)	RSI7.0 (R40)	RSI7.0 (R40)

*RSI (metric)and R (imperial) are measures of thermal (heat flow) resistance

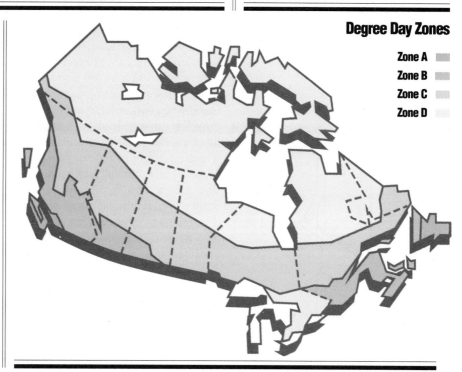

Degree Day Zones

Zone A
Zone B
Zone C
Zone D

As with most other products used in the home, decisions about insulation materials will involve an environmental trade-off. Most insulation materials are made from non-renewable resources and undergo an energy-intensive manufacturing process. The one exception is cellulose. The raw materials are recycled paper, sawdust, or wood chips, and processing is fairly simple. The one catch, however, is that cellulose can be installed only in attics and some walls. The other side of the environmental trade-off is, of course, substantial energy savings over the lifetime of a house. The best consumers can do is purchase the most appropriate materials for each area of the house and know what they are buying in order to ensure that the insulation materials are properly installed and sealed off from the interior of the house.

Insulation materials are manufactured from three primary types of ingredients:

1 Organic polymers. The nastiest of the lot, this group includes the now-banned urea formaldehyde foam insulation (UFFI), polyurethane and polyisocyanurate foam, and polystyrene boards. These materials use an expanding agent in the foaming process: Types 1 and 2 polystyrene use air; Type 4 polystyrene (also called extruded polystyrene), polyurethane, and polyisocyanurate use CFCs. Fortunately for the environment, CFCs will be banned substances soon; *how* soon was not clear at the time of writing. For both health and environmental reasons, these products should be avoided as much as possible.

2 Inorganic materials. This group includes another banned substance – asbestos-based insulation, now found only in houses built up to the early 1970s. (It should be examined by an asbestos-disposal specialist, who can tell you whether it is better to remove it or leave it in place.) Fibrous glass generally contains formaldehyde as a binder. The better choices among the inorganic-based insulating materials are mineral wool, vermiculite (made from expanded mica ore), and perlite (made from perlite ore). Their fine fibres and dust, however, can irritate the skin, eyes, and respiratory system. Careful installation and sealing, followed by thorough ventilation, are essential.

Most insulation materials are made from non-renewable resources and undergo an energy-intensive manufacturing process.

3 **Cellulose.** The best of the lot, insulation products in this category include sawdust, wood shavings, and cellulose fibre made from recycled newspaper – all renewable, non-toxic ingredients. They are the friendliest choices for wall cavities, ceilings, and attics.

All insulation products use various chemicals as binders, stabilizers, and fire retardants and to control mildew and pest infestations. These can cause health problems if the insulation is not thoroughly and properly sealed off from the interior of the house.

* *

Windows

In the average Canadian home, windows can account for as much as 25% of heat loss, which means that a quarter of your space-heating energy may literally be going straight out the window. You can recoup about half that loss by sealing the cracks and crevices where air rushes in and out (see pages 67-68). The other half gets lost in the flow of heat through the panes and frames of conventional windows. The only way of preventing that loss is by boosting the insulation value of your windows.

Standard double-glazed windows are very poor insulators; their R value is about one-tenth to one-sixth of the insulating value of the walls that surround them. The good news is that any effort you make to improve the R value of your windows translates directly into energy savings, not to mention increased comfort.

You can enhance the thermal resistance of double-glazed windows by installing "interior storm windows." One type is the *Window Insulator Kit* made by **3M**. It includes thin sheets of transparent polyethylene, which you cut to fit your windows. Each sheet is held in place by sticking the edges to the window trim or frame with adhesive tape, then shrinking it tight using heat from a hair dryer. The insulator adds another layer of dead air, between the glass and the plastic. A kit that will cover five 1-m by 1.6-m windows costs about $20. Most conservation stores and many of the larger hardware outlets now carry a range of these products.

A nother option is movable window insulation that you open during the day to trap passive solar energy and close at night to prevent heavy nighttime heat loss. Products include window shades and blinds that are outfitted with an insulated backing material and shutters that contain a polyurethane core. For best results, they should all have a vapour barrier, a reflective surface, and a device that provides a tight seal with the window frame or trim. When shopping for these products, ensure that what you are paying for is insulation and not fancy fabrics.

Insulating values for such products as Window Warmers and Window Quilts are about R 5.5 to R 5.8. A *Window Warmer* for a 1.3-m by 1.6-m window costs about $235, not including the decorator fabric for the outer layer; for a 1-m by 1.3-m *Window Quilt*, the cost is about $340 installed. Some manufacturers offer do-it-yourself manuals and kits.

If you are renovating an older home or building a new one, consider installing high-performance windows. There has been a leaps-and-bounds advance in window technology in the past 15 years. Researchers found that adding a very thin, low-emissivity (low-E) coating of metal and metal oxide to glass drastically reduced radiant heat loss in winter. To cut down on heat lost by convection and conduction, air spaces between panes were filled with a heavier inert gas (argon or krypton); low-conduction spacers (made from

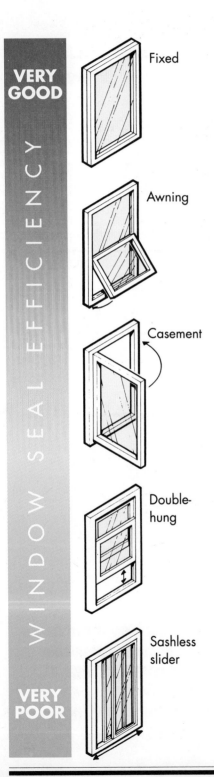

WINDOW SEAL EFFICIENCY

VERY GOOD

Fixed

Awning

Casement

Double-hung

Sashless slider

VERY POOR

polybutylene foam, fibreglass, or silicone) were inserted between the panes, replacing the highly conductive aluminum spacers used in conventional windows; a second sealant was added to guard against air leakage in the window unit; finally, frames and sashes were constructed from low-conduction materials such as wood. An added attraction of these high-performance windows is that the same technology that prevents heat loss in January also prevents heat gain in July.

The best RSI value you can expect from a top-of-the-line conventional double-glazed unit is 0.35 (R 2). With a high-performance double-glazed window, you'll get twice that, and twice again with a triple-glazed high-performance unit. Double-glazed high-performance windows cost about 8% more than conventional units; triple-glazed ones would cost 50% more than the comparable double-glazed models. Prices for high-performance windows are falling as the manufacturing technology improves, so your payback period will get shorter. Your savings in heating costs will vary according to the climate in your area, but there is no doubt that your bills will go down.

For more information, write **Repla Ltd.** (482 South Service Rd. E., Oakville, ON, L6J 2X6) or **Loewen Windows** (Box 2260, Steinbach, MB, R0A 2A0), considered by many to be Canada's state–of–the–art makers of high–performance windows. **The Insulated Glass Manufacturers' Association of Canada** (Box 1681, Brantford, ON, N3T 5V7) knows of others.

Whichever alternative you choose to upgrade the insulating level of your windows, if funds are limited, focus first on the windows that will make the most difference: those that trap solar energy (mostly south-facing windows) and those that are big losers of heat (large windows, north-facing windows, and windows in direct line with the prevailing winter wind).

* *

Retrofitting an Older Heating System

A conventional heating system can be inefficient for a number of reasons: incomplete combustion when the burner is not properly tuned; poor heat transfer when the heat exchanger is dirty; heat loss through the ductwork; air flow up the chimney when the furnace isn't running. You can improve your heating system's efficiency by following a regular maintenance program, by ensuring that the heat is being properly distributed, and by upgrading or downsizing the furnace.

Maintenance. All heating systems require regular maintenance for safety and efficiency. Oil systems should be serviced every year by an oil-burner mechanic; it's about a two-hour job that involves cleaning and lubricating parts, checking safety controls, and tuning up the burner. Because gas burns cleaner than oil, gas systems need to be serviced every two years by a certified gas fitter who inspects and cleans the pilot light, the main flame, and the burner, among other things.

Improving heat distribution. There are a few small, do-it-yourself steps that will help move the heat efficiently from the burner through the ducts to where it's needed. Dirty furnace filters restrict the flow of air; they should be cleaned or replaced once a month. Check the furnace fan belt to ensure that it's tight enough to drive the fan properly. Adjust the manual dampers in the heating ducts and the heat registers in the rooms to distribute the heat where you want it. Close dampers and registers in rooms and areas of the house where heat is not required. Seal the joints in the ductwork with duct tape or silicone caulking to prevent heat loss.

INDOOR INSECT PESTS

Even if you've never sprayed insecticide in your home, you probably have some – in your new or newly cleaned carpets, for instance, which are often treated, or in wallpaper (it's in the adhesive). If you'd rather not add to the toxic vapours in your home, you might want to use safer means of dealing with common insect pests.

First try prevention:

Follow strict sanitary practices, seal cracks and other possible entry areas, and fix plumbing leaks and other areas of undue moisture.

If defence tactics fail, try natural remedies:

Cedar oil, available in manual spray pumps, repels fleas and other insects; salt or red pepper sprinkled on counters and across doors or windowsills is a barrier for ants; freezing clothing or exposing it to hot sun for two days kills moth larvae; and a vinegar-water solution wiped on kitchen counters repels flies (the old-fashioned fly swatter works, too). A borax-type bait applied in traps or drops is a safer alternative for cockroach control, but don't use it around small children or pets.

It's also worth checking out some new biological pesticides, which target specific pests without affecting higher life forms or generally toxifying the environment (they break down easily). Methoprene, for instance, is an insect growth regulator that halts flea growth at the larva stage, thereby preventing reproduction.

Upgrading. There are a number of efficiency-enhancing devices that you can add to an older oil furnace to cut down energy consumption. Retention-head burners improve combustion and may reduce your fuel bill by 10% to 25%. A delayed-action solenoid valve ensures cleaner burning for greater efficiency, and a flue damper installed in the vent pipe prevents heat from escaping up the chimney. Consult a heating contractor before making any decisions about these devices; compatibility and the age and efficiency of your system may rule out this sort of upgrading.

Downsizing. If your oil burner is not running almost constantly on really cold days, you are probably wasting fuel on a furnace that produces more BTUs (British thermal units) than your home can use. Many of the furnaces installed in Canadian homes never reach their optimum level of efficiency because they are sitting idle most of the time. And when they are not running, indoor air and heat escape up the chimney. Downsizing involves reducing the furnace's firing rate or installing a smaller nozzle to restrict the flow of oil. Fuel savings can amount to 10%. To find out if these are feasible options for you, consult a heating contractor.

* *

Energy-Efficient Furnaces

If you have a cast-iron octopus in the basement or some other furnace that has clearly seen better days, it may well be time to begin hunting for one that uses a lot less energy to produce the amount of heat you need. An important point to keep in mind: eliminating the major sources of heat loss in your house by sealing air leaks and adding insulation will drastically reduce your home's heating requirements, and fewer BTUs mean less energy consumed.

How efficiently a furnace performs is measured by its AFUE (annual fuel utilization efficiency). For example, the AFUE of a conventional oil furnace is about 60%; the rating for a new mid-efficiency furnace ranges between 75% and 88%; and the AFUE of high-efficiency oil furnace is over 90%. These much higher ratings are partly attributable to what's known in the furnace trade as "efficiency-enhancing equipment" – things like flame-retention burners, delayed-action solenoid valves, automatic flue dampers, and condensing units. Other advanced features include ceramic or stainless steel combustion chambers and new, improved heat exchangers.

* *

Integrated Systems

If both your furnace and your water-heater are on their last legs, consider replacing them with an integrated space- and water-heating system. The integrated system has one heating unit that performs the work of two conventional units, with a lot less hardware – a big energy-saving advance for energy-efficient houses with relatively low space-heating requirements.

The *Habitair*, made by **Fibreglas Canada,** is an integrated system suitable for a 170- to 280-square-metre home with good insulation. The cost is $4,500 installed.

Furnace Efficiency
AFUE: Annual Fuel Utilization Efficiency (percent)

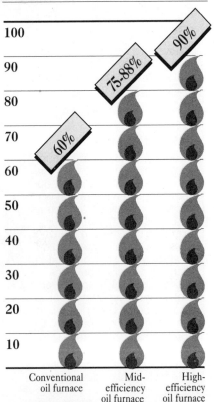

60%

75-88%

90%

| 100 | 90 | 80 | 70 | 60 | 50 | 40 | 30 | 20 | 10 |

Conventional oil furnace — Mid-efficiency oil furnace — High-efficiency oil furnace

Thermostats

By now, most consumers have acquired the habit of turning down their thermostats at bedtime and when no one is home. Lowering the thermostat just 5 °C during these periods can add up to a 14% reduction in your energy consumption.

A cost-effective investment for both old and new heating systems is a programmable device called a thermostat setback. With up to four setback adjustments possible in a 24-hour period, it allows you to automatically control the supply of heat – to keep your home at the lowest comfortable temperature throughout the day. There are a wide variety of automatic setbacks for each type of heating system; the more sophisticated ones offer weekday and weekend programming, weather monitoring, power reserves, and setback modules for a hot-water heater and air conditioner. Top-of-the-line purchases include: *Centratherm W*, a West German product distributed by **CanHort Engineering** (475 Mud Street West, Grassie, ON, L0R 1M0); *Pem Energy Myzer* from **Pem Energy Systems** (90 Pale Moon Crescent, Scarborough, ON, M1W 3H5); *Enerstat* from **Valera Electronics** (1733 St. Laurent Blvd., Ottawa, ON, K1G 3V4); and *Chronotherm Series 8000* from **Honeywell** (available from Honeywell dealers across Canada). Both Valera and Honeywell also offer heat-pump thermostats.

The location of your space-heating thermostat or automatic setback is important. It should be installed where it is not affected by direct sunlight, radiators, hot-air ducts, appliances, outside doors, or stairwells. The best place is on an inside partition wall where it can accurately register the temperature of the house.

* *

> **Lowering the thermostat just 5°C during certain periods can add up to a 14% reduction in your energy consumption.**

Heat Pumps

Because their energy source is clean, free, and inexhaustible, heat pumps are an exciting alternative to conventional heating and cooling systems.

Air-to-air heat pumps, the most commonly purchased variety, work best in the fall and spring; in most areas of the country you will probably still need a furnace for the coldest parts of winter. In warm weather the pump extracts heat from the inside and pumps it outside; in cool weather it extracts heat from the outside air and pulls it inside.

Ground-source heat pumps extract what's called "low-grade heat" (between -2° C and 10° C) from a few feet below the ground by passing a refrigerant gas through a compressor and two heat exchangers. In the first exchanger, the gas evaporates as it absorbs ground heat, and after moving through a compressor where its temperature is raised, it passes through the second exchanger where the heat is removed and pumped into the space-heating ducts. In the summer, the system is reversed to draw hot air out of the home. With the addition of another heat exchanger, this extracted hot air can be used for water heating. A groundwater heat pump operates on the same principle but extracts heat from underground aquifers.

If you are renovating an old house down to the bare bones or building a new one, installing a heat pump is worth considering, especially if you need a cooling system as well as a heating system. Annual energy savings with a heat pump in your home can be as high as 65%.

ANNUAL ENERGY SAVINGS WITH A HEAT PUMP CAN BE AS HIGH AS 65%

Air-to-air heat pumps cost $2,000 to $3,000 installed. Ground-source heat pumps range from $8,000 to $12,000 installed. **The Canadian Earth Energy Association** (228 Barlow Crescent, Dunrobin, ON, K0A 1T0) will answer all your questions about ground-source heat pumps and provide a list of suppliers.

* *

Ventilation

Ventilation isn't a problem if air leaks and draughts are common features of your housescape. Air moves very quickly and efficiently in and out of a leaky house; there's a complete change every 30 minutes to two hours.

To conserve energy, your house has to be as airtight as possible. But sealing all the sites where heat and cold exit and enter means that fresh air can't get in and stale air can't get out. You need to save energy; what you don't need is to be constantly inhaling a host of indoor pollutants.

Windows are the best indicators of whether a home is properly ventilated: if there is a lot of condensation on them, more ventilation is needed. If the ventilation problem isn't too acute, all that may be required is an intermittent running of kitchen and bathroom fans. Opening a window or two for short periods of time is not a good solution; it defeats all air-tightening efforts to conserve energy without necessarily providing adequate ventilation.

Consumers who want an accurate measurement of their home's airtightness should ask a heating or ventilation contractor to do a fan depressurization test (the cost is about $250). If the test results show less than two to three air changes per hour at a pressure differential of 50 pascals, the home needs a mechanical ventilation system that controls the flow of air in and out of the house.

Designers of energy-efficient homes have solved the air-quality and ventilation problems by installing heat recovery ventilators (HRVs). These air-to-air heat exchangers transfer as much as 75% of the heat from the stale air that is exhausted from the house to the controlled flow of air entering the house. The incoming fresh air reaches a temperature only a few degrees short of the household temperature. As an added benefit, a heat recovery ventilator also exhausts excessive moisture (from showers and cooking, for example) that can cause window condensation.

Heat recovery ventilators work equally well in new energy-efficient homes and in conventional homes that have been retrofitted for energy efficiency. In both, the recovery of heat from exhausted household air means a savings of at least $100 a year. An HRV that is approved for installation in R-2000 houses is your best bet. Look for a unit that has an efficiency rating of at least 75% at 0°C. A heating and ventilation contractor will steer you in the right direction. Best HRV buys include the *vanEE 2000 Plus*, the *AirChanger DRA 275*, the *Star 300 MPC-DV*, and the *Nutech Lifebreath 195-DCS* and *300*. These products cost $2,000 to $2,500 installed.

> Opening a window or two for short periods of time defeats all air-tightening efforts to conserve energy without necessarily providing adequate ventilation.

COMMON INDOOR POLLUTANTS

Pollutant	Source
Formaldehyde gas	Urea formaldehyde foam insulation, plywood, particleboard, carpets, furniture
Household chemicals	cleaning products, paint and paint solvents
Carbon monoxide, carbon dioxide, nitrogen oxides	furnaces, ranges, dryers, fireplaces, woodstoves

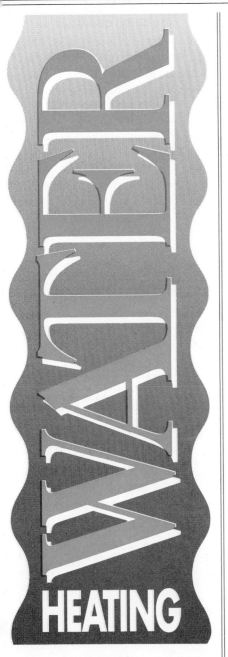

WATER
HEATING

Domestic water heaters are the second-heaviest users of energy in the average Canadian home. Between 17% and 20% of the energy consumed by most families goes to ensuring that an abundant supply of hot water is always available at the turn of a tap.

Conservative estimates of the daily hot-water use of a typical family of four range from 125 L to 250 L. Chances are pretty good, however,

that your family exceeds that limit just getting through its morning rush-hour routine. Running three five-minute showers, preparing breakfast, and turning on the dishwasher, for example, consumes 225 L of hot water – at an energy cost of 8.7 kWh of electricity.

HOW MUCH HOT WATER DOES YOUR FAMILY USE EVERY DAY?

Use	Litres
15-minute shower	160
Bath (half-full tub)	42-65
Whirlpool bath	400-1,200
Personal use (per day)	15
Hand dishwashing	7-16
Dishwasher	42-65
Laundry (1 hot-wash, cold-rinse load)	87

(Source: Ontario Hydro)

A sizeable portion of your energy-saving efforts should focus on reducing your family's hot-water demands. A quick shower uses a lot less water than a bath in a full tub, for example, and the warm-wash cycle gets clothes just as clean as hot water with less than a third of the energy. Running the hot-water tap is costly; for miscellaneous chores, like rinsing hands and dishes, reach for the cold-water tap and be sure to plug the sink first. When you need a basin full of warm water, add hot to cold rather than cold to hot.

an electric KETTLE

heats water far more efficiently than a pot or non-electric kettle. Fill it with only the amount of water you need, then switch it off as soon as it boils – or better, use a kettle that shuts off automatically when the water boils. Also descale the kettle regularly (rinsing well afterwards) to keep it operating efficiently.

ENERGY-EFFICIENT HOT-WATER TANKS

Replacing a hot-water tank is an expensive proposition. The first thing to sort out is matching the size of the tank to your family's needs. If each member of a family of four makes some energy-saving efforts and heat loss is cut to a minimum, a 180-L tank should be sufficient. The next step is to shop around for the most energy-efficient tank you can afford.

Performance standards for combustion units (gas and oil) are still being developed, so there's no guarantee that one type is more efficient than another. It's fair to say, however, that forced-draught and condensing-combustion hot-water heaters are the most efficient – and the most expensive.

Performance standards already exist for electric hot-water heaters sold in Canada. Each electric tank that meets the CSA C-191 performance standard carries a blue CSA (Canadian Standards Association) sticker that includes an efficiency rating. A good rule of thumb when purchasing an electric hot-water tank: a 180-L tank should have a rated standby loss of no more than 100 watts per hour; the rating for a 270-L tank should be no more than 115 watts per hour.

If you are interested in checking out state-of-the-art hot-water tanks, get in touch with **Rheem Canada**. The company, located in Hamilton, Ontario, produces tanks of varying sizes and types that use 40% less energy than conventional tanks.

After reducing your family's hot-water demands as much as possible, turn your attention to increasing the efficiency of your hot-water tank. Here are a few cheap and simple tricks.

Water Temperature

Check the thermostat on your hot-water tank. The setting should not exceed 54°C to 60°C. Unless you have a dishwasher requiring hot water at 60°C, you may be able to lower the temperature even further.

Pipe Insulation

Long stretches of hot-water pipes, especially those that pass through unheated areas, are major sources of heat loss. A quick and easy solution is pipe insulation, which is readily available in larger hardware stores.

Insulating Jackets

Hot-water tanks usually have 50 mm to 75 mm of insulation, but that won't prevent the tank from losing heat. You can add another 37 mm to 55 mm of insulation by purchasing a fibreglass jacket that is wrapped around the tank and secured with tape. If you have a gas water-heater, make sure that the blanket does not cover the opening at the bottom and that the jacket is taped tightly enough to prevent it from slipping down.

Heat Traps

Heat escaping from the tank up the hot-water supply line is a constant source of heat loss. Ask your plumber to install a heat trap, which is a simple device consisting of a few short pieces of sharp-angled pipe that traps the heat at the top of the tank.

ABOUT HOME W·A·T·E·R TREATMENT SYSTEMS

About 100,000 home water treatment devices are sold in Canada each year to householders who are concerned about the quality of their tap water. Unfortunately these costly and totally unregulated devices can't deliver what consumers expect of them, and many actually create more problems than they solve.

The variety of sources of impurity in water is so broad that no single system can remove all the undesirables: microorganisms such as bacteria, viruses, and parasites; metals such as lead, iron, and mercury; organic pollutants such as nitrates from fertilizer run-off; toxins and carcinogens such as benzenes, pesticide residues, and trihalomethanes.

The most common element in treatment systems is a carbon filtration unit. Filters are not very effective against organic pollutants; more alarmingly, they can actually increase the bacteria count in the water passing through them. There is some evidence that they can also increase the level of trihalomethanes. These unwanted results can be moderated if the filter cartridges are replaced when they become ineffective, but there is generally no way the consumer can tell that this point has been reached.

Similar problems plague reverse osmosis devices. The best ones do a good job of removing microorganisms and inorganic salts, as long as their internal membranes remain intact. Most units have no way to determine whether the membranes or the seals around them have been punctured, and even tiny holes dramatically reduce effectiveness. In addition, reverse osmosis devices return to the user only 10% of the water that flows through them. The rest is sent down the drain – a tremendous rate of water waste.

There are other types of water treatment systems – ozonators, distillers, ceramic filters, even ultraviolet irradiators – but none has so far been invented in which the benefits clearly outweigh the risks and costs, in financial, health, or environmental terms. If you're willing to spend hundreds or even thousands of dollars for better water in your home, why not invest some of that money (and some of your time) in the battle against pollution. Pressuring industry and government to clean up the sources of water contamination and improve treatment of the public water supply will help to assure good water quality for your whole community.

The water used in Canadian homes accounts for 44% of municipal water demand. That's 1% more than the combined water demand of the industrial, commercial, and public sectors. The remaining 13% is lost to leakage.

Toilets and showers consume most of the water that municipalities pump into the average Canadian household. But the most notorious, not to mention most annoying, waster of water is the leaky tap.

* *

Leaky Taps

A tap leaking only one drop per second wastes more than 25 L of water a day, or 9,000 L a year. The problem is often a worn-out washer, which costs less than 10 cents to replace.

* *

Water-Saving Toilets

A standard toilet consumes about 20 L of water with each flush. You can reduce that amount by placing a ceramic brick or a plastic jug in the tank to act as a dam. There are also water-saving toilets now on the market that operate perfectly well using 11 L to 13 L per flush. The following are manufactured in Canada, have CSA approval, and are available from most plumbing wholesalers: *Radcliffe* (model 3-147), manufactured by **Crane** in Montreal; *Trent* (model 101) and *Welland* (model 501), manufactured by **Waltec Bathware** in Cornwall, Ontario; *Plebe Water Saver* (model AF-2132-WS), manufactured by **American Standard** in Toronto. And then there's the state-of-the-art 303 *Royal Flush-o-matic*, a low-flush toilet that uses only 1 L per flush and performs as well as a standard toilet. It costs $150 and is available from **Sanitation Equipment Ltd.** (35 Citron Court, Concord, ON, L4K 2S7).

* *

Water-Saving Showerheads and Faucets

A great deal of hot and cold water is wasted by conventional showerheads and faucets. If you have a run-of-the-mill showerhead, it is probably spraying water at a rate of 15 L to 30 L a minute. Consider replacing it with a low-flow showerhead – such as *Nova* from **Ecological Water Products** (Ilderton, Ontario), *Shower Mate* from **Trans Continental Energy Saving Products** (Burlington, Ontario), *Niagara Shower Head* from **Niagara Products** (distributed in Canada by **20/20 Technologies**, Victoria, British Columbia), *Clear-Flo* from **Symmons** (distributed in Canada by **R.G. Dobbins**, Downsview, Ontario), or *Bubble Stream* from **Jenkinson and Company** (Toronto). These have flow rates that range between 7 L and 10 L per minute and are CSA-certified. If you're content to do without water at some point during a shower, attaching shut-off valves between the showerhead and downspout will save even more water and energy.

Average Daily Water Use (L)

	Switzerland	Britain	Canada
	350L	840L	5,000L

Canadians use an average of 5,000 L of water each per day; the British use 840 each and the Swiss just 350. How to account for this disproportionate consumption? Part of the answer is that most Europeans pay for their water directly via water metering.

Flat rates for water use encourage waste because they seem cheap: the rate is pitched unrealistically low, while the real costs are hidden in taxes. Studies have shown that installing water meters in homes, even without rate increases, permanently reduces water use 10% to 40%. An example: Edmonton meters all residential water, while Calgary is only partially metered. The result? Edmontonians use half as much water as Calgarians do.

If you care about throwing too much good water down the drain, consider lobbying for municipal water metering.

Today only a handful of Canadian homes are powered by the sun. But as conventional energy resources dwindle, solar and other renewable energy technologies will become increasingly important. The environmental group Friends of the Earth estimates that by the year 2025 Canada could be getting more than 80% of its energy from renewable sources.

Where does this leave the energy-conscious consumer now? If you live in a rural, wind-swept part of Saskatchewan, consider yourself lucky. At least some of your energy can be supplied by wind-powered generators. Small wind-powered electric generating systems are especially popular in cottage areas where the cost of installing hydro is prohibitive. For information about wind power, contact the Canadian Wind Energy Association.

The most practical renewable energy source for small-scale consumers, no matter where they live, is the sun – even in Canada. For example, there are enough days of year-round sunshine in Canada to make solar water-heating feasible. And the technology is in place. Canadians have been developing technology to harness solar power since the late 1970s. For a list of solar technology manufacturers, contact the Canadian Solar Industries Association.

One of the major principles behind the design of energy-efficient houses is taking advantage of passive solar energy, which can supply up to 40% of heating requirements. Canada's R-2000 houses, for example, trap passive solar energy by focussing on these measures: selecting a site that has maximum solar exposure and summer shade; concentrating window space on the south side of the house and minimizing the number of north-facing windows; installing high-performance windows; insulating to the maximum level to prevent heat loss; designing layout of rooms so that primary living areas receive as much direct sunlight as possible.

CONTINUED ON PAGE 79

It's the same story with faucets. Standard faucets flow at a rate of 11 L to 13 L per minute. Aerating faucets cut that rate in half, and the even more efficient units have cut flow rates to as low as 0.5 L per minute by using such water-saving technology as aeration, limiting maximum flow, and automatic shut-off. These features are unobtrusive, and it's likely you won't notice any difference in flow when you turn on the tap. Your plumbing wholesaler will be your best guide to water-saving faucets available in your area.

* *

MAJOR appliances

Few of us think of home appliances such as fridges, dishwashers, and stoves as polluters, but in fact they are. Apart from the raw materials and energy consumed in their manufacture, and the pollution produced as a result, such machines use large amounts of electricity to run them, to heat water, and to pump water into them. The typical refrigerator, for instance, produces over 13 kg of acid pollution a year and as much as a fifth of a tonne over a 17-year working life.

The six major appliances – fridge, freezer, dishwasher, range, clothes washer, and dryer – account for 14% of the total energy used in the home. In a year, conventional (low-efficiency) models would consume a total of about 6,500 kWh of energy. But if all six were energy-efficient, you could cut that figure by 50%. In dollar terms, that represents a saving of about $200 (assuming energy costs 5.5 cents per kWh, the national average). Over the lifetime of these appliances, savings could amount to more than $3,000.

L·I·F·E EXPECTANCY ·OF· APPLIANCES

dishwashers	13 years
clothes washers	14 years
refrigerators	17 years
ranges (electric)	18 years
freezers	21 years
dryers (electric)	28 years

* *

Energuide

Which is where Energuide comes in. In Canada, all models of the "big six" home appliances are tested for their energy use and rated in kWh per month. This rating must appear on an Energuide label attached to every new appliance (used appliances 10 years old or more should have the sticker too). The lower the figure, the more efficient the unit. This rating lets you compare models not only for energy consumption but also for actual price.

The energy cost represents a "second price tag" added to the purchase price of the appliance and should be part of your buying calculations:

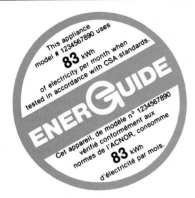

Second price tag = Energuide rating x 12 months x appliance life in years x local electricity costs (dollars/kWh)

This figure can sometimes make a big difference in determining what is really your best buy. Refrigerator A, for instance, priced at $800 with a high efficiency rating of 50, would over its 17-year lifetime cost about $560 to run, for a total of $1,360. Refrigerator B, costing $700 but with a low efficiency rating of 145, would end up costing $2,320, or $960 more. And it would use almost three times the energy.

The Energuide Directories list all "big six" appliances sold in Canada with their efficiency ratings. You can get free copies by writing to EMR Publications, 580 Booth Street, Ottawa, ON K1A 0E4.

❊ ❊ ❊ ❊ ❊ ❊ ❊ ❊ ❊ ❊ ❊ ❊ ❊ ❊ ❊ ❊ ❊

Refrigerators

The key issues here are energy consumption and the use of CFCs in refrigerator coolants and insulation. At this stage of the game there is little you can do to avoid the CFCs, apart from not buying a fridge: manufacturers have years yet to phase out CFCs in refrigerators. But you can save significantly in energy use.

After furnaces and hot-water heaters, refrigerators typically use the most energy in the home – up to 150 kWh per month. You can buy more efficient units that cut that figure by more than 50% – check the Energuide labels.

Besides choosing an energy-efficient model, there are some important tips to remember when buying and using a fridge:

▬ Buy the optimum size for your needs. A fridge that's too big obviously wastes energy, but one that's too small can use up extra energy too if it's always jam-packed. In general, 340 L (12 cu. ft.) is adequate for one or two people; 395 L to 400 L (14 to 17 cu. ft.) works for three to four people. Add 55 L (2 cu. ft.) for each additional person.

▬ The most energy-efficient style is a single-door, enclosed-freezer unit, while the least efficient is a two-or three-door unit with freezer chest beside the fridge compartment.

▬ Always load or unload a fridge as fast as you can, so that a minimum of cold air escapes.

▬ Regular defrosting cuts running costs. Contrary to what you might think, frost buildup (more than 7 mm) can make your fridge less – not more – efficient.

▬ Adjust your fridge to the most energy-efficient temperature, using a thermometer if necessary: 3°C for fridge compartments, -18°C for freezers (if separate).

▬ If possible, site the fridge well away from any heat source. At the very least, leave a good gap between them.

▬ Vacuum the cooling coils at the back of the fridge at least twice a year (unplug the fridge first). Grime can lower efficiency.

▬ Test the door seal occasionally by closing the door on a thin strip of paper, checking that it's held tightly in place. Worn seals can be replaced at fairly low cost.

CONTINUED FROM PAGE 78

Anyone can follow the same principles when renovating an older home or building a new one. Before calling in an architect or drawing up your own plans, get in touch with your provincial energy ministry or hydro supplier and ask for information on passive solar design.

RENEWABLE ENERGY ORGANIZATIONS

❑ Canadian Solar Industries Association, 67A Sparks Street, Ottawa, ON K1P 5A5.

❑ Canadian Earth Energy Association, 228 Barlow Crescent, Dunrobin, ON K0A 1T0.

❑ Canadian Wind Energy Association, P.O. Box 4165, Ottawa, ON K1S 5B2.

❑ Canadian Photovoltaic Industry Association, Suite 3, 15 York Street, Ottawa, ON K1N 5S7.

❑ Biomass Energy Institute, 1329 Niakwa Road, Winnipeg, MB R2J 3T4.

❑ Conservation and Renewable Energy Industry Council, Suite 209, 135 York Street, Ottawa, ON K1N 5T4.

❑ Solar Energy Society of Canada, 303 - 870 Cambridge Street, Winnipeg, MB R3M 3H5.

When your old fridge is carted off to the municipal dumpsite, its CFCs are eventually released into the earth and air. The solution may be new "vampire" technology that sucks out CFCs and renders them harmless.

Buying a new fridge poses another environmental problem: what to do with the old one. When it's carted off to the municipal dumpsite, its CFCs are eventually released into the earth and air. The solution may be new "vampire" technology that sucks out CFCs and renders them harmless. Facilities using this technique may be in place in some areas as early as fall 1989: watch for news.

One solution not recommended is retiring the old fridge to the cottage or garage to do service as a beer cooler – there are less expensive ways to keep your beer cold!

✳ ✳ ✳ ✳ ✳ ✳ ✳ ✳ ✳ ✳ ✳ ✳ ✳ ✳ ✳ ✳ ✳ ✳ ✳ ✳

Freezers

Most of the rules that apply to fridges also apply here. The most efficient models use about half as much energy as the least efficient units. And again size is important: don't buy a freezer that's too big for your needs. Generally, 130 L (4.5 cu. ft.) per person is about right.

Style is the next consideration, and here the choice is clear: chest freezers, with the door on top, are much more energy-efficient than upright models. Cold air leaks out around the door of an upright and rushes out every time you open it, but with the chest type, air tends to stay inside. Look for a unit that's well insulated: you can buy freezers with up to 7.5 cm insulation in the walls.

✳ ✳ ✳ ✳ ✳ ✳ ✳ ✳ ✳ ✳ ✳ ✳ ✳ ✳ ✳ ✳ ✳ ✳ ✳ ✳

Dishwashers

Key environmental question marks over dishwashers are the use of water and energy. According to a Science Council of Canada discussion paper on water, dishwashers account for an average of 1,200 L to 2,000 L of water per household per month. And during operation an average dishwasher uses about 100 kWh of energy per month, about 80% of it to heat the water

(each load uses 42 L to 65 L of hot water). Using efficient appliances and techniques can net significant savings in both water and energy.

Detergent use is also important, though your dishwasher is likely to require little more detergent than you would use in washing by hand. In Canada, most automatic dishwashing detergents are very high in phosphates, chemicals that can have a devastating effect on lakes and water life (see Chapter 3). Use a phosphate-free brand or make your own substitute, and experiment to find the smallest effective amount you can use under different circumstances.

When buying a dishwasher, compare the Energuide labels (ratings range from 83 to 121 kWh/m) and look for these features:

▬ A switch that turns off the heat-drying part of the cycle; air-drying works just as well and saves energy.

▬ A booster heater or "sani" setting that heats the incoming water to the recommended 60°C. You can then turn your water heater down to 55°C and save significantly in household water-heating costs.

▬ Extra-powerful spray action available on some newer units, which cuts down on water use.

Using your dishwasher wisely saves more energy. Try to wash only full loads and use the "econo" cycle when possible. Rinsing dirtier dishes by hand before loading can allow you to use the shorter cycle more often.

Ranges

Today's shopper faces a myriad of options in stoves – gas, propane, or electric, separate cooktops, self-cleaning and other special features, convection ovens, microwaves, and various configurations of any of these – that complicate the task of comparing specific models. Gas stoves are generally considered more energy-efficient than their electric counterparts (which use energy to heat up), but Energuide ratings are available for electric ranges only. Conventional electric stoves don't vary much in efficiency (59 to 73 kWh), but it pays to look for a low rating.

That said, these tips for choosing and using cooking appliances can help you save energy.

■ The main feature to look for in a gas range is electronic ignition. Pilot lights waste energy by constantly burning a small amount of gas. If you have a gas stove with pilot lights, consider turning them off and using matches. Good insulation and a tightly closing oven door also save energy in gas stoves.

■ Convection ovens are the most energy-efficient electric ovens available (although Energuide doesn't measure this feature). They incorporate fans that blow air around inside the unit, ensuring even heat and faster cooking at lower temperatures.

■ The self-cleaning option can be an energy-saver: it requires intense heat, but since stoves with this feature tend to be better insulated, they use less energy in cooking. You save even more energy by cleaning only when necessary and then right after cooking, to take advantage of the heat.

■ Smooth-surface elements use more energy than conventional ones.

■ Built-in exhaust fans tend to be energy-burners in winter because they draw heated air from the room, causing the furnace to work harder.

■ In cooking, use the right-sized pots (covered) and as little water as possible; don't overcook. The right small appliance for the job can save energy too – for example, cooking a stew in a slow-cooker rather than a saucepan consumes 80% less energy.

■ Use your oven to best advantage: don't preheat unless necessary (such as for baking) and then only for about 10 minutes. Try to cook several dishes at a time. Turn off the oven a few minutes early and let the trapped heat finish the cooking.

* * * * * * * * * * * * * *

If you have a gas stove with pilot lights, consider turning them off and using matches.

microwaves

Some 63% of Canadian kitchens now contain that supreme energy-saver the microwave oven. Not only does it save by accelerating cooking times, almost all the energy is used to cook the food, not heat the oven. For most cooking jobs, microwaves use less than half as much energy as do standard ovens. Most people who own a microwave oven, though, use a regular oven too. Your best bet could be a microwave with a convection feature, the most energy-efficient set-up of all. There is, however, an environmental problem associated with microwaves. The growing use of convenience foods that microwaves help encourage often means there are more packaging materials to throw away: boxes, disposable dishes, plastic wrap, and paper towels.

GARBAGE DISPOSALS

Garbage disposals waste water and electricity as well as putting more stress on the sewage treatment system. Compost heaps are much friendlier to the environment.

Clothes Washers

The same environmental factors applying to dishwashers - water and energy - apply here. But choosing carefully can make a dramatic difference to energy use and "second price tag" cost.

Energuide ratings vary from 54 to 136 kWh/m. Look for a low figure and these features:

- Front-loading machines (the laundromat type), which are common in Europe but can be hard to find here. They usually use much less hot water than top-loading models.

- Compact washers, which could save energy if your usual wash load is small; if not, however, you could end up using more energy by doubling up on loads.

- A cold wash and rinse cycle; using it as often as possible can reduce energy use significantly.

- Water-level control for small loads and shorter, gentler cycles for fine fabrics and less-soiled clothing.

* *

Dryers

By far the most energy-efficient method of drying clothes is, of course, to hang them up outdoors. If you find that suggestion impractical, the next best option is to find the most energy-efficient dryer you can. Energuide ratings for dryers vary from 74 to 111 kWh/m, a smaller difference than for some other appliances but still worth checking. When you're shopping for a dryer, consider these factors too:

- A compact model saves energy if it's sufficient for your needs; if not, a full-size unit probably saves more.

- A sensor that automatically shuts off the machine when clothes are dry saves energy and clothes.

- A cool-down or "permapress" cycle that switches the air from hot to cool near the end of the drying cycle is an energy-saver.

- If you buy a gas dryer, choose one that has electronic ignition rather than a pilot light.

- A couple of usage tips: avoid partial loads and clean the filter between loads.

* *

Air Conditioners

Keeping the heat out of the house in summer is a problem many Canadians attack with air conditioning. Unfortunately, even the most efficient air conditioners available are major energy users, and a really super one can't be found. "Efficient" room air conditioners consume some 7,200 BTUs per hour, while central units use up 24,000. Air conditioners going full-blast in the heat of summer can, in fact, force electrical generating plants to pump so much carbon into the air that they actually heat up a city.

But many natural, non-polluting methods exist for cooling the home that are cheaper and quieter than air conditioners and often just as effective. Before capitulating to machinery and adding CFCs to the atmosphere, consider trying some of these "greener" keep-cool alternatives.

■ Plant trees. Not only do they shade the house in summer, they also provide insulation against wind and snow in winter. Climbing vines, especially on east and west walls, can help shade windows.

■ If you've installed heat pumps for heating, you've also got free air conditioning (see pages 73-74).

■ Consider installing low-emissivity (low-E) windows (see pages 70-71). Their almost invisible metal coating reflects away outside heat and again has the double advantage of helping keep heat in during winter.

■ Pull down the shades. Awnings (look for cotton-fibreglass fabric) on south-facing windows help keep out the high midday rays, and vertical shading is effective for west- and east-facing windows, which get the morning and evening sun at low angles.

■ Sunscreen blinds, made of fibreglass and polyvinyl, reduce the sun's glare and heat by 70% to 85%, according to manufacturers. *Sun Project T-100* (**Sun Project Canada, Inc.,** 418 Hanlan Road, Unit 17 and 18, Woodbridge, ON, L4L 3P6) and *Lyverscreen* (**Altex, Inc.,** 3530 boulevard des Entreprises, Terrebonne, PQ, J6W 5C7) are available in drapery and design stores. A roller-type blind to cover a 1-m by 1.6-m window costs $140 to $185 installed.

■ Install low-speed ceiling fans. A fan that moves air at only about 3 km/h can make a big difference in comfort and is actually more efficient than a higher-speed fan, whose additional cooling isn't sufficient to justify the increase in noise and energy use.

■ Then there are the common-sense measures: keep the doors and windows closed until evening; shade east windows in the morning, west windows in late afternoon; as often as possible substitute your microwave, barbecue, and small electric cooking appliances for stovetop and oven.

LIGHTING

In most homes, lighting is not a major energy problem, accounting for 2% of total energy use (about 1,000 kW/h per year). But new technology can in some cases reduce that figure by 70% to 80% while providing other advantages, so it's well worth considering.

Compact Fluorescents

The big innovation in home and office lighting is compact fluorescent fixtures. Gone are the days when fluorescent meant long bulky tubes emitting poor-quality, flickering blue light. New compact fluorescent bulbs are not only far more efficient than regular incandescent ones but provide pleasant, comparable light quality for most purposes, and last 10 to 13 times as long. Some can even be screwed directly into standard fixtures, though most require an adaptor that fits into the socket.

They are also more expensive – $15 to $18 compared with less than a dollar for standard incandescent bulbs. However, this difference is usually cancelled out by huge savings on the second price tag, the energy cost.

Air conditioners going full-blast in the heat of summer can force electrical generating plants to pump so much carbon into the air that they actually heat up a city.

The key to energy efficiency in lighting is how much light is actually produced (lumens) in relation to the amount of power consumed (watts). Incandescent and fluorescent bulbs vary enormously in their lumens-per-watt ratios. Compact fluorescents, for example, produce four to five times as many lumens-per-watt as incandescents do. In other words, an 18-watt fluorescent can do exactly the same job as a 75-watt incandescent, while lasting 10 times longer.

Compact fluorescents are available in a variety of futuristic styles – circular, U-shaped, "quad cluster" – as well as the familiar globe, some requiring an adapter to plug into standard sockets. Before buying, be sure the lamp will fit the intended fixture; some may be too large.

Fluorescent technology is improving rapidly. Look for compact fluorescent bulbs that are unitized, incorporating a disposable electronic ballast built right into the base of the bulb. These newer units eliminate the annoying pulsing or flickering problem of earlier compacts with magnetic ballasts. Examples are the **Philips** *SL*18* and **Osram** *Dulux EL* series.

Finding compact fluorescents, however, can be a problem since they're not yet widely available. Check specialty lighting stores and electrical equipment outlets; if they don't have what you want, ask them to order it.

The major manufacturers of energy-efficient bulbs in Canada are Canadian General Electric, Osram Canada Limited, Philips Electronics Limited, and GTE Sylvania Canada Limited.

✳✳✳✳✳✳✳✳✳✳✳✳✳✳✳✳✳✳✳✳✳✳✳✳✳✳✳✳✳✳✳✳✳✳✳✳✳✳✳

Energy-Efficient Incandescents

Another option is a variety of new energy-efficient incandescent bulbs. For instance, tungsten halogen bulbs can cut power consumption by 50% over conventional ones and last up to two and a half times longer. In these bulbs, the tungsten filament is contained within a small quartz capsule filled with halogen gas, similar to an automobile headlamp. This gas enables the tungsten, which evaporates from the filament, to be redeposited back onto the filament instead of onto the inside surface of the bulb (the cause of darkening in regular incandescents). Consequently, the bulbs last longer and have a greater lumen output.

Parabolic-aluminized reflector (PAR) lamps, a tungsten-halogen type, can replace conventional pot or spot lamps in many decorative lighting applications in the home and will pay for themselves quickly. They last up to 6,000 hours and are available in strengths from 75 to 1,500 watts.

When you're buying incandescents, watch the terminology: "long-life" bulbs are in fact less efficient than standard incandescents, and "energy-savers" save energy by using lower wattage but aren't necessarily more efficient.

Lightbulbs aside, the way you use lighting can also make a big difference in energy savings:

▬ Use only as much light as you need for the purpose. A 25-watt incandescent bulb may work well for a porch light; save the bright lights for reading lamps and other special tasks.

▬ Consider installing energy-saving devices like timers, which automatically turn off lights at preset times, and photocells, which turn off night lights during the day.

▬ Install dimmer switches. Dimming is possible with fluorescents as well as incandescents, but ask for the newer bulbs with electronic ballasts. Unlike earlier

TURN LIGHTS OFF WHEN NOT IN USE

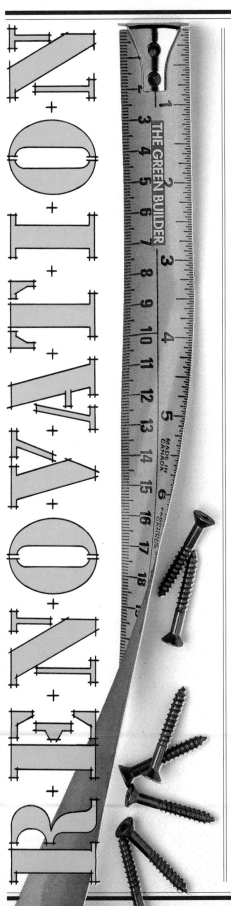

RENOVATION

types, they provide dimming without loss of efficiency. You can get them in several configurations: fixed dimming (preset at outputs of 85%, 70%, 50%, and 35%), manual dimming (with an output range of 100% to 35%), and automatic dimming (using programmed timers or photocell controls).

■■■ Don't forget the light switch – and don't hesitate to use it! Turn lights off as soon as you're no longer using them. This rule of thumb applies to both incandescent and fluorescent types. The energy you save will usually offset the reduction in lamp life caused by the increased frequency of switching.

■■■ A final, common-sense bit of advice: keep all bulbs and lampshades clean. The grubbier they get, the less light they emit.

Despite the hard work and hassles, few projects are ultimately more satisfying than renovating a home. But almost everything you tear down and everything you put up in its place is potentially harmful to the environment or to you. Modern homes are largely composed of synthetic materials, many of which are based on non-renewable resources or use these resources in their manufacture. Many require tremendous amounts of energy to produce. And many involve the use of toxic chemicals that can create pollution problems at every stage, from manufacture to disposal.

As an overall guideline for home construction, renovation, or repair: choose the natural rather than the synthetic, the product based on renewable rather than non-renewable resources.

The discussion and product choices in this and the following sections focus mainly on environmental impact, with health issues sometimes briefly mentioned. Some of our choices, however, would be inappropriate for people

---

TRY NOT TO BUY ENDLESS PACKS OF DISPOSABLE WORK GLOVES, whether for painting and decorating or for use in the kitchen or garden. Buy a sturdy, long-lasting pair, even if they're more expensive initially.

Most glues release **solvents,** which are an increasing pollution problem.

In a small way they help create the photochemical smogs that cause respiratory problems and kill trees. They also contain chemicals that can be toxic if you use them carelessly. Carpenter's glue and white glue are your best bets. When you're using any glue, make sure your home is well-ventilated.

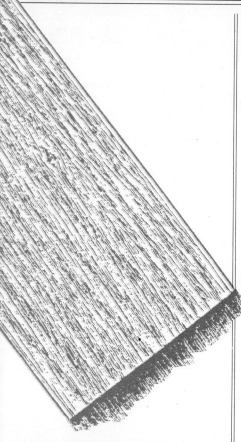

ASBESTOS
IN
OLDER HOMES

A potential hazard for renovators of homes built between 1900 and the early 1970s is asbestos, a then-common insulating, fireproofing, and strengthening agent used in roofing shingles, siding, pipe and boiler insulation, sheet and tile flooring, ceiling tiles (for soundproofing) – even as sprayed-on decoration in ceilings or walls. Asbestos, now infamous for causing lung cancer and asbestosis (there is no known safe exposure limit), can escape in microscopic fibres that hang in the air if the source is disturbed in any way. If you intend to remodel, it must be removed.

If you suspect you may have asbestos anywhere in your home, contact your provincial health department for advice on identifying it and arranging for a trained, licensed asbestos contractor to handle it safely for you.

with allergies or special chemical sensitivities. Even natural substances such as cotton and wood, for example, which are often suggested here as preferable from an environmental viewpoint, can be problems for certain individuals. If you have allergies, you might contact the **Allergy Information Association** (Suite 10, 65 Tromley Dr., Etobicoke, ON, M9B 5Y7) for help in sorting out your personal best bets.

* * * * * * * * * * * * * * * * * * *

Lumber and Wood

Few home renovators will choose a tropical hardwood for framing or a new deck. But if you're tempted by teak cabinets or doors, first read "Good Woods" (page 87). For wood used in basic construction, the main environmental issue is not tropical deforestation but hazardous chemicals.

Wood windows and door frames are often treated with poisonous insecticides, mildewcides, fungicides, or other chemicals that can outgas (give off fumes) into your home for months or even years. When disposed of as wastes, either during manufacture or after use by the consumer, these chemicals may contaminate water or soil.

An especially noxious chemical, formaldehyde, is an ingredient of the binding agent in indoor plywood, chipboard, and particleboard. Formaldehyde can cause cancer and affect the central nervous system. Dimensional lumber is safer, although more labour is required to use it.

However, manufactured lumber does have the advantage of making use of wood that would otherwise be wasted. If you choose manufactured wood, there are a few things to remember. Use exterior-grade plywood, since its binding agent is more stable and will cause less outgassing. You can prevent outgassing entirely by sealing the lumber. Don't burn the scraps.

Whatever framing lumber you choose, you can economize on the amount needed by using drywall clips, trusses, and other framing innovations.

* * * * * * * * * * * * * * * * * * *

Decks

Pressure-treated lumber is resistant to decay caused by moisture and insects, but the preservatives are highly toxic. If you do use preserved wood for a deck or fence, take precautions. Don't use it near a vegetable garden; wear protective clothing, a face mask, and gloves if you're treating cut ends with preservative; attach it with brackets to a concrete footing rather than sinking the wood directly into the ground where chemicals can leach into the soil; and don't burn the scrap.

Cedar, which is naturally decay-resistant, is an excellent alternative. Other softwoods work well outdoors, too, if you protect them with appropriate paint or stain. Protect outdoor wood from direct contact with the soil (attach it to concrete) to avoid wood rot.

* * * * * * * * * * * * * * * * * * *

Roofing

Slate, tile, metal, fibreglass, and asphalt roofing materials do not outgas chemicals, but they are all based on non-renewable resources. Of these, asphalt shingles, which are petroleum-based, have the shortest service life. Cedar shingles, though relatively expensive, are one roofing material based on renewable resources.

* * * * * * * * * * * * * * * * * * *

Siding

As is so often the case in trying to make environmentally sound buying decisions, the consumer faces trade-offs in choosing siding. Siding falls into four types: masonry, metal, plastics, and wood. The first three are all based on non-renewable resources.

Metal and vinyl sidings, though they have the advantage of being maintenance-free, are extremely difficult to repair if damaged. Aluminum is very energy-intensive in its production.

That leaves wood – probably cedar, which weathers well in most climates. But check local fire regulations: if non-combustible materials are required, choose stucco, brick, or stone.

* * * * * * * * * * * * * * * * * * * *

Flooring

Avoid such flooring materials as asphalt or vinyl tiles, which are based on petrochemicals, and choose those that are based on renewable resources and that require less energy to produce. Wood is your best choice. Other acceptable natural materials are ceramic tile, terrazzo, stone, brick, and quarry tile.

* * * * * * * * * * * * * * * * * * * *

Cabinets, Counters, and Interior Trim

For cabinetry, avoid particleboard and interior-grade plywood, which are certain sources of formaldehyde. If you have inherited some (check the sides, tops, bottoms, and shelves of "wood" cupboards and the base of countertops), seal exposed surfaces with special environmental sealers. Alternative cabinet materials are solid wood or metal.

Tropical hardwoods such as teak and mahogany are often used in cabinetry, doors, and interior trim. Don't use them unless you can determine that they came from managed forests (see "Good Woods," below). Also avoid plastic for baseboards and other trim; it's derived from petrochemicals. Use native wood for trim.

* * * * * * * * * * * * * * * * * * * *

Disposing of Wastes

Any kind of home repair or renovation creates a lot of waste, and getting rid of it in a way that causes the least environmental harm is sometimes the best you can do. Don't throw paints, solvents, varnishes, wood preservatives, or glues down the drain or into the garbage, where they can eventually leach into soil or water: dispose of them as hazardous wastes (see Chapter 7).

The same goes for scrap manufactured and treated wood. Never burn it, which sends chemical fumes flying into the air.

* * * * * * * * * * * * * * * * * * * *

Furniture and Decor

The environmental and health problems associated with furnishing and decorating your home can be summed up in two phrases: "bad" woods and hazardous chemicals. The cure is equally straightforward (though not always easy to apply): use "good woods" and prefer natural to synthetic.

The typical home is full of dangerous chemicals – they're in paints, solvents, stains, varnishes, wood glues, floor sealers, furniture, upholstery fabric and foam, carpets, wallpaper. If they can't be properly sealed in, many of these chemicals outgas into the air, where we breathe them in. And when we dispose of them, they're often released unsafely into the environment. The same hazards can exist during manufacture, if waste chemicals are unsafely dumped into the local soil or water supply.

* * * * * * * * * * * * * * * * * * * *

Good Woods

One of the key issues for Green Consumers is tropical deforestation. North America, Europe, and Japan are the major consumers of tropical hardwoods, most of which come from rainforests in the Philippines, Malaysia, Indonesia, South America, and West Africa. Every year millions of tonnes are exported to timber-hungry nations to make furniture, doors, window frames, construction materials, boats – even coffins.

use "GOOD WOODS" *and* *prefer natural to synthetic*

By the year 2000 it is expected that half the world's tropical forest will have been razed to supply the timber trade and make room for agriculture.

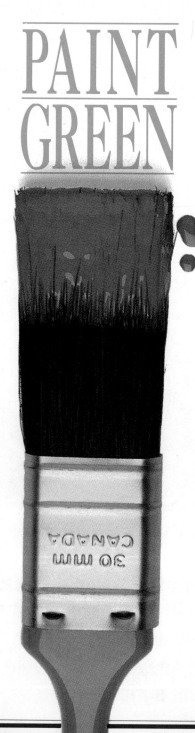

PAINT GREEN

Most of the supply of tropical hardwoods comes from badly managed and unsustainable sources – once the trees are gone, they're gone for good. Extracting the valuable timber species is a destructive process that also fells some nine times as many unwanted species, which are simply left on the ground; that compacts delicate forest soil and damages the roots of standing trees. Tropical forests are rapidly disappearing and with them the wildlife they sheltered, the soil they protected, the air moisture they produced. By the year 2000 it is expected that half the world's tropical forest will have been razed to supply the timber trade and make room for agriculture.

So what choices are there for the environmentally conscious Canadian consumer? Encourage the tropical timber industry to switch to sustainably grown tropical hardwoods by purchasing those woods, and use softwoods or temperate hardwoods whenever possible. Unfortunately, it's often difficult and sometimes impossible to determine the precise source of tropical hardwoods: for instance, some teak from Java, Thailand, and Burma, and some greenheart from Guyana is grown on sustainably managed plantations, but as yet you can't find out which. Malaysian rubberwood is a sure choice.

Look for temperate hardwoods like maple, cherry, oak, alder, apple, aspen, beech, birch, elm, hickory, and black walnut. Some softwood alternatives to hardwood are pine, spruce, hemlock, and Douglas fir. Where durability is a priority, however, the timber industry tends to treat softwoods with pentachlorophenol (PCP), Lindane, tributyl tin oxide (TBTO), and Dieldrin; ask for untreated.

* *

Veneers

You can assume that most tropical hardwood veneers come from unacceptable sources. Be wary of ebony, mahogany, African walnut, tulipwood, rosewood, and teak veneers (see above). Instead, ask for veneers made of apple, ash, aspen, beech, cherry, chestnut, elm, larch, maple, oak, pear, pine, poplar, or sycamore.

* *

Carpets, Upholstery, and Drapes

For carpets, rugs, upholstery fabric, and drapes, stick to untreated wool, cotton, and linen. One reason is that synthetic fibres are based on petrochemicals and do not decompose when disposed of. Another is that synthetic carpets and upholstery are typically loaded with noxious chemicals such as formaldehyde. The foam in cushions, mattresses, and carpet underlay often contains formaldehyde and is often made with CFCs. One foam that's CFC-free (though we don't know whether it contains formaldehyde) is **Union Carbide's** *Ultracel*. Furniture made with this urethane foam is prominently tagged. Other acceptable upholstery stuffing materials are polyester, feathers, and cotton.

* *

Paints and Solvents

Whether you should buy solvent-based or water-based paints is probably more a health than an environmental issue, and for most people, latex (water-based) is safer. Solvents (in strippers, oil-based paints, varnishes, thinners, sealers) contain chemicals that can be toxic enough that using them requires great care – adequate ventilation is a must.

If you're interested in natural or non-toxic products, look for the **Teekah** and

AFM Enterprises lines; both include a full range of home finishing products. *Crystal Aire* and *Crystal Shield* are non-toxic sealers, and **Color Your World** latex paint is relatively non-toxic.

A special word of caution: stripping paint can be one of the most dangerous of all do-it-yourself jobs. You're dealing with not only various stripping methods, all of which are hazardous, but also the old paint, which stands a good chance of containing lead if your home was built before 1950. If you can't avoid stripping the paint, be careful to use good ventilation.

And when you've finished any decorating job, dispose of all paints, varnishes, solvents, and strippers as hazardous wastes (see Chapter 7).

A variety of non-toxic home-decorating products can be ordered from these retailers:

■■■ Lowans and Stephan Environmental Products and Services, R.R. 1, Caledon East, ON L0N 1E0.

■■ Teekah Inc., 5015 Yonge Street, North York, ON M2N 5P1.

■■ Smith's Pharmacy, 3477 Yonge Street, Toronto, ON M4N 2N3.

■■ DeGroot's Only Organic, 1267 Weston Road, Toronto, ON M6M 4R2.

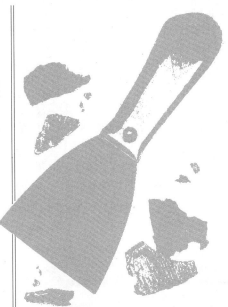

Energy to Go

Many batteries contain hazardous materials, including cadmium and mercury. About a third of world cadmium consumption, for example, goes into batteries. The incineration of wastes including batteries can pollute air and water (from the leftover ash and from landfilling). Indeed the Danes have banned mercury oxide batteries to ensure that they are not incinerated.

The various battery types are identified on the pack, although rarely in the case of zinc carbon batteries. They contain different levels of hazardous materials:

• Zinc carbon batteries, such as **Eveready's** *Classic* and *Super Heavy Duty* and **Mallory's** *Super Heavy* Duty, contain very small amounts of mercury in the form of mercuric chloride, and smaller amounts of cadmium. They are used in radios, bicycle lamps, flashlights, shavers, clocks, calculators, and TV remote-control units.

• Alkaline manganese batteries, made by manufacturers like **Duracell** and **Eveready**, are the most common small batteries in Canada and offer a far superior performance in most applications. They contain more mercury than zinc carbon batteries, although both Eveready and Duracell have recently reduced the mercury content in their alkaline manganese batteries by 90%.

Remember that when manufacturers claim that their alkaline batteries "last up to six times longer," they are comparing them to zinc carbon batteries. When used in less demanding applications, where zinc-based batteries tend to perform better, alkaline batteries last up to three times as long. Alkaline batteries are used in portable stereos, cameras, and camera flash attachments.

• Button cells require materials of the highest energy density because they are so small. Mercuric oxide and silver oxide are preferred materials. Silver oxide is more expensive, however, and can have a shorter shelf life, so mercury oxide wins out. Button cells are not recycled: the silver contained in a silver oxide watch battery is worth no more than two cents. Mercury cells are used in hearing aids and some cameras and should be properly disposed of.

• Nickel-cadmium rechargeable batteries obviously contain toxic cadmium. Rechargeable batteries can be recharged as often as 500 times. Although more expensive initially, rechargeables can work out to be cheaper in the long run. They have to be recharged several times during the normal life of an equivalent alkaline battery, however. And they must also be used very carefully or their life is shortened. As a result, they have so far won only a small share of the consumer market.

• Lithium batteries, such as **Eveready's** *LithEon* and **Duracell's** *XL*, are more expensive but hold promise for the long term. Lithium offers higher voltages in small batteries than do such materials as silver and mercury.

So what to do? Difficult. The best advice is probably as follows:

1. Use plug-in power rather than batteries when you can. Manufacturing batteries can take 50 times more energy than they produce.
2. Second choice: rechargeables, especially for equipment that's a heavy user of batteries.
3. If you must use batteries, pick the type most suitable to the appliance you are using. Whichever batteries you use, don't mix new batteries with old. The new batteries try to recharge the old ones and their life is cut significantly as a result.

6. GARDENING

Louis Dudek

"There is some hidden wisdom in all gardens."

GREEN CONSUMERS

look for gardening methods and materials that produce tasty tomatoes and ravishing roses without hurting the environment or our own health.

▲▲▲▲▲▲▲▲▲▲▲▲▲▲

This chapter focusses on organic gardening. Hydroponic gardening – another environment-friendly approach – is best left to the specialists. If you live where produce is both

▲▲▲▲▲▲▲▲▲▲▲▲▲▲

scarce and expensive, and where garden plots are in short supply, the hydroponic way is worth trying, and you'll find there's a good body of literature available.

The same basic elements are needed to grow lawns, fruit, vegetables, or flowers: soil, seed, and care and protection.

SOIL

> **"We pump in chemical fertilizers to get quick results or showy blossoms, but fail to nourish the soil to foster its long-term health"**

Twentieth-century gardeners tend to treat outdoor green space as we do our indoor flowerpots: we pump in chemical fertilizers to get quick results or showy blossoms, but fail to nourish the soil to foster its long-term health. Fertilizers give the soil a boost, but ultimately they weaken its constitution. In time, the soil becomes dependent on its "drug fix." We strip the earth of its natural nutrients and leave it vulnerable to the ravages of pests and erosion.

Fortunately, there's a simple solution at hand for home gardeners:

* * * * * * * * * * * * * * * * * * *

Composting

The soil in your garden, under your lawn and around your flowers, is a living organism. It takes up nutrients and excretes waste. The cycle of soil is the ages-old tale of new life from old. Organic matter ages, dies, decomposes, and is absorbed into healthy young life. Last autumn's crimson maple leaves will, next year, be the green shoots of a new forest fern or wild flower. Green gardeners simply accelerate nature's cycle by composting.

Like commercial fertilizers, compost supplies the three main nutrients needed for plant growth: nitrogen, phosphorus, and potassium. But it supplies them in a natural, "trickle release" system, so plants aren't burned by too much fertilizer, too fast; nor is the bulk of the fertilizer, like many commercial products, simply flushed away into the water table. You can have your soil tested (see pages 92-93) to find out what nutrients your garden particularly needs.

Liberal composting also dramatically improves the structure of the soil in your garden by improving both drainage and aeration. With each passing year of composting you will find the soil darker, richer, easier to work, and more free of pests.

These overall advantages of composting have been known for centuries. But in our polluted age, compost takes on special importance. Compost actually protects your plants from heavy metals in the soil and air, such as lead in the exhaust from passing traffic. Well-rotted compost "binds" or collects any lead in the soil, so that it cannot be taken up by your garden produce. It's a natural safety filter.

While it "imprisons" lead in the soil, compost releases other essential mineral nutrients to your plants. In addition to nitrogen, phosphorus, and potassium, compost has all the trace elements plants need – elements your garden seldom gets from commercial products. These include calcium, magnesium, sulphur, iron, manganese, zinc, copper, boron, molybdenum, and vanadium.

1 m

RAIN COVER

WOOD SIDES

EARTH

YARD WASTE

KITCHEN WASTE

BRICKS, STONES, OR TWO-BY-FOURS

YOU CAN MAKE YOUR COMPOST BIN YOURSELF

* *

Compost Bins

You can make a compost bin yourself or buy one ready-made.

Your bin should be about 1 m square, at a minimum, and 1 to 1.6 m high. If it's smaller, it may not generate enough heat inside to decompose the material efficiently. If it's too much higher, the stuff on top may compress material on the bottom, and squeeze out the oxygen needed to keep the process cooking.

customized composting

Just as chemical fertilizers are designed with varying balances of nitrogen, phosphorus, and potassium, you can customize your compost to boost whichever nutrient is lacking in your garden soil. See below for a list of soil testing services that can tell you what help your soil needs.

	Nitrogen	Phosphorus	Potassium
beet roots	low	low	high
bone meal	high	high	low
coffee grounds	high	low	medium
corncobs (ground)	—	—	very high
eggshells	high	medium	low
feathers	very high	—	—
hair	very high	—	—
lobster shells	very high	high	—
oak leaves	medium	medium	low
peanut shells	medium	low	high
pine needles	low	low	low
pumpkin flesh	low	low	low
rhubarb stems	low	low	medium
seaweed	high	medium	very high

S·O·I·L TESTING SERVICES

Expert advice on what's in your soil now can help you to determine how to improve its quality. Soil testing services can tell you whether you need to boost the nitrogen, the phosphorus, or the potassium; whether your soil is too acid or too alkaline; and whether you have excess salinity. Some services can test for the presence of toxins and contaminants, such as lead.

Write to one of the services listed below, telling them what you want to find out. Their fees vary.

ALBERTA

Alberta Agriculture
905 O.S. Longman Building
6909 - 116 Street
Edmonton, AB T6H 4P2

Alberta Environmental Centre
P.O. Bag 4000
Vegreville, AB T0B 4L0

CONTINUED NEXT PAGE ☞

The sides can be wood, a circle of snow fencing, even wire fencing lined with cardboard cartons (to hold in the heat and moisture). If you use wood or cinder block, leave some air spaces or gaps. Put a few bricks, stones, or two-by-fours at the bottom to allow air to circulate underneath. Leave an opening in the front so you can turn the material over while it's cooking and remove the finished compost. Put a shed roof of wood or fibreglass sheeting on top to keep heavy rain off, or cover the top of the pile with plastic sheeting. If you can, build a double bin; you can continue to add to one side while the other is finishing off.

Ready-made compost bins are usually made of plastic, with a lid, and doors at the bottom to remove the finished compost. They are generally about 75 cm high and 60 cm square.

A Canadian model called the *Soil Saver* is the most popular bin sold in Canada; it's available at gardening centres across the country. Made by **Barclay Horticultural Manufacturers**, it retails at $129.95. It was given the highest rating of all bins on the market in the April 1988 issue of *Organic Gardening* (published by Rodale Press).

✳✳

Compost Pits

Compost "pits" work every bit as well as compost bins. So if you are a lousy carpenter, or don't demand geometric perfection in your garden, follow the example and advice of Mary Perlmutter, president of Canadian Organic Growers: "Just dig a hole and throw your wet garbage into it. Cover it with leaves or grass clippings and a bit of the soil you removed. Dig some out from underneath when you want to use it."

Your compost pit should be kept moist. The compost is just right if it forms a ball (like cooked short-grain rice) in your hand. If there's a very heavy rain, and it gets too soggy, you could cover the pit with plastic until it dries out a bit.

✳✳

Making Compost

Start with a layer of coarse compost – small branches pruned from your shrubs and trees, straw, or grass cuttings, for example – on the bricks or loosely spaced wooden slats at the bottom of your bin. To get the process going well, add a layer of old compost, rotted manure, good garden soil, or seaweed, which is one of the richest sources of nutrients.

Now you are ready to add a layer of kitchen garbage. Any green kitchen wastes, such as vegetable tops and salad leavings, are terrific. Add coffee grounds and tea leaves, eggshells, fruit peels, and even scraps of paper, if they're not too big. Don't be afraid to pitch in shells from lobster and other seafood; they'll biodegrade more quickly if you break them up first by wrapping them in paper and hitting them with a hammer.

Don't include plastic, glass, foil, or metal. If you don't want frequent visits from animals, skip fish scraps, meat scraps, grease and oil, bones, and milk products, too.

When you add kitchen garbage to your compost pile, you're recovering a lot of nutrition that you used to waste. For instance, the average Canadian family throws away every year as much iron as is contained in 500 eggs, as much protein as they'd get from 60 steaks, and a volume of vitamins equal to the contents of 95 glasses of orange juice – just in discarded potato peelings. When you throw them into the bin or pit, you'll get the nutrients back in next year's backyard vegetables.

Now keep adding layers, with some soil, leaves, or grass cuttings between layers of kitchen garbage. If you are going to eat the garden produce next summer, don't use any leaves or grass cuttings that have been sprayed with herbicides or pesticides. If you run out of material, collect hair clippings from your local barber shop – no joke, they're rich in nitrogen. (Avoid, if you can, clippings with a lot of chemical colouring or conditioning on them.)

If you are in a hurry, and the weather is warm, you can have completely digested compost in two weeks by turning it with a pitchfork every two or three days, to keep it aerated and cooking evenly. If you just leave it alone, you'll have dry, crumbly, utterly inoffensive humus in eight weeks to six months. Poke at it and tumble it about occasionally, when adding new layers.

The speed of decomposition will depend on how much moisture and air is getting into the bin. You can help by mixing coarse and fine materials. A heavy layer of leaves, for example, can bond together like thick, wet cardboard and slow down the process. Punch holes in them with a sharpened broomstick or, better yet, put them through a leaf shredder in the fall. (If grass and leaves are stored in paper bags, they can be tossed directly into the pile – the paper will biodegrade, too.)

You can tell whether things are working properly by the temperature. Once the compost pile is well started, the temperature inside (about 25 to 30 cm down from the top) should rise from 40°C to between 60 and 70°C, as decomposition starts the compost "cooking." It's "done" when the temperature falls back to about 40 to 45°C. The compost pile will steam as it's finishing the process, giving off moisture and heat. It will be hot to the touch while cooking and just warm when it is done. (If you want a precise measuring tool, garden centres sell soil thermometers.)

Put the finished compost on your house plants, your garden plants, and, after shaking or pushing it through a 0.5-cm screen, onto your lawn. There is no better fertilizer or soil replenishment.

✳ ✳

Composting Tips

■ If your compost bin smells, it's too wet. Turn it over and mix in some dry material.

■ If the temperature fails to rise, you might have too little moisture; sprinkle it with the garden hose. Or there might not be enough nitrogen to start the cooking: add some bone meal, blood meal, seaweed, grass cuttings, or manure.

■ Composting works through the winter, too. Keep adding your kitchen garbage. If the scraps freeze, they'll break down into good soil all the faster in the spring.

■ There are commercial "accelerators" for compost, but they should be unnecessary if you have followed all the instructions above. As a last resort, a carton or two of fishing worms should do it.

Norwest Labs
9938 - 67 Avenue
Edmonton, AB T6E 0P5

BRITISH COLUMBIA

Griffin Laboratories
1875 Spall Road
Kelowna, BC V1Y 4R2

Norwest Labs
203 - 20771 Langley Bypass
Langley, BC V3A 5E8

MANITOBA

Manitoba Soil Testing
Room 262, Ellis Building
University of Manitoba
Winnipeg, MB R3T 2N2

NEW BRUNSWICK

New Brunswick Department of
  Agriculture
Provincial Agricultural Lab
P.O. Box 6000
Fredericton, NB E3B 5H1

NEWFOUNDLAND

Agriculture Canada Research
  Station
P.O. Box 7098
St. John's, NF A1E 3Y3

NOVA SCOTIA

Nova Scotia Department of
  Agriculture and Marketing
Soils and Crop Branch
P.O. Box 550
Truro, NS B2N 5E3

ONTARIO

Agrifood Labs
503 Imperial Road, Unit 1
Guelph, ON N1H 6T9

PRINCE EDWARD ISLAND

Soil and Feed Testing Lab
PEI Department of Agriculture
Box 1600
Charlottetown, PE C1A 7M3

QUEBEC

Soil Testing Lab
Macdonald Stewart Building,
Room 2-099, Macdonald College
Ste-Anne-de-Bellevue, PQ H9X 1C0

SASKATCHEWAN

Saskatchewan Soil Testing Lab
Department of Soil Science
General Purpose Building
University of Saskatchewan
Saskatoon, SK S7N 0W0

Mulch

Mulch is nature's compost system. You won't see much bare earth on a late-autumn stroll through any stretch of Canadian bush or forest. That carpet of leaves and needles is next year's soil nutrients – and this year's protection against wind and water erosion. It shelters the earthworms and other burrowing insects as they tunnel near the surface, aerating and draining forest soil and protecting tree roots from rot and exposure. As the birds and small animals poke at the mulch, winkling out insects and seeds, the matted leaves are broken up. Gradually they merge with the forest's topsoil.

Mulch is just as rich a bonus for your lawn and garden as for any forest. Providing mulch, or ground cover, for your garden has many benefits.

■ Mulch smothers weeds, saving you the trouble of pulling them up. You'll have to take out the big ones, though – over 7.5 cm – before you put down the mulch.

■ Mulch keeps water and nutrients in your soil by reducing evaporation, run-off, and wind erosion. It also adds more nutrients as it decomposes.

■ By providing a layer of insulation, mulch reduces temperature shifts. The soil stays cooler in summer, warmer at night and in autumn. In winter, mulch reduces frost boils and breaks in the topsoil.

■ With mulch you get earthworms, which provide aeration and drainage as well as the richest fertilizer of all: worm castings. Similarly, mulch encourages "good guy" bacteria and fungi, which nourish your plants, break down organic matter into rich new soil, and help repel pests or disease.

■ Mulch protects the tender roots near the soil surface. It also keeps vine crops, such as cucumbers and melons, from rotting on the wet ground – and keeps them clean. Indeed, all your ripening vegetables will be cleaner, as the mulch prevents rain from splattering them with bits of soil.

■ All the activity in and around mulch will help attract birds, foraging for stray seed, insects, and worms.

What are the drawbacks? Mulch can attract some unwanted visitors, too: slugs and mice.

To be rid of slugs, just turn back the mulch, collect them, and drop them into a pail of boiling water. See page 99 for more bug-repellent ideas. Mice usually leave if you roll back the mulch carpet and make loud noise.

If you find your ground cover encourages crown rot in perennials, keep the mulch away from the base of perennials during their growth season. Don't let it rest too close to them in wet weather, either.

* * * * * * * * * * * * * * * * * * * *

Mulch Ingredients

Availability, cost, and appearance are factors to consider when you select your mulch or ground cover.

■ Grass clippings or leaves: The leaves should be shredded. Run them over with the lawn mower and put down a layer 5 to 8 cm deep.

■ Seaweed: Terrific, if you can get it – it's full of useful minerals. Needs to be 5 to 8 cm deep. Apply after a rain, if you can, to avoid making the soil too salty.

■ Sawdust or wood chips: Both leach nitrogen from the soil, so put a nitrogen-rich dressing down first. Both are high in carbon. Sawdust improves soil structure when it breaks down. Make certain it's not from chemically treated lumber. Wood chips are pretty; let them weather a year before you use them. Make a layer 2 to 5 cm deep.

■ Corn cobs: Mills will provide these free; some mills will crush or grind them for you, so that they biodegrade faster. They, too, steal nitrogen from the soil. Spread about 10 cm deep.

Straw and hay: The most common mulches. Straw depletes nitrogen. If you use hay, look for last year's: you'll be less likely to spread a lot of nuisance seeds. Needs to be 10 to 15 cm deep.

Peat moss: It's clean, tidy, and attractive, and it greatly helps the soil hold moisture. But it's expensive and very acidic. Peat moss has to be wetted down when applied or it may blow away. Put down 2 to 5 cm.

Paper products: Cardboard is functional, if not brightly decorated with printing. It will eventually biodegrade. Newspapers are a bad idea: the inks have metals and chemicals you don't want in your food.

Black plastic film: Plastic keeps the soil hot and wet, lasts a long time, and is cheap. It's not very attractive, though. Punch some holes in it to allow for air circulation.

Boards, stones, old carpeting: All are functional. Avoid carpets treated with chemicals, which means most carpets not made of pure cotton, wool or silk. Take these covers up in the fall so you can cultivate.

For cool-weather plants such as peas, beets, radishes, and lettuce, apply mulch in early spring, to keep the soil moist and cool. For plants that need warmth – tomatoes, peppers, eggplants – apply it after the first growth spurt.

* * * * * * * * * * * * * *

Commercial Fertilizers

Buy products that will spare your environment while they nourish your garden. Most garden centres now stock composted manure, blood meal, bone meal, fish emulsion, and seaweed – all acceptable alternatives if you can't make your own compost.

These companies produce safe garden products:

C-I-L, in common with most gardening suppliers, markets an apparently chemical-free bone meal. It also makes *Fortified Organic* fertilizer.

Loblaws, with the endorsement of Pollution Probe, is now marketing *Nature's Choice 100% Natural Source Fertilizer* for lawns and gardens. The supermarket chain has several other environment-friendly garden products.

Safer Ltd., a Canadian company, makes "natural" plant care roducts, including several organic plant foods, mainly for house plants. Safer's herbicides, pesticides, and fertilizers are sold through health food stores as well as by several large hains.

The **Wen-Hal** company markets everything from composted sheep manure (great for strawberries) to black earth and potting soil, under the trade name *Organix*.

So-Green, which also uses the trademark names *Lawn Pro* and *Nature's Garden*, concentrates on fertilizers and emphasizes products with "natural and organic fertilizers." Their lime, bone meal, and blood meal are "natural," as is their *High Organic Lawn Pro* fertilizer.

Most of these products are available in gardening supply centres as well as hardware stores, supermarkets, and other chain stores. Always check the labels: the material that makes up the biggest part of the package is listed first. If in doubt, ask at your gardening centre, or write to Canadian Organic Growers (see page 101) for their source list of organic fertilizers.

> Always check the labels: The material that makes up the biggest part of the package is listed first.

* *

"In the natural world, diversity is the key to survival." David Suzuki

Most seeds sold through catalogues and at gardening centres are *hybrid* seeds, bred by artificial techniques at seed houses. These engineered varieties have little or no resistance to insects and disease, so they are dependent on chemical fertilizers, herbicides, and pesticides for survival. Most do not reproduce well, so you must buy new seed every year.

TREES
are more than just a pretty garden's face:
trees produce oxygen. The more of them we all nurture, the healthier our planet.

They also, of course, provide you with a shady spot on scorching days. And they shelter the birds that will eat up the insects you'd just as soon do without.

IF YOU WANT A FULLY ROUNDED GARDEN

– a private ecosphere – put in a perennial patch to attract the birds and insects you need to keep pests down, give your garden variety and colour, and give those helpful creatures the sanctuary they need.
Select a space you don't need for other purposes (the larger the better) and seed it with perennials: daisies, cornflowers, poppies, chamomile, columbines, and astors. Once established, this meadow will seed itself; you needn't mow it, and it will need minimal cultivation and tending. Let it "go wild" – that's the whole point.

Not surprisingly, the major manufacturers of chemical pesticides and herbicides now own the world's biggest seed houses, which supply farmers and gardeners alike. Rather than working to develop naturally resistant seed stocks, they manufacture fragile seeds that need the protection of their chemical products.

The dominance of hybrids thus ensures that tonnes of chemicals will continue to be introduced into the food chain and washed into the water supply. At the same time, natural seed varieties are disappearing – and with them, the natural capacity for resistance that they have carried for thousands of years. Some scientists believe the decline in a wide variety of seed stocks is a more serious global problem than the destruction of the world's rainforests. To take only one example of shrinking variety in seeds, there were more than 8,000 apple varieties catalogued in North America at the turn of the century; today fewer than 1,000 remain.

Green Consumers prefer untreated, open-pollinated, or heritage seed. *Untreated* seeds are simply those that haven't been coated with chemicals to preserve them or to act as pesticides. *Open-pollinated* seeds are those that can reproduce themselves. That means you can save seed from your vegetables or flowers and use it next year. *Heritage* seed is handed down from generation to generation. Many gardeners have joined heritage seed groups to encourage the preservation of seed species and to exchange seeds, thus preserving diversity in our seed stocks.

For home gardeners, the goal is seed that is "region-specific" (appropriate to conditions in one's area) and that has built-in, natural resistance to pests and disease. Most of Canada's seed for farms and gardens is imported from multinationals, but the major companies in Canada do produce some of their own, with regional varieties.

The two biggest Canadian seed houses, **Stokes Seeds** (39 James St., St. Catharines, ON, L2R 6R6) and **Dominion Seed House**, Georgetown, ON, L7G 4A2), sell some untreated and region-specific seeds along with their full range of conventionally grown seeds. Among the alternative growers, **William Dam Seeds** (P.O Box 8400, Dundas, ON, L9H 6M1) is the largest dealer in untreated seed; **Richter and Sons** (P.O. Box 26, Goodwood, ON, L0C 1A0) sells organically grown herb seed.

There are many smaller seed companies, from Newfoundland to Vancouver Island, specializing in organically grown, open-pollinated, and untreated seed. Many sell and ship organically grown seedlings and plants, too. Many health-food stores also carry non-hybrid and untreated seeds, as well as organic fertilizers and organic pesticides.

The *Garden Seed Inventory* lists all the Canadian and U.S. seed catalogues that include non-hybrid vegetable seeds. It's available for $17.50 from the Seed Savers Exchange (see page 101); members of Canadian Organic Growers can borrow the book from their library. The January issue of *Harrowsmith* magazine is another useful reference. Every year it provides a good overview of Canada's seed industry and describes the varieties best for where you live, wherever in Canada that may be.

You can get involved in producing heritage seeds in your own backyard. When you have a good crop of anything – or your neighbour does – save some seeds to try again. Maybe you've stumbled on just the right strain for your soil, your climate, your sunlight orientation in the garden. After collecting the seeds, dry them out somewhere dry and warm (but never above 35°C, or you'll bake and kill them). Seal them in airtight containers, and put them somewhere as cool and dark as possible. You can even freeze seeds; the cooler and darker the storage area, the better. Heritage Seed Program (see page 101) can give you more information.

Don't hoard all the seeds, though. Leave a few sunflowers, gone to seed, for the blue jays and the chickadees. They make great emergency rations in early winter.

care &
PROTECTION

To the conventional gardener, "care and protection" means pesticides, herbicides, and artificial fertilizers. Green Consumers can replace most of these chemicals with composting, mulching, weeding, and cultivation.

Caring for your garden also involves taking the time to pay attention to it. Walk through it, every evening. Consult with it. Look for pests, for dryness or over-moisture. Pull the weeds as you go by.

Lawn care is easier once your lawn is mulched, aerated, and properly watered. Choose the best seed for the light you have. When mowing, leave the grass 5 to 8 cm high. It will shade – and kill – most weeds.

To remove any remaining weeds that you find unattractive, dig instead of spraying. But consider keeping some of the plants on your lawn. Many people consider clover a weed, but others find it pretty. Besides, the greater the diversity in your garden, the healthier the soil, and the better the ecological balance. Hedge rows, ditches, and marshes are what keep the farm fields of Normandy and Kent healthy, by encouraging diverse populations of wild plants and animals and by controlling erosion.

Watering Lawns and Plants

If water shortages are not a problem in your area, soak your lawn once every week to ten days. That means a solid watering of two to four hours for each section. You've watered enough if it "slurps" when you walk over it afterwards.

If water is in short supply, talk to your gardening centre about a "drip irrigation" system for your lawn. They can be expensive, and they need annual maintenance – but they save a lot of time and are very efficient without wasting water.

In addition, sprinkle your plants several times each summer, to wash off the residue from smog and traffic. Soot and grime on leaves interfere with photosynthesis and reduce both growth and crop yields.

If conditions are very dry, use the "clay pot" system for your plants, trees, and shrubs. The Chinese have used this method for over two thousand years, and many dry areas around the world continue to rely upon it.

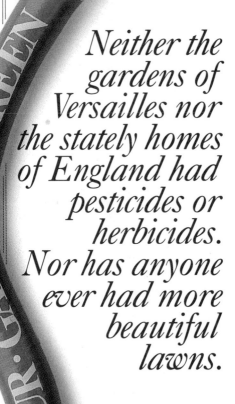

KEEP · YOUR · GARDEN · GREEN

Neither the gardens of Versailles nor the stately homes of England had pesticides or herbicides. Nor has anyone ever had more beautiful lawns.

THE CHINESE CLAY POT SYSTEM

BEWARE OF 2,4-D

IT HAS BEEN IN USE FOR DECADES; RECENTLY IT HAS BEEN IDENTIFIED AS THE POSSIBLE CAUSE OF NON-HODGKIN'S LYMPHOMA, A CANCER OF WHICH CANADIAN CASES DIAGNOSED HAVE DOUBLED SINCE 1950.

Dig a hole beside each fruit tree or shrub that you want to irrigate, or every 2 to 3 m along a row of plants that you wish to water. Place an unglazed earthenware pot or jug in each hole. (Use old flowerpots if they are porous. To test them, stand them in water for a while; if they become moist inside, they are porous.) If the pots have drainage holes in the bottoms, plug or caulk them. Fill them with water and cover them to prevent evaporation. You'll find you need to fill them only once every four to eight days.

* *

Pest Control

As for protection, gardeners need not resort to chemicals. There are biological means of combatting or preventing most garden hazards. Besides, not enough is known about the health hazards of most common pesticides and herbicides.

What we do know is that several chemical garden products contain organophosphates and carbamates, likely cancer-causing agents. One extremely common weedkiller called 2,4-D has been in use for decades; recently it has been identified as the possible cause of non-Hodgkin's lymphoma, a cancer of which Canadian cases diagnosed have doubled since 1950. This form of cancer causes tumours in the lymph glands; it is fatal in half to two-thirds of cases.

Used to kill common weeds, including dandelion and clover, 2,4-D is the most popular weedkiller in parks, on golf courses, and on suburban lawns. Metropolitan Toronto stopped using 2,4-D in its parks in 1980. Some chemical fertilizers have 2,4-D; see page 95 for some brands that don't.

When we use pesticides, 60 to 90% (by volume) of what we spray misses the intended targets entirely. Most goes directly into our air or our water table, and thence into our kitchen taps. We have little understanding of what effects result when the various pesticides and herbicides combine with one another in the environment. Sometimes they may destroy plants, animals, and insects that we want to keep alive.

In fact, most insects in the garden are worth keeping; only 0.1% are "pests." The rest either are working for us or are entirely uninterested in our ambitions and gardening schedules. When we kill off a helpful insect, we have to find another way to consume or destroy the mites or aphids that it was eating.

* * * * * * * * * * * * * * * * * * * *

Birds

Mary Perlmutter of Canadian Organic Growers says, "Birds are a wonderful - an extremely beneficial – part of our ecosystem. They eat their weight in insects every day." Entice birds into your garden and you'll have a natural control mechanism for insects.

However, too many birds are occasionally a nuisance themselves – eating your berries, for example, or pecking at the fruit in your backyard orchard. Scarecrows, foil pie plates, streamers, and wind chimes are often effective, but if stronger measures are required:

■■■■ Buy some netting (with a 1-cm weave) from your garden centre, and cover the berry bushes or trees you want to protect. (The birds are afraid of getting their feet caught in the webbing.)

■■■■ Buy a fake owl from your gardening centre. Perch it on a conspicuous branch. But move it every few days – birds are not as brainless as they seem.

Killer Insects

Lots of insects eat other insects. The praying mantis, for example, loves mosquitoes, and can eat about as many as it can catch. You can buy the mantis and other "white hat" insects by mail. Write to Pat Coristine at **Better Yield Insects** (P.O. Box 3451, Tecumseh Station, Windsor, ON N8N 3C4).

Insects, like gardeners, specialize, and are even finicky about their diets. So Better Yield can recommend the best warrior bugs, for example, to take on your whitefly, spider mites, aphids, thrips, or whatever insects you need rounded up.

✱✱✱✱✱✱✱✱✱✱✱✱✱✱✱✱✱✱✱✱✱✱✱✱✱✱✱✱✱✱✱✱✱✱

Do-It-Yourself Remedies

Tools and ingredients from the kitchen and the potting shed can be put to work against unwanted insects.

▄▄▄ Slugs love to congregate under a board on the ground. Leave a couple in the garden. Flip them over every morning, scoop up the slugs, and drown them in some soapy water or boiling water.

▄▄▄ Snails seek shade, so they'll be delighted to shelter inside a cool, shady clay flowerpot turned upside down. Gather them in the early evening and drown them.

▄▄▄ Slugs and snails are also partial to warm, stale beer. Put a shallow dish in the garden and watch them die happy.

▄▄▄ Other insects can simply be hosed off sturdy plants – or wiped off with warm, soapy water. If you use the latter, rinse the leaves with the hose afterwards.

▄▄▄ To post "keep out" signs for ants, sprinkle a line of paprika, red chili powder, dried peppermint, or cream of tartar across their entrance.

▄▄▄ If you have a strong stomach, collect the slugs and other insects from your garden, run them through your kitchen blender with some water, and pour the "purée" back on the beds. No one knows why, but bug soup is the most effective and biologically safe bug repellent.

▄▄▄ Vegetable gardens can be protected from nighttime assaults by rabbits and groundhogs by planting rows of garlic and chives around them.

▄▄▄ You can make your own pesticide by chopping rhubarb leaves and brewing them in boiling water. These leaves, like the leaves of oleander, contain toxic oxalic acid. Rhubarb leaves, in fact, are about the deadliest poison in your garden. The brew you distill from them is a concentrated poison, so make very certain none of the "tea" you produce is left where children might mistake it for a beverage.

▄▄▄ For another natural pesticide spray, throw some garlic and green onion tops in your blender or food processor. Strain this purée and mix the juice with soapy water. Pour into an old pump spray container.

Even when you use compost,

you'll still need to take measures against airborne lead that is deposited on the surface of your garden foods.

Fortunately lead is not absorbed through the skins of vegetables and fruit. But if they're grown within 100 m of busy traffic, you should wash them very carefully before serving them. Water alone won't remove all the lead deposits. Add a little vinegar or dish detergent to the water; scrub the food thoroughly, and rinse.

A windbreak – a fence or hedge – can greatly reduce the lead fall-out onto your garden from passing traffic. Just don't use the hedge cuttings in your compost for next year.

SLUG "PURÉE" KEEPS THE SLUGS AWAY.

Safer Pesticides

If all else fails, the products listed here are the least dangerous pesticides commercially available.

■■ ***Bacillus thuringiensis:*** BT is as safe as any pesticide can be. It will kill cabbage worms, cutworms, gypsy moth, and all caterpillars, including tent caterpillars. It's also been used successfully to destroy potato beetles and the larvae of black fly and mosquito.

You must apply BT directly to the plant or the soil (in the case of cutworms). Sunlight breaks it down, so use it in the evening. Rain washes it away; so applications must be repeated, if it rains.

BT is sold under many trade names, including *Botanix, Dipel, Thuricide,* and *Envirobac.* Many garden centres sell it in boxes marked "organic garden spray." **C-I-L** markets *Thuricide* in a container labelled *Organic Insect Liquid Killer.*

■■ ***Diatomaceous earth:*** Not "earth" at all, this product is made of natural skeletons, like coral, whose crushed remains consist entirely of very sharp splinters. The splinters punch holes in the waxy shells of insects, so they die of dehydration. However, diatomaceous earth is not discriminating: it kills all the insects that encounter it. So it's probably best used indoors – where you don't want even beneficial insects – against earwigs, silverfish, ants, and cockroaches.

Look for the brand names *Insectigone,* in Quebec (made by **Chemfree Environment Ltd.**), and *Fossil Flower* elsewhere in Canada (distributed with the *Green Cross* trademark by a **Ciba-Geigy** firm).

Roach and Crawling Insect Killer, a powder or dust distributed by the **Safer** garden products company, contains both diatomaceous earth and pyrethrum, a natural pesticide (see below).

■■ ***Rotenone and pyrethrum:*** Both are "broad spectrum" insecticides (that is, they kill all the insects in their path). Extracted from plants, they are considered non-poisonous to people and pets where used as directed. Both will quickly despatch any cold-blooded animals, however, including frogs and fish, so don't use them near waterways.

Rotenone is available under its own name and under the brand names *Atox* and *Deritox* (the *Green Cross* brand), which comes in both liquid and powder. Brand names for pyrethrum include *Schultz Instant* and *Wilson's Vegetable and Garden Spray.* Synthetic pyrethroids with the same qualities are available, too.

■■ ***Dormant oil spray:*** Used by commercial orchards, it suffocates mites, scales, and other insects if applied to fruit trees before budding.

■■ ***Tanglefoot:*** This well-named product protects trees from caterpillars, ants, canker worms, and other climbers. One paints it around a tree, and they get stuck in it, so can't climb any higher – or lower for that matter. But it shrinks as it dries, so to avoid strangling the tree, paint a swatch of white latex around the trunk first. Then paint the Tanglefoot over the latex. You'll find Tanglefoot at most any gardening centre.

Like other multinationals, CIBA-GEIGY, distributor of Green Cross products, is aware of the brewing consumer demand for safe products. But the green cross is merely a trademark and does not necessarily indicate organic or non-toxic formulas. So sensible organic gardeners check the labels and consult a garden centre manager.

For More Information

In addition to the organizations listed below, ministries and departments of agriculture across the country will happily send you literature on composting and other features of organic gardening. Several **Rodale Press** publications, including the monthly magazine *Organic Gardening*, are worth investigating.

* * * * * * * * * * * * * * * * * * * *

Canadian Organic Growers,

Box 6408,
Station J,
Ottawa, Ontario
K2A 3Y6
COG has a nationwide network of members and offers excellent information services. It also publishes a very informative quarterly newsmagazine on organic gardening, called *COGnition*. Membership in COG costs $10 ($5 for seniors and students) and includes a subscription to *COGnition*.

* * * * * * * * * * * * * * * * * * * *

Civic Garden Centre of Metropolitan Toronto

(416) 445-1552
In Toronto, the Civic Garden Centre operates a Master Gardener's Hot Line from noon until 3 p.m., Monday through Friday. They specialize in answering questions on home organic gardening.

* * * * * * * * * * * * * * * * * * * *

Ecological Agricultural Staff,

Box 225,
Macdonald College,
Ste. Anne de Bellevue, Quebec
H9X 1C0

* * * * * * * * * * * * * * * * * * * *

Friends of the Earth,

Suite 701,
251 Laurier Avenue,
Ottawa, Ontario
K1P 5J6
Friends of the Earth has published a book on environment-friendly gardening. Called *How to Get Your Lawn & Garden Off Drugs*, the book is being sold in bookstores, at Loblaws, and directly by Friends of the Earth, at $12.95.

* * * * * * * * * * * * * * * * * * * *

GROW

National Farmers Union,
7th Floor,
222 Somerset Street West,
Ottawa, Ontario
K2P 2G3
GROW – "Genetic Resources for Our World" – is a clearinghouse and lobby formed to help preserve plant genetic variety, and to fight plant-breeding patent laws. Its members include the Canadian Labour Congress, the Canadian Environmental Law Association, Friends of the Earth, the United Church of Canada, and Oxfam Canada.

* * * * * * * * * * * * * * * * * * * *

Heritage Seed Program,

c/o Heather Apple,
R.R. 3,
Uxbridge, Ontario
L0C 1K0
The Heritage Seed Program is dedicated to saving unique seed varieties, fighting to preserve seed variety, and exchanging data. It has an excellent reference library and information base. You can join for $10 ($7 if you live on a fixed income).

* * * * * * * * * * * * * * * * * * * *

The Recycling Council of Ontario,

P.O. Box 310,
Station P,
Toronto, Ontario
M5S 2S8
Canadian Organic Growers highly recommends the Council's free booklet *Be Good to Your Compost! Your Guide to Backyard Composting*.

* * * * * * * * * * * * * * * * * * * *

The Seed Savers Exchange,

Route 3,
Box 239,
Decorah, Iowa
52101
The Seed Savers, a "mothership" for Canadians and Americans eager to preserve diversity of seed strains, publishes an annual list of over 4,000 "heirloom and endangered seed species." Founded and operated by Ken Wheatly, Seed Savers publishes the *Garden Seed Inventory* each year and operates an information clearinghouse.

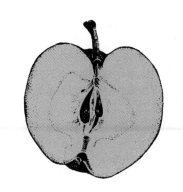

7. WASTE MANAGEMENT

HOME SWEET HOME

S. Quinlan

THOSE OF US WHO LIVE IN CITIES

and towns rarely have the opportunity to realize just how much garbage each of us produces. It's whisked away regularly by our municipalities, and our surroundings become neat and ordered again. Only during garbage strikes do we begin to get some sense of the amount we throw away. And then it's only a few weeks' worth at most.

▲▲▲▲▲▲▲▲▲▲▲▲▲▲▲

If somehow we had an entire year's castoffs dumped back on our doorsteps, they probably would overflow the living room, creep into the kitchen, and possibly need bathroom space as well. There would sit our discarded bags, wrappings, food leavings, cans, bottles, junk mail, shoes, cosmetics, ornaments, papers, broken glass, appliances (large and small), cleaners, boxes, old dishes, razors, weedkillers, cardboard, furniture

▲▲▲▲▲▲▲▲▲▲▲▲▲▲▲

(soft and hard), disinfectants, batteries, grass clippings, magazines, clothes, toys, paint strippers, medicines, suitcases, wood preservatives, tools, diapers, cat litter, jewellery, posters, games, umbrellas – all leftovers of our lives.

Until recently, most of us never worried about our mountains of trash. It's a big country, after all; surely there will always be space in which to hide our garbage. Trouble is, apart from the very serious environmental impact of landfill sites, getting rid of Canada's waste costs a great deal of money. And it isn't "government" money, of course – it's our money.

The garbage crisis of which we're becoming ever more aware is not really a problem of waste management. What we should be concerned about is our mismanagement of used materials and the fact that we produce garbage at all. But before we tackle those problems and offer some alternatives, let's consider how we handle our garbage now.

"Whatever befalls the earth, befalls the sons of the earth. Man did not weave the web of life; he is merely a strand on it. Whatever he does to the web, he does to himself. Continue to contaminate your bed and you will, one night, suffocate in your own waste."

Seattle, Chief of the Dwamish (1851)

Incineration

Burning our garbage seems like a good idea to many Canadians. Some even argue that we can solve two environmental problems at once: dispose of our waste and produce energy at the same time. Our garbage would simply go away and we'd have found a substitute for coal-fired and nuclear-powered generating stations.

Unfortunately, this is not a workable solution. The first law of thermodynamics gets in the way. It says that "matter is neither created nor destroyed." In other words, chemicals and waste won't simply go away, and they certainly won't disappear in an incinerator's fire. About 30% of them become ash, but the remaining 70% sail up the stack and out into the atmosphere. There they stay, building and building as we add to them each day, until they work their way back through the environment, into our soil, vegetation, and water, then back up the food chain to us.

The gases and particles that go up the stack are by no means safe for our environment, although proponents of waste incineration often claim that they are. The gas is almost entirely carbon dioxide and water vapour. True enough, the carbon dioxide we all breathe out naturally is good for the environment. But too much is bad for the environment. Carbon dioxide is the main gas causing the greenhouse effect. Essentially what an incinerator does, then, is convert used materials into greenhouse gases.

The problems with the air emissions don't end there. Because our garbage is such an incredibly mixed bag, incinerators belch out innumerable dangerous chemicals, some of them very dangerous. They fall into three categories: toxic organic chemicals, heavy metals, and acid gases.

Dioxins are the most toxic of the organic chemicals; in fact they are widely regarded as being among the most poisonous substances in our world. And they are surrounded by the greatest uncertainty. The uncertainty starts with the identification of sources, continues through questions of formation, dispersal, and the existing levels in the environment, and increases when the effects on environmental and human health are considered.

Incinerators were thought to be one of the major culprits when a Toronto Department of Public Health study found in 1986 that a balanced daily diet of food grown in Ontario (including fruit, cheese, meat, and milk) would contain 66 times the "acceptable" daily intake level of dioxins. Even worse, many scientists fear that the current acceptable level doesn't reflect the actual toxicity of dioxins and is probably much too high.

In addition to dioxins, incinerators produce a wide range of other hydrocarbons that are harmful to both humans and the environment. These include polyaromatic hydrocarbons (PAHs), chlorobenzenes, and PCBs. Although hexachlorobenzenes are less toxic than dioxins, they're emitted in far larger quantities, and very little information is gathered on those emissions.

Mercury is just one of the heavy metals that gets into our atmosphere from incinerators. (In Sweden, the government has calculated that 55% of all the mercury in the country's environment comes from incinerators.) The growing acidification of our environment increases the mobilization of mercury – acid rain washes it out of the soil and into the water. Not only is this believed to

Mercury from incinerators is believed to contribute to forest decline, and it is almost certainly the reason why fish in many areas of the world are accumulating mercury at unsafe levels.

contribute to forest decline, but it is almost certainly the reason why fish in many areas of the world are accumulating mercury at unsafe levels. Of all the heavy metals emitted from incinerators, mercury is the most difficult to reduce because it's discharged in gaseous form; other metals are bound to flyash particles.

Of the other heavy metals emitted in significant quantities, cadmium is the most toxic. While government regulations usually address only human health risks, a scientist at West Germany's University of Göttingen has reported that it takes no more than a very low level of cadmium to damage the roots of spruce trees.

The group of acid gases produced by incinerators – sulphur dioxides, nitrogen oxides, and hydrogen chloride – also has come under public scrutiny. Hydrogen chloride receives the most attention because incinerators are its largest source and, unlike the other two acid gases, it isn't transported great distances. Consequently it poses a health risk to everyone living within about 50 km of the plant. Emissions of sulphur dioxide and nitrogen oxides are low in comparison to other sources, but they can only add to our problem of acid precipitation.

Toxic heavy metals and organic chemicals are troublesome even when they aren't sent up in smoke. Ironically, the better the pollution control equipment is at keeping the toxins from leaving the stack, the higher the levels will be in the residual ash left over from incineration. Our provincial governments are now struggling with the question of how to dispose of this residue.

In the most recently approved Canadian incinerator, in Brampton, Ontario, the ash will be tested for a variety of toxins. When it fails to meet acceptable standards, it must be sent to a licensed hazardous waste facility for safe disposal. This procedure is costly, however, and despite the concerns of environmentalists, Canada's ash is generally sent to regular garbage dumps that are not designed to handle toxic wastes.

****

The potential energy savings from recycling paper, metals, glass, and other materials is far greater than the amount of energy we get from incinerators.

Energy from Garbage?

In a perfect world we could replace polluting non-renewable energy sources like coal with garbage that would otherwise just be dumped. The main concern with burning coal is that it contributes to the greenhouse effect by emitting carbon dioxide. In this imperfect world, however, it must be pointed out that carbon dioxide is also the main emission from garbage incinerators.

As well, incinerators are a highly inefficient way of producing energy. Because our garbage contains such non-combustibles as metal, a tremendous amount of the incinerator's heat is wasted simply heating up the metals. Energy must be used to boil off all the moisture in food, glass, and similar materials, too. In the end, only about 40% of the energy we get by burning used materials can be recovered to make steam: only about 15% can be recovered to make electricity.

In fact, steam and electricity produced by incinerators are created so inefficiently that we actually lose energy by burning garbage. The potential energy savings from recycling paper, metals, glass, and other materials is far greater than the amount of energy we get from incinerators.

****

Landfilling

Obviously, incineration of mixed garbage is not the solution to our waste disposal problems. Why, then, can't we just bury it?

Landfills are no solution, either. For one thing, the sites chosen for them are usually on agricultural land, so landfilling contributes to the shrinkage in our farmland. It's estimated that Ontario alone loses 0.6 hectares of land to garbage every day.

For another thing, no thinking person wants a landfill anywhere near his or her home. Landfills leak. Their seeping liquids contaminate water supplies. They give off toxic gases. These often result from fires that can smoulder for years, feeding off the combustibles in used materials and the methane gases produced as wet garbage rots. There has been little study of these gases, but it's acknowledged that methane is probably the second most significant gas in the creation of the greenhouse effect.

Given the uncontrolled nature of these burns and the lack of pollution control equipment, it's reasonable to assume that landfill gases may be at least as dangerous as those emitted from incinerators. In addition, methane is highly explosive. The gas has been known to migrate from old landfills into the basements of houses. And, not surprisingly, it has been known to explode underneath people's living quarters.

Methane is highly explosive. It has been known to migrate from old landfills into the basements of houses.

solving the garbage problem

T he solution to our garbage problem – our used materials mismanagement – is straightforward: stop creating garbage that must be disposed of and find ways to make the best use of the materials we do produce. In short, stop wasting resources and start conserving them.

A tin can doesn't become garbage until you throw it away. Up to that point, it was a highly refined and processed piece of tin and steel, one that was produced at an environmental cost (mining, energy for smelting, water for industrial processing, and so on). Turning some metal-bearing rock into a throwaway container is not only costly to the environment, it will become increasingly difficult to repeat as our resources run out.

Given that we can't replace that tin can effortlessly, it remains a valuable object even when it has been used. Its value, indeed, is equal to the total resources, capital, labour, and pollution expenditures that would be needed to replace it. It takes two to three times as much energy to make a new can as it does to recycle one. If we simply "burn" the can and turn it into incinerator ash and emissions, we squander all that energy. There are energy savings to be made from all recyclable materials, sometimes huge savings. Recycling plastics and aluminum, for instance, uses only 5% to 10% as much energy as manufacturing new plastic or smelting aluminum.

Long before most of us even noticed what we now call "the environment," Buckminster Fuller said, "Pollution is nothing but the resources we are not harvesting. We allow them to disperse because we've been ignorant of their value." To take one example, let's compare the throwaway economy with a recycling economy as we feed a cat for life.

Say your cat weighs 5 kg and eats one can of food each day. Each empty tin of its food weighs 40 g. In a throwaway economy, you would discard 5,475 cans over

A tin can doesn't become garbage until you throw it away.

A cat may use up to 40 times its body weight in steel in 15 years.

the cat's 15-year lifetime, not counting leap years. That's 219 kg of steel – more than a fifth of a tonne and more than 40 times the cat's weight.

In a recycling economy, we would make one set of 10 cans to start with, then replace them over and over again with recycled cans. Since almost 3% of the metal is lost during reprocessing, we'd have to make an extra 10 cans each year. But in all, only 150 tins will be used up over the cat's lifetime – and we'll still have 10 left over for the next cat.

Instead of using up 219 kg of steel, we've used only 6 kg. And because the process of recycling steel is less polluting than making new steel, we've also achieved the following significant savings:

SAVINGS	
In energy use	47%-74%
In air pollution	85%
In water pollution	35%
In water use	40%

So much unnecessary pollution, lost resources, and wasted land for garbage dumps happens as the result of a simple decision repeated over and over again: we decide to ignore the valuable material left over after each feeding, and call it garbage. That decision compounded in every aspect of our home life results in 10 million tonnes of household garbage per year in Canada, and about that amount again of garbage from our workplaces. This does not include hazardous waste, liquid waste and sewage, bio-medical waste, and air pollution emissions.

Between where we live and where we work, then, we throw out 20 million tonnes of used resources per year. That's almost a tonne for every man, woman, and child in Canada. A cat may use up 40 times its body weight in steel in 15 years; we throw out 150 times our average body weight in garbage during the same length of time.

* *

Cutting Down on Garbage

If you have the average household (and of course few do), your garbage would break down this way.

Wet Waste	% by weight
Yard and lawn waste	25
Food scraps	10
Paper	
Newspapers	15
Mixed paper	10
Corrugated cardboard	3
Fine paper	2
Box board	1
Other paper	5
Glass	9
Metals	5
Plastic	5
Composite materials (two or more materials fastened together, as in blister packs)	4
Wood	2
Disposable diapers	2
Textiles (clothing, etc.)	1
Miscellaneous (hazardous household wastes, kitty litter, ceramics, etc.)	1

You might expect that plastic would be a large part of our trash. But as you'll note, it accounts for only 5% – paper accounts for 36%. And our yard waste and food scraps account for more than a third.

Let's say you rethink your attitude to used materials. No longer is an empty glass, metal, or plastic container garbage, now it is a resource that can be recycled. No longer are grass clippings, leaves, and vegetable peelings garbage, they're a valuable mix of nutrients that can be composted and returned to the soil. Paper too can be recycled. That leaves you with the following:

Some plastic	3%
Composite materials	4%
Disposable diapers	2%
Textiles	1%
Miscellaneous	1%

If you also start using cloth diapers instead of disposables (see Chapter 4), avoiding bad packaging, using hazardous waste depots, sending old clothing and furniture to charitable organizations, renting the items you use rarely and repairing others, you could cut the list of things you throw away to almost nothing. All that would remain would be odds and ends like lightbulbs (the glass of which can't be recycled), a few food scraps that can't be composted, food-stained paper (unless you composted it), and items that could no longer be repaired.

It can be done. In Seattle, Washington, where households are charged a certain rate for each garbage can they put out for collection, some homes have been granted a no-fee status because they produce no garbage!

It can't be done, of course, unless your municipality provides recycling services, your supermarket provides good packaging, and manufacturers make longer-lasting products. (Beware, for example, of throwaway cameras and disposable razors – especially the new electric ones.) If you've never even thought about your garbage before, you can get started right away by composting at home (see Chapter 6), by choosing refillable soft-drink containers, and by following the three Rs of waste management.

Wherever possible:

1. Reduce
2. Reuse
3. Recycle

These three are known as the waste management hierachy – reduction is better than reuse, and reuse is better than recycling.

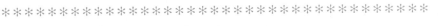

Reduce

The most misunderstood of the three Rs, "reduce" doesn't mean doing without. To an environmentalist it merely means avoiding the purchase of wasteful products and packages. Reduction means not buying what you don't need. In the supermarket, for instance, are you going to buy pre-wrapped produce and carry it home in yet another plastic bag? Or are you going to choose loose produce and take it home in your own shopping bag?

This point is important. The Federation of Canadian Municipalities has called for a 50% reduction in packaging by the year 2000. It points out that one-third of household garbage is packaging and that more money is spent by consumers on packaging than farmers receive for growing the food.

Composting
is
Catching On

Many towns across the country now encourage individual or central composting. In Peel Region, in Ontario, there's been an especially felicitous outbreak of common self-interest. A local industrial plant had several thousand steel drums to dump at considerable expense. Instead, local Boy Scouts are drilling holes in the drums for aeration, at $10 per barrel. The municipality is giving the drums to local householders, to use for composting kitchen garbage and lawn cuttings.

The bottom line? The industry is getting rid of the barrels, at no cost. The Scouts are raising money. The householders are starting to compost. And the municipality is saving greatly on garbage disposal costs, thanks to the composting.

Reuse

This R is often confused with recycling, but it means something different and is even better environmentally. Simply put, reuse is the act of making the same item serve over and over again. This sounds very basic, yet many of us miss a lot of reuse opportunities that would benefit the environment. Most of us have good intentions; we reuse yogurt containers for food storage and plastic grocery bags for carrying lunches or putting out garbage. How many people do you know with a drawerful of old plastic bags and a shelf laden with empty yogurt containers?

The other chances we miss include renting and repair. Rentals go far beyond cars, videos, and office equipment; just take a look at the Rentals section of your Yellow Pages. If you don't find what you want there, look under the item you're interested in, because just about anything for the home, garden, or repair shop can be rented. Whether you look at tools or tuxedos, society gets more value per item when consumers rent. One item is made, then used or worn many times by different people, and eventually retired after a job well done. Instead many tuxedos – and even more tools – are bought and used only a few times before being discarded.

Repair is another valuable form of reuse that is often overlooked. Not everything can be repaired once it's broken, but often it's worth trying; having shoes mended and resoled, for instance, means that we get more footwear with less waste. A good further step would be to give shoes you no longer want to such charities as the Salvation Army and Goodwill for repair and resale.

We can donate clothes of any description, old bicycles and children's toys, books, magazines, appliances, furniture, and all sorts of other things to any number of charities. We can sell our used materials, too, and buy those that other people have grown tired of. Again, check your Yellow Pages; most cities, for example, have very popular secondhand book stores, as well as clothing stores that resell anything from children's outfits to designer originals. If the word "secondhand" bothers you, consider the prevalence of garage sales and that an antique may be sixth-hand or more.

Another important way to reuse involves packaging. Despite our best efforts, we will still need some containers. Pouring shampoo or ice cream into your shopping bag is obviously a silly notion. But it is equally silly to take home a different container every time you buy one of these products. It makes no sense to go to the time and expense – and resource use – to make a plastic shampoo bottle that could be used for years and have it thrown out in days or weeks.

Many stores now sell foods in bulk dispensers. We should go the next step and bring back our old containers for a refill at the bulk bins. If we can return beer and pop bottles, we can carry a clean, empty container to a food store. Even ice cream can be bought by the litre in some shops.

✳✳

Recycle

What makes recycling different from reuse– and not quite as environmentally sound – is that the item involved must be reprocessed. Paper gets repulped and made into new paper, but obviously the processing results in some pollution. Also, reprocessing is not something you can do yourself. Your municipal and provincial governments need to be involved, along with some industry. Programs like the Ontario Blue Box emphasize recycling beverage containers rather than the more environmentally desirable path of refilling them.

But they also allow for recycling of other containers made from glass, plastic, and metal, as well as newspapers; indeed, soft-drink containers are now only a small percentage of the total material collected.

However, the savings to be gained from recycling are considerable. For instance, 2.2 tonnes of wood are needed to make a tonne of new paper, along with considerable quantities of energy, water, and chemicals. Paper made from recycled fibre uses up 40% less energy. Glass can be recycled forever and every tonne of crushed waste glass used saves 135 L of oil and 1.2 tonnes of raw materials. A tonne of aluminum uses up four tonnes of bauxite, and all metal smelting is energy-intensive. The energy used to make one tonne of virgin aluminum could recycle 20 tonnes of aluminum from scrap.

Here is just a brief list of what is already being recycled in some parts of Canada.

RECYCLABLE MATERIALS		
Newspaper	Glass	Used oil
Fine paper	Metal	Cotton
Computer paper	Wood	Plastic and rubber
Cardboard	Food waste	Yard scraps

If you're not getting the opportunity to recycle all of these materials, pursue the issue with your local governments. Most Canadian municipalities now go through a planning process for used materials management, which includes input from and participation by the public. Get involved, and be prepared by taking note of the following examples of what can be done.

* *

Recycling Programs

The "Blue Box" program in Ontario is the largest and most successful recycling effort in North America. About 1.5 million households in the province have each been given a heavy-duty plastic box for regular pickup of cans, glass bottles, plastic soft-drink bottles, and newspapers. Some municipalities are also collecting corrugated cardboard (the type that has a ruffled layer sandwiched between two flat layers), used motor oil, and all hard plastic bottles. The programs are expanding gradually to include more households.

The Blue Box program came about as a result of an amendment to the Ontario soft-drink container law. Almost every province has long had regulations governing these containers, generally limiting the use of various types and stressing that a certain percentage must carry a deposit and a certain percentage must be refillable.

The best example is Prince Edward Island, where all soft-drink containers must be refillable.
Manitoba and Newfoundland, however, have no regulations at all. The original purpose of these laws, most of which were drafted in the early 1970s, was to reduce the amount of roadside litter. It has only been in the last four or five years that governments have begun to see the implications for used materials management inherent in their soft-drink container laws.

The success of the Blue Box program has helped convince other governments that recycling can work on a large scale and that even more can be done. Similar programs are springing up all over. British Columbia, Nova Scotia, New Brunswick, and Quebec are taking a serious look at the Blue Box idea. Each should have a number of programs operating by 1991. Some Alberta cities are already using the Blue Box.

Neunkirchen, a county in Austria, recycles two-thirds of all household and commercial/industrial used materials.

*There is
no question
that we're an
overpackaged
country.*

Despite its success, the Blue Box hasn't solved the problem of used materials mismanagement. The best examples of the program – Ottawa, Peterborough, Mississauga, and Guelph – are getting only about 15% of the garbage from single-family homes. And that is only about 5% of the total garbage volume in those cities.

So environmental organizations are drawing the attention of Canadian governments to vastly more intensive efforts in Japan, West Germany, and Austria. The most successful program, in Neunkirchen, a county in Austria, recycles two-thirds of all household and commercial/industrial used materials. It's worth noting that Europe produces fewer and smaller packages than North America does, and Europeans tend to be less wasteful in what they buy. Austrians throw out only a third of the garbage we do; with two-thirds of that being recycled, their total waste is one-ninth of ours.

Many municipalities are considering the Austrian system, which relies on a simple separation of garbage. Each household receives two containers, one of them a sort of super Blue Box

for dry used materials like cans, glass, and all paper. Its contents go to a separating plant, where metals are taken out by magnets, paper is separated out by air clarifiers (blowers) and gravity, and other materials are pulled out by other means.

The second bin is for wet garbage: food scraps, lawn clippings, and other yard waste. This material is collected and composted centrally, either in a plant or in large "windrows" out of doors. The compost is sold to plant nurseries and parks, and is acceptable for agricultural use under Austria's quite rigorous standards. But the preferred route is that individuals compost in their own backyards where possible; this saves collection and processing costs and produces a cleaner compost. Private industries can deliver their wastes to the sorting or composting plant for a fee that's lower than the cost of disposal elsewhere.

The village of Ryley, Alberta, already uses a similar system. Guelph, Ontario, is expected to introduce a composting/recycling program this year, and a number of other Canadian municipalities are considering pilot programs.

✳✳✳✳✳✳✳✳✳✳✳✳✳✳✳✳✳✳✳✳✳✳✳✳✳✳✳✳✳✳✳✳✳✳✳✳✳✳

Packaging Laws

There's no question that we're an overpackaged country. This issue may be one of the most difficult to tackle, however, because there are jurisdictional problems in the Canadian system. The federal government regulates packaging, and municipal governments are responsible for garbage collection and disposal. In other words, the federal government doesn't suffer the pressure of finding new landfills or incinerators, which might drive it to attack overpackaging. It's the municipalities, and their taxpayers, that pay the consequences of something over which they have no control.

The jurisdictional problem is not the only big hurdle to overcome. Another lies in the fact that no one has ever implemented large-scale packaging reduction regulations before. The closest we've come has been the soft-drink container laws, which were designed to reduce litter, not waste. Just writing package-reduction regulations could prove an enormously difficult task. Try to imagine a regulation that can distinguish, in legal terms, between packaging that's necessary and packaging that's unnecessary. Government consultations with the packaging industry and the environmental community won't make it any easier; the two groups are far from agreement on what constitutes necessary packaging. Nevertheless, three models have so far emerged in other jurisdictions:

1. Austria has passed a law stating that by 1992 it will be illegal to sell a package that can't be recycled. Its definition of recyclable is that there must be an operating program to collect and recycle the material.

2. Palo Alto, California, has a pilot program to label all packages with colour-coded price stickers that reflect where the product or its package will end up. Canadian cities might adopt a similar system: blue stickers on items for the Blue Box; green stickers on items for the compost bin; red stickers on hazardous household products that should go to a special depot; grey stickers on products or packages that will wind up in general garbage.

3. The state of Massachusetts is considering legislation that would put a 6-cent tax on each package. The tax would be waived entirely if the package is reusable; 3 cents would be waived if it's made of recycled material; and 3 cents would be waived if it's recyclable.

* *

Degradable Plastics

Many Canadians are concerned about the amount of plastic we add to our garbage – 16 to 18 kg per person per year. We know those plastics will pile up over the centuries as a lasting monument to our throwaway society. All of us have seen too the many plastic items that aren't put out in the garbage; they litter our roadsides, parks, and campgrounds. And so the new biodegradable and photodegradable plastic bags seem on the surface to be very beneficial. But we may have to think again about these wonder products.

Biodegradable plastics are made by including cornstarch with the polyethylene in the manufacturing process. When the plastic item is discarded, the cornstarch is eaten by bacteria, which causes the polyethylene to break down into pieces too small to see. Another chemical added during manufacture helps provide oxygen to the bacteria, which also aids in the decomposition of the plastic.

Photodegradable plastics are used in bags and in the plastic rings used to hold six-packs of cans together. In this case, a light-sensitive additive is mixed with the plastic to help break the product down into small particles in the presence of sunlight. This is important environmentally not only because of the despoiling of nature by litter, but also because seabirds often choke or strangle on plastics.

Plastics that will degrade in a few years, or even a few months, seem to be promising solutions. However, let's apply two of our rules for managing waste and see how they come out.

* *

> The plastic in biodegradable bags is weakened by the addition of starch, so 5% to 10% more plastic must be added to strengthen the bag.

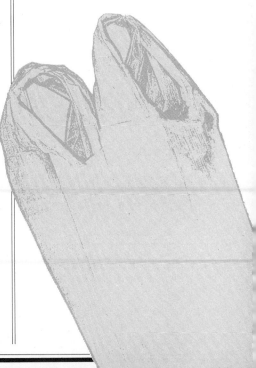

Reduce, Reuse, and Recycle

RULE ONE

Do degradable plastics reduce the volume of garbage we generate? Not at all. In fact, the plastic in biodegradable bags is weakened by the addition of starch, so 5% to 10% more plastic must be added to strengthen the bag.

Are degradable plastics reusable? Obviously not, since they're designed to fall apart.

As to whether they're recyclable, the answer on one level is yes. At least one company recycles the scrap and trimmings from manufacturing

A Return to the Old Ways

Vancouver residents now have a special opportunity to reduce waste . It isn't anything new or fancy, but it's something most Canadians seem to have forgotten about. The era of milk deliveries has returned to Vancouver, and it has brought back the refillable glass milk bottle. During 1988, **Avalon Dairy Ltd.** sold 75,000 L of milk in returnable glass bottles.

Not many communities have dairies like Avalon, but plastic jugs for milk are fairly common. Those jugs can be recycled (if not refilled), but in fact most of them aren't.

Becker's, a jug-milk chain with more than 700 corner stores in southern Ontario, recycles its two-litre jugs when customers return them to the stores. And 98% of jugs do come back, largely because Becker's charges a deposit on each jug. To encourage buyers to choose the recyclable jugs rather than disposable milk bags, Becker's sells the jug milk at a lower price than the bags.

biodegradable bags into new bags. This recycling of in-house scrap is standard practice in the manufacture of regular plastic bags, but it is an expensive new technology in the biodegradable field. Although this may change in time, as of now it means that more of the scrap from these plastics will go to the dump.

On another level, the issue is even more complicated. In recent years we've started to get good news about the recycling of "post-consumer" plastics (meaning those you have already disposed of). Guelph, Ottawa, and North York, Ontario, have begun to recycle some hard plastics such as soft-drink bottles, jugs, and margarine tubs; many other municipalities are expected to follow suit shortly.

In Korea, West Germany, and some other countries, they are recycling film plastics, including plastic bags. And in the U.S. and Belgium there is a promising young technology called the ET1, which can fuse together all kinds of different plastics and make a wood substitute for fence posts and park benches.

The problem is that degradable plastics may interfere with some of these recycling technologies. The degradables may be difficult to recycle themselves, and they make it difficult or impossible to recycle other plastics with which they are mixed. Plastics manufacture is an extremely precise business, and recyclers must meet exacting standards of purity. Degradable plastics will only complicate the process.

The key question with degradable plastics, then, is whether they make recycling easier or whether they hinder the process. Since they cause problems, it makes more sense to stick with the regular plastics in the hope that improvements in technology will make them fully recyclable.

Nothing is Destroyed

RULE TWO

You'll recall from the incineration section that one of the great environmental myths is that we can make unwanted chemicals and wastes "go away" through one method or another. The truth is that atoms in a molecule may re-form into new molecules under certain conditions, but they do not go away. So what happens to the plastic bits after the additives in degradable plastics have done their job?

Stop for a moment to think about degradation in an ecological sense: biodegradation. In the food chain we can trace nutrients in the soil through plants to herbivores and through herbivores to carnivores and potentially through one carnivore to another. Through the action of bacteria, flies, worms, and moulds, the plants and animals that aren't used for food by other organisms are decayed or degraded back into a complex mix of nutrients. That mix, of course, becomes part of the soil that we began with.

There are serious questions about the role of plastics in this process of nutrient cycling. For various species to be able to eat, digest, and excrete organic matter and so aid in its decomposition, the molecules of any given matter must be below a certain size. But the particles left after the new plastics have degraded are hundreds of times bigger than what scientists consider digestible.

So while these individual pieces of plastic may not be visible to our eyes, they may still be with us for centuries. Even if we replace all ordinary plastics with these special new plastics, we will still be collecting and transporting the same amount of discarded packages to landfill sites. And once they are buried, we will have wasted forever the resources used to make them. Whether they are dust or bags, they will have cost us dearly.

As with all other materials, the best route to take is still:

Reduce. Don't accept plastic bags you don't need, not even for clothing purchases. Think about getting permanent shopping bags of sturdy cloth or canvas.

Reuse. Use any bags you do collect again and again.

Recycle. Urge your municipality to adopt a plastics recycling program – and when you get it, use it faithfully.

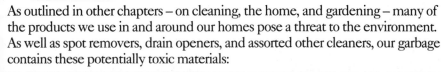

THE DISPOSAL OF
HAZARDOUS
WASTE

As outlined in other chapters – on cleaning, the home, and gardening – many of the products we use in and around our homes pose a threat to the environment. As well as spot removers, drain openers, and assorted other cleaners, our garbage contains these potentially toxic materials:

HOUSEHOLD HAZARDOUS WASTE		
Pesticides	Pool chemicals	Photo-developing chemicals
Medicines	Paint stripper	Batteries
Rug shampoo	Paints and paint thinners	Used oil
Upholstery cleaners	Stains and finishes	Metal polishes
Furniture polishes	Bleach	Floor wax

The best way to make sure these products cause no harm is to avoid using them in the first place. However, if you do use them, or if you find old containers of them gathering dust in storage areas around your home, it's vital that you dispose of them in the safest possible manner. Never pour them down a drain or put them out with your garbage. Municipal landfills aren't designed to cope with hazardous materials, and incinerators may just hasten these chemicals' entry into the environment.

In most areas, you can take these products to a household toxic waste depot set up by your provincial or municipal government. There trained chemists sort the hazardous waste into different groups. Some wastes can be reused or recycled, others can be chemically neutralized. Some, however, must be sent to properly licensed facilities that can dispose of them safely.

The following list will tell you if your area has such a program for hazardous waste, and whom to contact. (You'll note that some provinces have no programs, and you might like to ask why.) If you don't have a car to get you to the waste depot, combine forces with a friend or neighbour who does have transportation. That way you can dispose of all the chemicals from two (or more) homes at once.

Alberta

For the times and locations of Toxic Waste Roundup days, call the Alberta Special Waste Management Corporation, (403) 422-5029 or (800) 272-8873. Edmonton operates its own roundup for three days once a year.

British Columbia

Special Wastes and Emergencies Unit, Waste Management Branch, Ministry of Environment, (604) 387-9952. Eight regional offices operate depots: Vancouver Island, 758-3951; Cariboo, 398-4532; Lower Mainland, 584-8822; Skeena, 847-7260; Thompson-Nicola, 374-9717; Omineca-Peace, 565-6135; Kootenay, 354-6121; and Okanagan, 493-8261.

Manitoba

The Manitoba Hazardous Waste Management Corporation, (204) 945-5781, and the City of Winnipeg run a depot for three days during Environment Week. Other communities may run programs in conjunction with MHWMC, as Snow Lake did in October 1988. Ask your municipality or call MHWMC at the above number.

New Brunswick

The province has no program at present.

Newfoundland

No program at present.

Nova Scotia

There has been a collection day in Halifax.

Ontario

Household Hazardous Waste Program, Waste Management Branch, Ministry of Environment, (416) 323-5154. Peel Region permanent depot, 791-9400, ext. 372; Metropolitan Toronto (four permanent depots), 392-8285. The province has a cost-sharing program to encourage other municipalities to run single-day depots. For information, contact your local office of the Ontario Ministry of the Environment.

Prince Edward Island

Contact the Supervisor of Air Quality and Hazardous Waste, Department of Environment, (902) 892-0311. The province offers a one-day depot during Environment Week. Citizens should call the above number for information.

Quebec

There is no program for the province as a whole, but there has been one successful depot day in Montreal. The event is likely to become annual; residents should contact the Montreal Urban Community at 280-4330.

Saskatchewan

Call the Chemicals Management Section of the Ministry of Environment and Public Safety, (306) 787-6185. The province has no householders' program at present.

5 BAD PACKAGES

Until our various levels of government start to work together on reducing our packaging and hence our garbage, do your best to avoid the following examples of environment-unfriendly product wrappings.

1 Juice boxes: Those little boxes full of everything from apple juice to soya milk that you see in vast numbers on supermarket shelves. They can be neither reused nor recycled because they have an outer layer of plastic, a middle layer of cardboard, and an inner layer of aluminum foil.

2 Blister packages: These cardboard-backed packages with a plastic bubble on the front to hold the product do let you see the contents. Again, however, the different materials can't be separated efficiently for recycling, and so they become general garbage.

3 Individually wrapped snacks: A package of cookies that has each cookie separately wrapped may seem "hygienic" at first glance, but is the second wrapping truly necessary? And do we need individually wrapped restaurant portions of butter, sugar, salt, pepper, ketchup, and other condiments?

4 Single-serving microwaveables: Here too the layers of packaging are excessive. We could easily buy a larger package, take out the appropriate serving size, and heat or cook it on a plate or pan.

5 Polystyrene foam egg cartons: The issue here isn't so much one of reducing packaging as it is replacing a harmful package with a benign one. Cardboard egg cartons can be make from recycled paper, which saves resources. The foam packages can contain and are made with CFCs, which harm the ozone layer.

8. TRANSPORTATION

"The car has become a secular sanctuary for the individual, his shrine to the self, his mobile Walden Pond."

E.C. McDonagh

Transportation Uses of Energy (%)

Passenger Travel	Freight
60%	40%

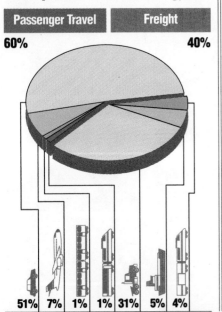

| 51% | 7% | 1% | 1% | 31% | 5% | 4% |

IN CONQUERING CANADA'S VAST SPACE, *modern transportation has done nothing less than make our national life possible, but at considerable environmental cost. Second only to industry in its consumption of energy, transportation accounts for one-quarter of all energy used in the country, with road vehicles responsible for 83% of that share.*

▲▲▲▲▲▲▲▲▲▲▲▲▲▲▲

It's also the country's largest source of air pollution, every year spewing into the atmosphere some 13.6 million tonnes of noxious fumes that poison forests, lakes, and marine life, contribute to global warming, and endanger human health. According to Environment Canada, transportation sources produce 64% of total nitrogen oxides (a cause of acid rain), 42% of hydrocarbons and 66% of carbon monoxide (both of which cause smog), 32% of the lead, 30% of the carbon dioxide, 76% of the benzene (a carcinogen), and unknown

▲▲▲▲▲▲▲▲▲▲▲▲▲▲▲

quantities of toluene, xylene, and ethylene dibromide.

Transportation also takes up space. To build all the necessary highways, roads, docks, railway tracks, and airfields, millions of hectares of forest, farmland, and cityscape have been sacrificed to the bulldozer.

By far the biggest players in the scenario are gas-powered motor vehicles, especially the automobile. Cars and trucks are much more damaging to human and environmental life than any other form of transport. A Swiss study, for example, found that, compared with trains, motor vehicles accounted for almost three times as much land use, 3.5 (cars) and 8.7 (trucks) times the energy consumed, nine times the pollution, and 24 times the accident rate. (Canadian figures would probably be similar or even worse for motor vehicles.)

> **"Cars and trucks are more damaging to human and environmental life than any other form of transport"**

We may all want to go back to nature, but we want to go back in a car. In the six decades since it became available to almost any North American over 16, the car has not only transformed the way we move about but assumed an almost sacred place in our lives and psyches. We have come to regard its gift of unprecedented individual mobility as a basic right. In 1986, Canadians owned 11.5 million cars, one for every 2.23 people. In global terms, the allure of the car has proven contagious: since 1950, the number of cars worldwide has jumped from 50 million to 386 million, and the total is continuing to rise. In the Soviet Union and Eastern Europe, car fleets jumped 500% from 1970 to 1985; and even in the developing countries the number of cars, though comparatively small, is growing at twice the rate as in the industrialized nations.

Yet the car's very success has brought a Pandora's box of modern ills that would have appalled Henry Ford: air pollution, used resources, noise, congestion, destruction of land and wildlife, human death and injury – all on a grand scale.

The following are some of the particular issues the Green Consumer should consider in assessing the environmental effects of the car.

* *

Losing Ground

The environmental group Friends of the Earth estimates that each kilometre of road or highway takes up about 6.5 hectares of land. In Ontario alone there are 155,000 km of highways, roads, and streets, adding up to a million hectares of land given over to motor vehicles. Our cities devote one-third of their area to roads and streets. Highways consume the largest amount of space per kilometre, but even relatively small roads can cause major controversy where they run through environmentally sensitive areas.

* *

Fuel Efficiency

Consumer pressure has been a key factor behind the trend to more fuel-efficient automobiles. Fifteen years ago, with the world still reeling from the shock of the first OPEC oil crisis, the motor industry was slowly forced to recognize that it would have to junk its gas-guzzlers and produce thriftier cars. And it was successful: the average car's fuel efficiency improved from 22 L/100 km to 15 L/100 km, with much higher ratings achieved by some Japanese and Western European car manufacturers. Between 1972 and 1982, the total amount of vehicle fuels consumed in the leading car-producing nations fell by 4%, even though the number of cars in use jumped by a third.

Each kilometre of road or highway takes up about 6.5 hectares of land.

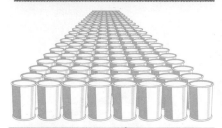

1,500 L OF OIL

TO MANUFACTURE THE AVERAGE CAR

10,000 L OF GAS

FUEL USED UNTIL THE VEHICLE IS SCRAPPED

Yet we still need enormous quantities of fuel to keep us on the move:

▬ Because other sectors have reduced their reliance on oil since the two OPEC crises, cars, which operate almost exclusively on petroleum-based fuels, actually account for a larger portion of oil use now (about a billion tonnes per year) than they did then.

▬ World gas consumption has edged up again since 1982, thanks to cheaper prices and a false sense of oil security. The truth is, all known oil reserves are expected to be used up in about 30 years.

▬ In Canada and the U.S., generally lower fuel-efficiency ratings and more hours on the road mean the average car burns up twice the amount of gas that its counterpart in Western Europe or Japan does.

▬ Even today, the average car takes the energy equivalent of 1,500 L of oil to manufacture and uses at least 10,000 L of fuel before it's scrapped.

The fuel economy of new cars is now a key selling point, and designers have achieved a great deal in making cars more efficient. The car industry's challenge for the 1990s will be both to maintain and improve on these achievements and to design cars that are safer, cleaner, quieter, and longer-lasting. The challenge for the Green Consumer will be to help persuade the industry that cleaner, quieter, and longer-lasting cars are what the customer wants.

Pollution

As factories, power stations, and other industrial sources of air pollution begin to clean up their acts, motor vehicles in all industrialized nations have emerged as the worst offenders. The average car, for instance, pumps five or six times its weight in carbon into the atmosphere each year. Despite get-tough environmental regulations and technical improvements in fuel economy over the past 15 years, the volume of most pollutants produced continues to grow. Many of the positive effects are being offset by an increase in sheer numbers of cars and kilometres of driving.

Cars produce six major forms of pollution:

1 **Hydrocarbons.** These gases react primarily with nitrogen oxides in the presence of sunlight to produce photochemical smog, the familiar urban haze that causes respiratory disorders and erodes buildings. Smog's principal component is ozone, a greenhouse gas and a suspected cause of forest damage. Gas-powered motor vehicles produce almost half of all hydrocarbon pollution in Canada.

2 **Nitrogen oxides.** Produced by all combustion processes, from power stations to motor-scooters, nitrogen oxide emissions are implicated in smog and, with sulphur oxides and unburnt hydrocarbons, in acid rain.

3 **Carbon monoxide.** The gas that kills you if you leave your car running in a closed garage, carbon monoxide is actually increasing in volume in most industrialized countries. Environment Canada says it's increasing here, too, although the share accounted for by transportation sources is actually decreasing.

4 **Particulates.** Road vehicles, especially diesel-powered ones, have overtaken the coal fire as the major source of soot. Particulate matter reduces visibility, blackens buildings, damages plants, and is implicated in the onset of cancer and other diseases.

5 **Lead.** Among the most ubiquitous of pollutants, lead at sufficient blood levels damages the brain and central nervous system; children are particularly vulnerable. However, lead is the one exhaust emission for which there is real hope of a dramatic reduction, as stringent lead restrictions are being enforced in many countries, including Canada.

6 **Carbon dioxide.** Although carbon dioxide is not a regulated automotive emission, as a greenhouse gas it is associated with perhaps the most serious long-term environmental threat of all, global warming.

What is being done – and what could be done – to control these pollutants?

Getting the Lead Out

Gasoline is a blend of up to 400 hydrocarbon chemicals. The exact recipe is juggled to produce varying levels of fuel economy or performance. Lead was first added to gas in the 1920s to stop engines from "knocking" and as a lubricant, to help improve the durability of exhaust valves and seats. But lead in gas inevitably meant lead in exhaust emissions, and that meant lead – lots of it – in the environment.

Lead is highly toxic and, unfortunately, does not break down naturally in the environment. The lead poured out from motor exhausts each year simply adds to the lead already in the atmosphere. However, gasoline in Canada is being steadily purged of lead and the effects are dramatic. In the decade after 1974, when unleaded gasoline became widely available in this country, automotive lead emissions dropped from 12,980 tonnes to 7,278 tonnes.

Environment Canada has taken steps to get rid of the rest. In 1987, the Clean Air Act lowered permissible lead content in leaded gasoline to 0.29 g/L. Dovetailing with this act were regulations limiting emissions of hydrocarbons, carbon monoxide, and certain oxides of nitrogen, which required the use of catalytic converters (see below) and, by extension, unleaded gas in all new light-duty vehicles (cars with catalytic converters run only on unleaded gas). And on December 1, 1990, leaded gas will no longer be sold in Canada.

On December 1, 1990, leaded gas will no longer be sold in Canada.

Catalytic Converters

Two-way catalytic converters (presently the most common) help eliminate up to 90% of exhaust pollutants by converting hydrocarbons and carbon monoxide into water vapour and carbon dioxide. Three-way converters, which also oxidize certain nitrogen oxides, became mandatory with the 1988 models. Contrary to myth, they do not affect either your car's fuel economy or its engine performance.

Pollution abatement devices in use to date, however, tend to come with some strings attached, in this case the slightly increased levels of carbon dioxide and sulphur dioxide they produce. But it's a worthwhile trade-off, at least until better fuels – renewable and non-polluting – come along.

Similarly, lean-burn engines, which have higher-than-average air-to-fuel ratios, burn fuel more efficiently and reduce nitrogen oxide and carbon monoxide emissions at the expense of tending to increase hydrocarbons.

Contrary to myth, catalytic converters do not affect either your car's fuel economy or its engine perfomance.

The Diesel Deal

D iesel cars are good examples of environmental trade-offs. On the one hand, in urban conditions they're much more energy-efficient than gas-powered vehicles, they're sturdier, they normally emit much less carbon monoxide and hydrocarbons, and they're lead-free. On the other hand, they produce more particulate pollution (soot or dark smoke), nitrogen oxides, and sulphur dioxides than gas engines with pollution devices, and they're noisier.

Overall, however, diesels still come out well – as long as you don't do a lot of highway driving. And if you opt for a diesel, be sure to have it regularly serviced.

* *

Alternative Fuels

E ventually we'll have to replace the gas in our cars with a non-polluting, renewable energy source. In the meantime, a number of alternate fuels with some advantages over gas are being tried, at least experimentally, with varying degrees of success. But so far all have drawbacks that chip away at the gains. It's a tricky issue.

The two alternatives most widely available in Canada are natural gas and propane. These high-octane fuels burn more cleanly than regular gas (they cut carbon monoxide and hydrocarbon emissions by 90% and are lead-free), are 6% to 15% more efficient, and are easier on engines. They may be an option for you if you do a lot of driving and live in an urban area where supplies and prices are good. The cost of converting a car ($1,500 for propane, $2,300 for natural gas) is often soon recovered in fuel savings.

Dedicated engine systems (those that run only on propane or natural gas) are somewhat cleaner than dual-fuel systems (those that also run on regular gas or blends): they reduce carbon dioxide emissions, whereas a dual system may actually increase them. However, in the case of natural gas, the carbon dioxide reduction may be partly offset by higher discharges of methane, a potent greenhouse gas.

A number of "biomass" fuels – those derived from plants – have been tried, most of them alcohols such as methanol ("wood alcohol") and ethanol (the kind in alcoholic drinks). In this country, methanol is usually manufactured from natural gas (Canada has a plentiful supply), but it can also be made from wood, coal, oil, or organic wastes. On the plus side it's a high-octane fuel that cuts noxious fumes in half and to some extent reduces carbon dioxide emissions (unless derived from coal, which would double them); and it can be blended up to 5% with gas without requiring changes to a car's fuel system or engine. On the minus side, it's currently very expensive to produce and is unlikely to be made in significant amounts from renewable sources.

Ethanol is distilled from various renewable feedstocks including corn, grain, and wood. In Canada it's selling mostly in the west in various "gasohol" blends that are much cleaner than gas but, like methanol, can emit appreciable amounts of carbon dioxide. Unfortunately, production is expensive at present (although the technology exists to make it much more cheaply) and requires vast areas of land to yield significant quantities.

Electric-powered vehicles, which are quiet and release no pollutants, are being tested experimentally. Here, the net environmental effects depend on what's used to generate the electricity. If it's coal, for instance, cars would release substantial amounts of carbon dioxide. Electricity is also likely to be expensive.

Methanol is usually manufactured from natural gas, wood, coal, oil, or organic wastes.

Ethanol is distilled from various renewable feedstocks including corn, grain, and wood.

Experiments with solar power have so far yielded cars that are as light as bicycles and go about as fast. Solar power also requires a sunny sky – for the foreseeable future, you can probably forget it.

Hydrogen, which you get by separating water, via electricity, into hydrogen and oxygen, may be our best hope for the (distant) future. It releases no pollutants, and unless the source of the electricity is fossil fuels, no carbon dioxide – its only emission is steam. It's also 15% to 45% more energy-efficient than gas. The catch, again, is the source of the electricity. If it's photovoltaics, wind, hydropower, or geothermal power, the environmental cost would be minimal.

* *

Cars of the Future

Improved car design has already made lighter, sleeker, more efficient models available to Green Consumers. But the fuel consumption of even the latest and best cars could be halved with the use of such innovations as more light materials like fibre-reinforced plastics and aluminum in bodywork, more ceramic components in the engine, and microprocessor-based fuel management systems. The fuel saved by using lightweight materials would probably not be offset by increased energy consumption in manufacture.

Several major car manufacturers (such as Volkswagen, Peugeot, Toyota, and Volvo) already have prototypes ready for production that can reach fuel ratings as low as 2.3 to 3.5 L/100 km. The problem is, they're still just prototypes. It seems that lower oil prices are encouraging car companies to slow down the incorporation of advanced fuel-economy technologies into mass-produced cars.

* *

The Environment-Friendly Driver

The car – whether gas-wasting behemoth or the most squeaky-clean model on the market – is only half the environmental equation. The other half is the driver. If you want to reduce to a minimum your car's negative impact on the environment, how you drive can be as important as what you drive. These driving and handling tips can help save not only the planet but your car and perhaps your life.

■ Slow down. It's the simplest way to save energy and reduce pollution. An aggressive driving style characterized by high speeds and lots of sudden stops and accelerations drastically increases exhaust emissions and fuel use. Cutting your driving speed from 112 km/h to 80 km/h reduces fuel consumption by 30%; reducing speed also cuts nitrogen oxide emissions.

■ Keep your car properly tuned and serviced to ensure maximum efficiency and minimum pollution. Despite the fact that manufacturers have designed better cars to comply with government emission standards, studies show that most Canadian cars still fail to meet them simply because they are not being adequately maintained.

■ Fit radial tires and keep them inflated. By cutting tire drag, radials give you a 6% to 8% fuel saving. Under-inflated tires (check your owner's manual for the recommended pressure) wear out faster and can cost you 4% more for fuel.

An aggressive driving style can drastically increase exhaust emissions and fuel use.

▬ Avoid air conditioning, which uses CFCs and increases fuel consumption by 8% to 12%, especially in stop-and-go city traffic. Use the air vents and windows instead. A folding cardboard shade for the windshield will help keep the car cooler when it's parked in the sun.

▬ Consider car pooling as a cheaper, cleaner, energy-saving way to get to work. If you only need a car occasionally, rent one or take a taxi.

▬ Cover several errands in one car trip by doing some advance planning.

▬ Drive less. Most car trips are within five or ten kilometres of the driver's home. Whenever possible walk, bike, or take public transit.

* *

GREEN CONSUMER RECOMMENDED BUYS

These cars have the best fuel-efficiency rates in Canada, according to the *1989 Fuel Consumption Guide*, from Transport Canada.

	Transmission	City L/100 km	Highway L/100 km
Chevrolet Sprint	M5+	5.5	4.4
Chevrolet Sprint	A3	5.9	5.3
Ford Festiva	M5+	6.0	5.0
Ford Festiva	M4+	6.2	5.4
Honda Civic CRX	M5+	6.9	5.3
Mercury Festiva	M5+	6.0	5.0
Mercury Festiva	M4+	6.2	5.4
Nissan Micra	M5+	6.4	4.7
Pontiac Firefly	M5+	5.5	4.4
Pontiac Firefly	A3	6.0	5.4
Subaru DL Justy	M5+	6.9	5.7
Subaru GL Justy	M5+	6.9	5.7
Suzuki Swift	M5+	6.2	4.8
Volkswagen Golf Diesel	M5+	6.5	5.0
Volkswagen Jetta Diesel	M5+	6.5	5.0
Volkswagen Jetta Diesel Turbo	M5+	6.4	5.0

Codes: A3 – Automatic, three gears
M4+ – Manual, four gears plus overdrive
M5+ – Manual, five gears plus overdrive

Urban Planning for a Greener Future

The automobile has transformed a lot more than our atmosphere; it has changed the face of our cities and suburbs, and the way we live in them.

Modern subdivisions, usually built on former farmlands, would be unlivable without the cars that their residents use to escape them. Subdivisions have few large parks, no corner stores, no neighbourhood pubs or restaurants. Instead they have malls, and recreation areas that the kids have to be driven to. Their lack of sidewalks gives the game away: no one is expected to walk in these non-neighbourhoods.

Forward-looking planners can design new communities to reduce automobile use by adding sidewalks, local gathering places of all kinds, and public transit routes.

In the process they'll be encouraging the neighbourly interactions that make residential areas safe and attractive, as well as reducing traffic jams, car accidents, smog, and the acceleration of global warming.

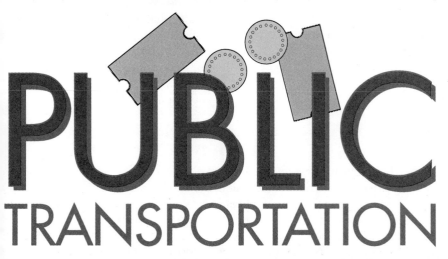

PUBLIC TRANSPORTATION

Ranking right up there among the country's major polluters are those who live – and drive – in the fast lane: Canada's urban motorists. They consume over 40% of the transportation sector's petroleum, making a sizeable contribution to acid rain and global warming.

More than 75% of Canadian municipalities have a public transportation system, which doesn't leave city drivers with much of an excuse. If just one out of ten switched to public transit, annual global oil production could be cut by 17%. Mass public transit consumes far less energy than the automobile. According to Transport 2000 Canada, this is how the figures stack up:

Vehicle	BTUs/passenger-km
Subway or light rail (200 passengers)	175
Bus (67 passengers)	285
Small car (1 passenger)	2,570

Most drivers rolling along city streets are en route to work or the hardware store; in other words, taking short trips around the corner or across town. The assumption is that the car is faster and more convenient than a bus or streetcar. In Canada's big cities, that's not true any more. Traffic jams and congestion have slowed urban drivers down to a stop-and-go gridlock on most major streets and roadways. That means more stress on the gas

Traffic congestion means more stress on the gas tank, on the environment, and certainly on the human spirit.

Passenger-kilometres from one litre of gas or energy equivalent

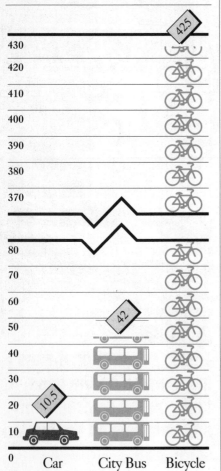

	Car	City Bus	Bicycle
430			425
420			
410			
400			
390			
380			
370			
80			
70			
60			
50		42	
40			
30			
20	10.5		
10			
0			

tank, on the environment, and certainly on the human spirit.

Public transportation has other advantages. Per passenger, a bus takes up about one-ninth of the road space occupied by cars, which means less congestion and less pollution. As well, building and maintaining city thoroughfares requires enormous quantities of land and resources, two more environmental problems that could be greatly reduced if more drivers were to abandon the car for short, in-city trips. The expansion and maintenance of a public transit system also requires land and resources, but it's certainly one of the better trade-offs.

In some of the country's urban centres, public transportation systems are just as congested as the city streets. For instance, in Toronto and Montreal the systems are already overtaxed, and city buses in Edmonton and Calgary are reaching a saturation point. It's hard to attract more riders to these overcrowded and often unreliable transit systems. What's needed is some lobbying for improvements on the part of riders and some vision and foresight on the part of city planners and politicians. To encourage the switch from private to public modes of transportation, the goal should be an efficient and integrated transportation system that offers commuters as many alternatives as possible.

For downtowners, walking and public transit are the best choices. For people who live in the suburbs, it may be a little more complicated. Ride-sharing and driving to the closest transit centre are possible alternatives. And one option that needs more serious consideration by both commuters and planners is the bicycle.

* *

The Bicycle

With the automobile destroying the environment and the quality of urban life, it's time to reconsider the advantages of the bicycle. Topping the list is its energy efficiency, which far outshines anything else on the road. A 25-km round trip on a bicycle burns 350 calories of energy, about as much as a person consumes in a hearty breakfast. The same trip by car requires 18,600 calories of energy (and in a less renewable form than bacon and eggs).

Another fact: in a car, one litre of gasoline provides 10.5 passenger-kilometres; in a city bus, about 42 passenger-kilometres; on a bicycle, the energy equivalent of more than 425 passenger-kilometres.

North Americans unfortunately consider the bicycle child's play. Obviously, we have lessons to learn from elsewhere. In Asia, the bicycle is the major mode of in-city transportation, and a few European countries launched national campaigns in the 1980s to encourage commuters to make the conversion from four wheels to two. In the Netherlands, for instance, there are almost 20,000 km of well-used bicycle paths; about half of all trips in the country are now made on two wheels. When the town of Erlangen in West Germany created 250 km of two-wheel paths, bicycle commuting doubled.

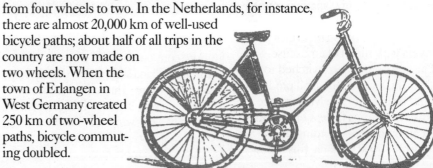

The same kind of effort and commitment has to be made by planners and politicians in Canadian cities. Right now, bicycle commuting is simply too dangerous on congested city streets. Besides bicycle paths, we also need bike-and-ride centres to encourage suburbanites to make the switch. What would also help are two-wheeler parking areas, as well as shower facilities. Once again, the bottom line is an integrated transportation network that provides space and facilities for the cyclist.

* *

Intercity Travel

How we travel from Moncton to Moose Jaw is as environmentally important as how we travel from home to work. Once again, energy efficiency per passenger-kilometre is the key issue:

Vehicle	BTUs/passenger-km
Train	270
Bus	320
Small car (2 passengers)	1,000
Boeing 767	1,990

It's clear from this chart that buses and trains are the most efficient modes of cross-country travel. Unfortunately, we've been abandoning them in droves in the last few years. Here are some alarming statistics from Transport Canada.

▬ From 1984 to 1987, the number of passengers choosing air travel steadily increased, reaching 18.9 million in 1987.

▬ In 1981, 8 million Canadians travelled by Via Rail; in 1987, the number of passengers had fallen to 5.9 million, a decline of 26.3%.

▬ The total number of intercity public transportation passengers declined from almost 60 million in 1980 to about 46 million in 1987, with buses losing about 90% of the shortfall.

Cheaper fares and better service from the airlines, as well as more money in the pockets of passengers, account for part of the decline in train and bus travel.

But something else is afoot here. Most Canadians find travelling more than about 500 km by bus too cramped and uncomfortable; their mode of choice is Via Rail, which stops in 900 Canadian cities, towns, and isolated communities (only 200 of these have airports). But with Via's service steadily deteriorating over the last decade, ridership has dropped. A large part of the problem is the federal government, which has abandoned Via for more energy-intensive modes of public transportation, especially air and road travel.

According to Transport 2000 Canada, studies indicate that 85% of Canadians believe that improving Via Rail is a "federal obligation." What it will take is some intense and relentless public lobbying for improved service and modern equipment. For the average consumer, a good start is to support Transport 2000's ongoing campaign to get the country back on the rails (**Transport 2000 Canada**, P.O. 858, Station B, Ottawa, ON, K1P 5P9).

The motor oil that your car can't use any more can be re-refined for reuse. That saves a non-renewable resource, as well as sparing the environment the effects of improper disposal. Used oil should never be burned, poured into a sewer, or dumped into landfill: along with oil go toxic and carcinogenic chemicals such as benzene, lead, cadmium, and polynuclear aromatic hydrocarbons.

If you have your car's oil changed at a service station, ask the manager what happens to it. Many stations have their oil collected by a contractor; will the contractor dump it or refine it?

Only a few Canadian communities have public collection systems for do-it-yourself oil-changers who want to have their used oil re-refined. Ottawa residents can pour their oil into a clean, sealed plastic container and put it out beside their Blue Box. In Metropolitan Toronto and in Alberta, certain service stations collect the oil; for the one nearest you, call the Recycling Council of Ontario at (416) 960-1025 in Toronto, or the Alberta Environment Department at (403) 427-5838.

If you do your oil change yourself and you don't live in Ottawa, Toronto, or Alberta, it will be harder to get the used oil into the hands of re-refiners. Most contractors who do this for service stations will not deal with individual consumers. But at least you can ensure that your oil is disposed of properly. Put it with your other household hazardous waste and treat it accordingly (see Chapter 7). And when you need more oil, look for a re-refined oil such as **President's Choice** *Green High Performance Motor Oil,* endorsed by Pollution Probe and available at **Loblaws** and other stores, or *SGX Motor Oil,* made by **Oil Canada Ltd.**

9. WORKING and INVESTING

S. Quinlan

F

OR MANY YEARS IT'S BEEN SAID *that the only business of business is to make money. Other sectors could worry about social or ethical issues; the best way for business to benefit society was to be successful. But lately, business has begun to realize that the companies that do good also tend to do well. Although they may not have perfect records, many of the most successful corporations in the world are also known for having good employee relations, supporting the arts, or sponsoring community projects.*

▲▲▲▲▲▲▲▲▲▲▲▲▲▲▲▲▲

"Enough, if something from our hands have power
To live, to act, and serve the future hour."

William Wordsworth

Now the old view of the role of business is being challenged by the new philosophy of "sustainable development." "The traditional economic view of the world," says David Powell, a consultant in corporate social performance, "is that social responsibility wastes money, hurts the company, and punishes shareholders. But that argument doesn't stand up under scrutiny." As government and the public become increasingly concerned about pollution, and the fines begin to

mount, "it's a sign of stupidity if a business refuses to take environmental issues seriously," says Powell.

There are substantial initial costs in being an environmentally responsible company – costs that are not incurred by less responsible corporations, especially those operating in countries where pollution laws are lax. Canadian industry feels that companies that take costly environmental measures should be compensated by tax breaks. That suggestion is controversial: should the public pay for what companies should be doing anyway? But we've all benefitted from the success of these companies, counters business, and bought their products. And if prices rise to pay for pollution controls, Canadian business will lose out to international competitors. It's not an easy issue to solve.

> **"** Canadian industry feels that companies that take costly environmental measures should be compensated by tax breaks. Should the public pay for what companies should be doing anyway? **"**

Fortunately, some companies have found that investments in pollution control have paid off generously. One of the first companies to discover this was Minneapolis-based **3M**. In 1975 3M instituted its "3P" program – "Pollution Prevention Pays." It did. Through recycling, the early introduction of pollution-control equipment, and eliminating pollution from the production process, the company saved $235 million over the next 11 years.

Even though pollution-control devices are a heavy investment, many companies are finding ways to allay the cost. Through the **Canadian Waste Materials Exchange** in Mississauga, Ont., hundreds of companies are saving money by swapping waste chemicals, solvents, and other pollutants. **Inco Ltd.** designed its own system to cut sulphur dioxide emissions and is now selling the design to other firms. In Owen Sound, Ont., **RBW Graphics**, a printing company, decided to take a hard look at its waste management after the city announced that landfill rates would double. After about a year of recycling waste paper, ink, and other garbage, the company found it had saved $280,000 at a cost of $60,000.

So doing the right thing environmentally doesn't necessarily mean losing money. In the past, both business and environmentalists tended to believe that the only way to preserve the environment was to limit growth. Now the concept of sustainable development, as outlined by the Brundtland Report, has suggested that, if we work at it hard enough, economic success and good environmental practices can go together. In fact, environmental needs can even stimulate business. For example, a large part of the international success of Japanese automakers stems from the more fuel-efficient engines they were obliged to develop in order to meet tough government emission standards at home. (American automakers responded to a similar situation by fighting the pollution controls in court.)

In fact, there are indications that preserving and cleaning up the environment will become a big money-making industry. Experts have predicted a growth rate of as high as 20% to 30%. One leader in the rapidly developing field of environmental problem-solving is **Eco-Tech Inc.** This wholly owned Canadian company designs and manufactures systems that recover chemicals and minimize hazardous waste in the metal-finishing industry. From a small company with only a couple of full-time employees, Eco-Tech has grown to become a leading supplier in its area, with 75 employees in Canada and a plant in Britain, exporting to 28 countries. Meanwhile, among new consumer products, "green" products have outperformed regular items, and industry experts estimate the North American market for environment-friendly products could be worth over $1 billion by the early 1990s.

There are indications that preserving and cleaning up the environment will become a big money-making industry. Experts have predicted a growth rate of as high as 20% to 30%.

Labour unions in particular can be effective in alerting employers and the public to environmental problems.

But where does this leave the individual? We tend to think of corporations as huge faceless organizations that we cannot possibly influence. We forget that those companies are made up of employees and rely on investment by individuals to operate. In short, those companies cannot exist without us. So by influencing the decisions made by the companies we'll invest in, we can make real improvements in the way Canadian corporations treat the environment.

✳ ✳ ✳ ✳ ✳ ✳ ✳ ✳ ✳ ✳ ✳ ✳ ✳ ✳ ✳ ✳ ✳ ✳ ✳ ✳

Influencing Decisions

If you're the general manager of a petrochemical refinery, then of course you have the opportunity to make good environmental decisions. But even less exalted employees can take responsibility for their company's environmental policies.

Employees can lobby their companies to set up environmental committees to monitor the company's performance. Employees can also implement purchasing policies that consider the environmental records of the companies they purchase goods and services from. You may also want to encourage your company pension plan not to invest in companies that harm the environment.

Labour unions in particular can be effective in alerting employers and the public to environmental problems. As Rick Coronado of the Environmental Committee of the Windsor and District Labour Council pointed out in a report to the Labour Education Institute, workers are often the first to feel the effects of chemicals and products that will later cause environment and public health problems.

Moreover, because of their power in the workplace and their experience in organizing and negotiating, unions can be particularly effective in promoting better environmental legislation and encouraging employers to practise environmental safety in the workplace. For example, the environment committee for Local 444 of the Canadian Auto Workers has urged members to monitor materials being sent from their plants to the landfill sites, and to inform the committee if toxic materials or items that could be recycled are being dumped. Coronado recommends that union locals set up their own environment committees and cooperate with community groups to combat pollution problems. For example, union members in the Windsor area helped to collect 40,000 names on a petition protesting the giant Detroit garbage incinerator, which is expected to release cancer-causing toxins.

There are also steps you can take in any office or factory, regardless of what your company actually does, to make your workplace more environment-friendly. If your premises are ripe for renovation, you will have even greater opportunities to implement energy-efficient improvements in such areas as heating, air conditioning, and ventilation; see Chapter 5.

* *

Recycling

Paper, cardboard boxes, plastics, cans, glass bottles, and food waste can all be recycled. One of Toronto's large downtown office complexes, the Sun Life buildings, recycled 180 of 780 tonnes of waste in 1988, reducing their disposal costs by $25,000.

If you want to start a paper recycling program, contact one of the following organizations or government offices.

BRITISH COLUMBIA

Policy and Program Development, Government Management Services, 2nd Floor, 4000 Seymour Place, Victoria, BC, V8X 4Y3. (604) 389-3375.

ALBERTA

Director of Marketing, Paper Chase Recycling, 11941-73rd Street, Edmonton, AB, T5B 1Z7. (403) 477-9391.

SASKATCHEWAN

Air and Land Protection Branch, Saskatchewan Environment and Public Safety, Walter Scott Building, 3085 Albert Street, Regina, SK, S4S 0B1. (306) 787-6209.

MANITOBA

Recycling Council of Manitoba, 1329 Niakwa Road East, Winnipeg, MB, R2J 3T4. (204) 257-3891.

ONTARIO

Ministry of the Environment, Waste Management Branch, 40 St. Clair Avenue West, 5th Floor, Toronto, ON, M4V 1M2. (416) 323-5195.

QUEBEC

Department of Recycling, Ministry of the Environment, 3900 Marly Street, Saint Foy, PQ, G1X 4E4. (418) 644-3376.

NEW BRUNSWICK

Waste Management Planner, Sanitary Engineering Section, Environmental Protection Branch, P.O. Box 6000, Fredericton, NB, E3B 5H1. (506) 453-2861.

NOVA SCOTIA

Recycling Officer, Ministry of the Environment, P.O. Box 2107, Halifax, NS, B3J 3B7. (902) 424-5300.

Clean Nova Scotia Foundation, P.O. Box 2528, Station M, Halifax, NS, B3J 3N5. (902) 424-5245.

NEWFOUNDLAND

Manager of Environmental Quality and Assessment, Environment Canada, P.O. Box 5037, St. John's, NF, A1C 5V3. (709) 772-4087.

Nova Recycling, P.O. Box 5128, St. John's, NF, A1C 5V6. (709) 579-7466.

PRINCE EDWARD ISLAND

Information and Assessment Coordinator, Recycling, Department of the Environment, P.O. Box 2000, Charlottetown, PE C1A 7N8. (902) 368-5024.

Paper, cardboard boxes, plastics, cans, glass bottles, and food waste can all be recycled.

Recycled Paper

Naturally you'll want to purchase recycled paper as well. The paper you are dropping into the office recycling bin – the industry calls this "post-consumer" waste paper – isn't yet being recycled into new office paper, at least not in Canada. It's made into tissue and boxboard. But increasing demand is encouraging papermakers to invest in the equipment that will make it possible for Canadians to close the recycling loop.

In the meantime, lots of office paper with "recycled content" is on the market. Most manufacturers use the term to include a combination of two main categories of fibres. The first category is the paper and fibre that is left over during the regular milling process, which has always been reclaimed and recycled. These materials make up at least 10% of the content of most "new" paper. The second principal source of recycled content is "post-commercial" waste paper: printed paper from printing plants and similar pre-consumer sources.

Fraser Inc. is the only Canadian papermaker that uses de-inked post-commercial fibre in its fine (printing and writing) papers. On average, about 10% of the fibre going into its fine papers is recycled from this source.

Domtar Fine Papers calculates its "waste fibre" content as a combination of reclaimed manufacturing waste, forest residues, post-consumer waste, and fibrous material from municipal wastes. By this definition, all bond paper produced by Domtar Fine Papers has 40% to 60% recycled content. Domtar also is marketing 100% recycled paper made at its mill near St. Catharines.

Rolland Inc., which uses the same definition, includes an average of 45% waste fibre in its business papers.

The Paper Source (Fallbrook, ON, K0G 1A0) sells only paper with a minimum of 50% recycled content. Since no office paper with that much recycled content is currently available in Canada, The Paper Source distributes only U.S. papers, including some with substantial amounts of post-consumer fibre.

Conservatree Paper Company (2107 Van Ness Avenue, San Francisco, CA, 94109) also supplies American-made papers with high levels of recycled content.

Lots of office paper and fine paper with "recycled content" is available in the market.

Lighting and Furniture

Use compact fluorescents in both overhead and desk lamps, and make sure there are accessible switches so they can be turned off when they're not needed. Lower the lighting levels where possible. Look for furniture that is not made from tropical hardwoods (see Chapter 5).

* * * * * * * * * * * * * * *

Cleaning

Substitute less toxic cleaners for the usual commercial products (see Chapter 3). See that the old cleaners are treated as hazardous waste when they're disposed of.

* * * * * * * * * * * * * * *

Washrooms

Make sure you have aerated faucets (see Chapter 5) and reusable cloth roll towels. Tank dams in toilets will save water.

* * * * * * * * * * * * * * *

Kitchens and Cafeterias

Use washable dishes and cutlery instead of disposables. Even if you've only got a coffeemaker, you can do your part by using mugs and spoons instead of disposable cups and stir sticks. Make sure your refrigerator is efficient, and generally follow the same rules as for your kitchen at home (see Chapter 5).

Landscaping

If you're lucky enough to have lawns and flowerbeds around your workplace, discourage the use of chemical fertilizers and pesticides. Food waste from the cafeteria can be composted to improve the garden's soil.

* * * * * * * * * * * * * * *

Transportation

If your company supplies cars to employees, encourage them to purchase fuel-efficient vehicles with good pollution controls. To encourage cycling, install a bike rack, and hire a bicycle courier where possible.

* * * * * * * * * * * * * * *

Different offices will have different sorts of environmental problems to deal with, and it's amazing how many changes you can make. One excellent example of a workplace that can do a lot to clean up its environmental act is a school. Not only do schools employ thousands of people and buy huge amounts of products, they also influence the attitudes of young people. The possibilities for science projects that focus on environmental issues are innumerable: try planting an ecology park one year, for instance.

* *

WHMIS

The Workplace Hazardous Materials Information System (WHMIS), recently passed by the federal government, provides guidelines for ensuring that workers know how to handle hazardous materials safely. It applies to all workplaces in which such materials are used. The basic elements of a WHMIS program are strict regulations for labelling every hazardous material used in a plant; data sheets for every hazardous material, giving further information on how to use it safely; and education for *every* worker in the plant.

Through WHMIS, all workers should know what equipment they need to use the material (gloves, safety glasses, etc.), what special precautions they need to take, and how to store it or dispose of empty containers safely.

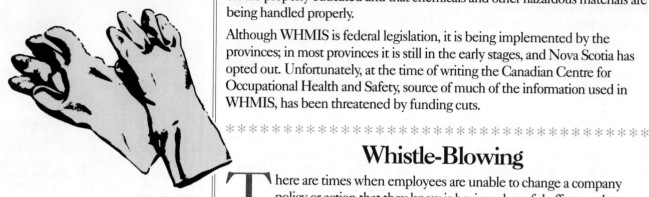

A symbolic labelling system makes sure that even workers who are illiterate or who do not read English will be able to understand the dangers of the materials they're handling. Although WHMIS puts personal responsibility in the hands of the workers, it does not absolve companies of their duty to make sure that workers are properly educated and that chemicals and other hazardous materials are being handled properly.

Although WHMIS is federal legislation, it is being implemented by the provinces; in most provinces it is still in the early stages, and Nova Scotia has opted out. Unfortunately, at the time of writing the Canadian Centre for Occupational Health and Safety, source of much of the information used in WHMIS, has been threatened by funding cuts.

✳✳✳✳✳✳✳✳✳✳✳✳✳✳✳✳✳✳✳✳✳✳✳✳✳✳✳✳✳✳✳✳✳✳✳✳✳

Whistle-Blowing

There are times when employees are unable to change a company policy or action that they know is having a harmful effect on the environment. If you find yourself in that situation you may want to consider whistle-blowing – informing the public and/or the government of the company's misbehaviour.

Think carefully about that decision. All provinces have legislation protecting whistle-blowers – an environmental protection or health and safety act – *if* they take their information to the government. But your legal situation if you're caught and punished by the company is far from clear-cut, and it may prove expensive to defend yourself.

If you don't belong to a union and if there's any other good excuse for firing you – the company is overstaffed and you're the least senior person, for example – then you're particularly vulnerable. Moreover, people who inform on their company, even in the most righteous cause, are often ostracized by co-workers, friends, and relatives and may suffer serious financial and personal problems. The name Karen Silkwood is enough to remind us how serious the consquences can be for a whistle-blower. Nor are results guaranteed. As one whistle-blower said, "If you have God, the law, the press, and the facts on your side, you have a 50-50 chance of winning."

Whistle-blowers and the people who counsel them give the following advice.

▬ Count the cost. If informing on your company or government department could cause devastating problems for you and your family – for example, if you're close to retirement and could lose your pension – maybe someone else should take the responsibility. If you do decide to take the risk, make sure you and your family are prepared emotionally and financially for the consequences.

All provinces have legislation protecting whistle-blowers if they take their information to the government.

▬ Get advice – from a lawyer, your professional association, your union, your provincial environment ministry, from fellow employees you trust, from other whistle-blowers.

▬ Check your rights. You may be protected under provincial legislation – but there may also be qualifications. For example, you are protected by legislation if you complain to the government, but not if you talk to the media.

▬ Prepare your case thoroughly. You're taking a big risk, and you don't want to fail to make your point just because you don't have all your facts straight. The worst-case scenario is that you'll lose your job and still not expose the danger.

▬ Send the information where it will do the most good. Don't assume that someone higher up in the company will be as shocked as you are and immediately resolve the problem. Some whistle-blowers advise you to work through the system, taking your case higher and higher until someone will listen. Others say put your own safety first and "brown envelope" – send the information anonymously to the media or a governing organization that's in a position to investigate and force changes. You may also want to wait for the appropriate moment to expose the problem – a change in management may mean a better chance of changes. Some people feel that brown-enveloping and waiting for the right moment are cowardly. But the important thing is not for you to play the hero, it's to expose the danger. Perhaps the most successful whistle-blower of all time was Deep Throat, the media source who helped uncover the Watergate scandal, and his identity is still secret.

T he case of Alex Karamanchuri, a chemist at the Liquor Control Board of Ontario, illustrates the persistence necessary for effective whistle-blowing. In 1978, Karamanchuri began finding high levels of a cancer-causing chemical, ethyl carbamate, in Ontario wines. When his superiors failed to take effective action, Karamanchuri continued his tests and bombarded them with memos. Meanwhile, he was passed over for promotions. It wasn't until a new government was elected in Ontario that he was finally able to force his superiors to take action, by threatening to go over their heads to the new officials. Karamanchuri's memos and carefully documented experiments prompted a major investigation and a clean-up in the wine industry – seven years after his initial discovery.

For further information and advice on whistle-blowing, you can contact Dave Bennet, at the **Canadian Labour Congress** (2841 Riverside Drive, Ottawa, ON, K1Z 8X7).

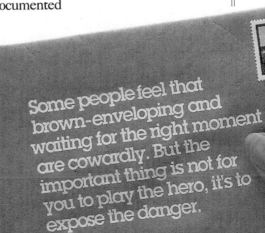

Some people feel that brown-enveloping and waiting for the right moment are cowardly. But the important thing is not for you to play the hero, it's to expose the danger.

Ethical Investing

O nce we recognize that environment-saving companies are not necessarily money-losing enterprises, the idea of "ethical investment" becomes very attractive. There are many different ways of investing your money, from leaving it in a bank account to buying a home. But usually "ethical investment" refers to buying stocks and bonds of publicly owned companies. Ethical investors refuse to invest in corporations whose policies they disagree with and may also try to encourage responsible corporations by buying their bonds and shares.

Of course, deciding which companies are environmentally responsible is not easy. Should you invest in a company that continues to pollute the environment but is making measurable changes to improve its environmental record? Or should you keep yourself pure and invest only in non-controversial companies – while continuing to drive your car and use unrecycled paper products? Do you simply want to avoid companies with a bad environmental record? Or do you want to actively encourage companies that are showing environmental initiative? Since environmental concern has become very fashionable, how do you tell the sincere corporation from the one that's cynically donned a few flashy improvements to cover a less-than-impressive performance? And do you really have the financial security, temperament, and interest to invest in corporations? Perhaps you'd be better off making your own ethical statement by investing in a community co-operative fund or a credit union.

An invaluable guide for dealing with all these issues is *The Canadian Guide to Profitable Ethical Investing* (Lorimer, 1989). The guide points out the ethical implications of every kind of investment, from savings accounts at your local bank to credit unions to stocks and bonds, as well as explaining how those investments work.

Some investors take a more proactive approach and buy stock in a company in order to have a say in how that company is run. Churches, universities, and other concerned organizations have often used their stock holdings to try to influence a corporation's policies. Certain types of stock entitle you to voting rights at a company's annual meeting. It's highly unlikely that you as an individual will ever have enough stock to vote down a bad policy, but your votes do give you the right to speak at the annual meeting.

If you've really got big bucks to play with, then you might want to consider lending "venture capital" – start-up funds – to companies with exciting environmental technology. You could be funding the ecological equivalent of the Gutenberg press, but you could also lose everything you've invested, so this idea is obviously only for people who are financially secure.

Envestment Corporation is attempting to match investors with environmental companies that need venture capital. You can write to them at 260 Queen's Quay West, Suite 1202, Toronto, ON, M5J 2N3.

If you do want to invest in corporations, then you have to decide whose stocks and bonds you want to buy. In response to public interest, the financial community is becoming more sensitive to ethical issues. **EthicScan Canada Ltd.** (P.O. Box 165, Postal Station S, Toronto, ON, M5M 4L7) is one company that will provide information on companies related to a variety of issues, including the environment, for a fee. The company also publishes a bi-monthly newsletter, *The Corporate Ethical Monitor.*

Another book that can help you decide what companies you want to invest in is *Rating America's Corporate Conscience*, written by the Council on Economic Priorities (Addison-Wesley, 1986). (A shorter guide from the Council, *Shopping for a Better World: A Quick and Easy Guide to Socially Responsible Supermarket Shopping*, contains similar information, but with much less detail.) Although the book deals only with American corporations, many of these companies have branches or subsidiaries in Canada. Be aware, however, that a company's environmental record may be different here than it is in the U.S. The Council also plans to publish in the spring of 1990 an ethical investing sourcebook, tentatively titled *Investing in America's Corporate Conscience*, to be distributed in Canada by Prentice-Hall. For further information you can contact: **Council on Economic Priorities**, 30 Irving Place, New York, NY 10003.

There are also a few environment companies listed on stock exchanges. But remember that many new technologies, such as biodegradable plastics, are controversial. Moreover, these stocks can be volatile, especially when some new environmental crisis is at the top of newscasts. The June 1989 issue of *Moneywise*, a magazine published by *The Financial Post*, contains a good summary of publicly listed companies that are involved in environmental technology.

If you feel you don't have the time or expertise to decide what companies you should invest in, consider a mutual fund.

When you buy shares in a mutual fund, the fund takes the money placed in it by investors and invests it in a variety of companies. Mutual funds have become popular recently because they are seen as a relatively safe way for investors to play the stock market, and they have a fairly good rate of return. And since someone else makes the decisions about what companies to invest in, the mutual fund saves the investor a lot of research time. (Remember, however, that unlike a savings bond or bank deposit, there is no insurance on a mutual fund. If the fund declines drastically in value or the fund's managers prove unscrupulous, you have no protection against losses.)

For many years there have been special "ethical" mutual funds that did not invest in firms that made liquor or weapons. More recently, funds have been developed that tackle other ethical concerns, including corporations' environmental records.

Ethical mutual funds in Canada still have only a tiny percentage of the market for mutual fund investments, but members of the **Canadian Network for Ethical Investment,** an association that includes brokers, investment advisers, and investors, say the movement is fast-growing and could eventually control 10% of the $150 billion in Canadian pension funds – not to mention individual investments. For more information, write to Box 1615, Victoria, BC, V8W 2X7.

Mutual funds are seen as a relatively safe way for investors to play the stock market and have a fairly good rate of return.

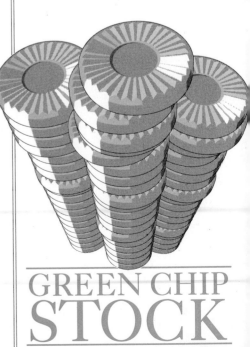

GREEN CHIP STOCK

Some good ethical mutual funds have decided not to include environmental factors in their criteria for companies they will invest in, because they feel the issues are too complicated. Instead, they stick to issues such as a corporation's dealings with South Africa and Third World countries or its involvements in military contracts. (They may also decline to invest in companies involved with nuclear power.) However, the mutual funds listed below do screen companies for their environmental policies. Some funds simply avoid companies with bad environmental records, while others actively seek out corporations with innovative environmental programs. (You will probably need to make special arrangements through your broker to purchase the U.S. funds.)

✳ ✳

These mutual funds do screen companies for their environmental policies.

▰▰▰ Environmental Investment Canadian Fund/International Environmental Investment Fund (sponsored by Energy Probe), Environmental Investment Funds Ltd., 225 Brunswick Avenue, Toronto, ON
M5S 2M6

▰▰▰ Investors Summa Fund Ltd., 280 Broadway, Winnipeg, MB
R3C 3B6

▰▰▰ Dreyfus Third Century Fund, 767 Fifth Avenue, New York, NY
10153

▰▰▰ New Alternatives Fund, 295 Northern Boulevard, Great Neck, NY
11021

▰▰▰ Pax World Fund, 224 State Street, Portsmouth, NH
03801

In addition, the following funds are open to group investors, such as pension funds.

▰▰▰ Canadian Ethical Dynamic and Responsible Balanced Fund (CEDAR), #1, 10005 – 80 Avenue, Edmonton, AB
T6E 1T4

▰▰▰ Crown Commitment Fund, Crown Life Insurance, 120 Bloor Street East, Toronto, ON
M4W 1B8

Theoretically, ethical investment funds should not perform as well as funds with no restrictions, because they have a narrower range of companies to invest in. Contrary to theory, however, most of the funds have performed quite well. But the performance of particular funds or of mutual funds in general may change over the years, so make sure you check a fund's recent performance before investing and track it carefully once you have invested. A broker or financial planner may be able to help you.

✳ ✳ ✳ ✳ ✳ ✳ ✳ ✳ ✳ ✳ ✳ ✳ ✳ ✳ ✳ ✳ ✳ ✳ ✳

For further information on ethical investing and the environment, you can contact the following organizations.

▰▰▰ The Social Investment Forum, 711 Atlantic Avenue, Boston, MA
02111

▰▰▰ Taskforce on the Churches and Corporate Responsibility, 129 St. Clair Avenue West, Toronto, ON
M4V 1N5

▰▰▰ Social Investment Study Group, c/o Ted Jackson, E.T. Jackson and Associates, Suite 712, 151 Slater Street, Ottawa, ON
K1P 5H3

If you decide to get involved in ethical investing, remember that good intentions are no guarantee that you won't lose money. Investments you consider ethical are subject to the same fluctuations as any other investment. So do your research, get expert advice from a stockbroker or financial planner, and be aware of any risks you're taking.

* *

GREEN C·A·R·D

5007 6630 0-299 5790

AFFINITY CREDIT CARDS

Another way to send money in the right direction is through "affinity" credit cards. These are special Visa cards or MasterCards that direct a portion of your payments to a designated charitable organization. Every time you purchase something with the card and every time you pay an annual fee, a percentage of that money is donated by the bank, trust company, or credit union to the organization. For example, both Bank of Montreal and Canada Trust now offer affinity MasterCards that provide funds to environmental groups. Ducks Unlimited has netted more than $45,000 from the Bank of Montreal, and the Canadian Wildlife Federation hopes to receive over $50,000 by September 1990. World Wildlife Fund (in Canada) uses the money it gets from Canada Trust to help pay its administrative costs, freeing up donations for field projects. Canada Trust gives the WWF $10 from each new affinity MasterCard application and $20 for each renewal, as well as a percentage from each card transaction. If your credit card funds an operation you want to support, why not switch your card to an affinity card? If it doesn't, then encourage your bank, trust company, or credit union to fund that organization – or switch your credit card to one that does.

INVEST IN GREEN

10. TRAVEL and LEISURE

DESPITE THE FAMOUS INJUNCTION to *"Leave only your thanks, take nothing but photographs,"* it's all too easy to leave crushing footprints wherever we travel. Whether you're spending an afternoon at the zoo or travelling for a year in the Far East, there are environmental issues to be considered. Your choice of transportation is important; see Chapter 8. How will you affect the cultural and physical environment you're entering? And while you're having fun, are you supporting practices and organizations you'd rather not be involved with?

"It appears that many people when they travel really see nothing at all except the reflection of their own ideas."

Stephen Leacock

▲▲▲▲▲▲▲▲▲▲▲▲▲▲▲

Three hundred million people now travel internationally every year. Canadians are eager members of this globe-trotting family. In 1988, we took more than 105 million trips outside the country. Exotic destinations are becoming increasingly popular. By 1984 about 17% of all international travellers were visiting the Third World – twice the proportion of 10 years before. Nor is it only young backpackers who are trekking in Nepal or cruising the Galapagos Islands. Third World countries are becoming standard destinations for more conventional travellers. This trend is causing problems for both the physical environment and the people who live in those countries.

" At its best tourism can be an instrument of greater understanding, breaking down the barriers among people and informing them about one another's culture, society, and philosophy "

Contours, the newsletter of the **Ecumenical Coalition on Third World Tourism** (P.O. Box 24, Chorakhebua, Bangkok 10230, Thailand), outlines the problems this trend is creating:

The geographical direction of tourism, on an international level, consists of people from the First World travelling to visit islands, beaches and picturesque towns of the Third World. But though we opt for the "tropical paradise," we demand it come with all the comforts of home. So we drop glass-and-steel hotels next to peasant villages or fishermen's huts, creating luxuriant, forbidden facilities that no resident would dare enter… Though we may be only modestly well-off, we pay prices of a staggering size in local terms… In the course of our stays, we make no use at all of the lodgings that residents use, or of their transportation or dining spots.

Although tourism is often promoted as a way of bringing money into poorer nations, it may actually be economically disadvantageous for a Third World country. Consider that money has to be sent out of the country to pay for elevators, cars, buses, air conditioners, Western-style food, and the other amenities that tourists demand. Much of the money tourists spend is paid up front to foreign tour companies, airlines, and hotel chains before they even leave home. But meanwhile the government is spending huge sums on tourism development in the hopes it will bring in foreign currency – sums that might better be spent on health care and education or other forms of development. Land must be cleared – often without proper recompense and sometimes with violence – for hotels, airports, and tourist sites. Farmers and fishermen give up their traditional livelihood and become dependent on the tourist trade; but the best jobs usually go not to local people but to staff imported by the international companies. Traditional social structures and ways of life vanish, resulting in social problems. And if there's a hurricane, political unrest, or simply a change in fashion, the tourists stop coming and suddenly the community is bereft of the business it's come to rely on, with little to fall back on.

The incidence of economic dislocation, prostitution, and other havoc wreaked by tourism in the Third World is enough to make you feel you should just stay home. But at its best, tourism can be an instrument of greater understanding, breaking down the barriers among people and informing them about one another's culture, society, and philosophy.

One way to make travel a method of international diplomacy rather than economic exploitation is to live more like the locals. Instead of staying in the big international hotels and eating in expensive Western-style restaurants, stay in local lodgings and experiment with the local food. That way, you're supporting the local economy.

Make travel a method of international diplomacy: stay in local lodgings, experiment with local food – support the local economy.

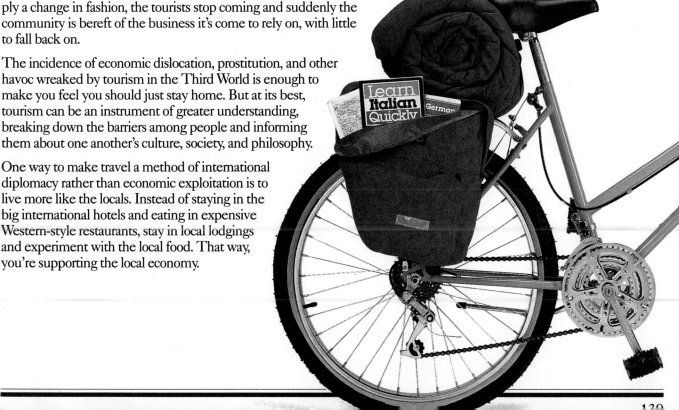

Travelling closer to the ground is not only cheaper, it's more stimulating. You're exposed daily to a different culture, a different way of looking at the world. No less a person than Arthur Frommer of *On $5 a Day* fame has come to the same conclusion. "After 30 years of writing standard guidebooks," writes Frommer in the introduction to his latest guidebook, "I began to see that most of the vacation journeys undertaken by Americans were trivial and bland, devoid of important content, cheaply commercial, and unworthy of our better instincts and ideals."

In his *The New World of Travel* (General, 1988), Frommer takes a more authentic approach to travel, covering everything from ethical, pro-environment travel and study vacations to discount travel and tours. Other travel books, such as the *Lonely Planet* series, give good advice on travelling cheap in the Third World. You can get *Alternative Tourism: A Resource Guide* and other publications on responsible travelling from the **Center for Responsible Tourism,** 2 Kensington Road, San Anselmo, CA, 94960, USA.

Let's not be naïve, however. Travellers who stay and eat in local establishments are just as capable of bad behaviour as those staying in air-conditioned international hotels – and the local people are forced to put up with *both* groups. So if you're going to travel that way, be on your best behaviour. Improper dress, stinginess (or extravagance), rowdiness, bad language, sexual promiscuity, arrogance and just plain rudeness, and impatience with local customs and sense of time are just a few of the characteristics some Western travellers have become known for.

Some of that behaviour occurs because travellers are not prepared to encounter a totally different culture. They may behave badly out of ignorance or because they're overwhelmed and confused – suffering from "culture shock." Preparing yourself by researching the country, its history, culture, and religious beliefs will make the travel experience easier for you and your hosts.

* *

Travelling closer to the ground is not only cheaper, it's more stimulating.

The Ecumenical Coalition on Third World Tourism recommends the following code of ethics for travellers:

▬ Travel in a spirit of humility and with a genuine desire to meet and talk with local people.

▬ Be aware of the feelings of the local people; prevent what might be offensive behaviour.

▬ Cultivate the gift of listening and observing, rather than merely hearing or seeing, or thinking you know all the answers.

▬ Realize that other people may have concepts of time and thought patterns that are very different – not inferior, only different.

▬ Instead of seeing the beach paradise only, discover the richness of another culture and way of life.

▬ Get acquainted with local customs; respect them.

▬ Remember that you are only one among many visitors; do not expect special privileges.

▬ When bargaining in the shops, remember that the poorest merchant will give up a profit rather than give up his or her personal dignity.

▬ Make no promises to local people or to new friends that you cannot deliver on.

▬ Spend time each day reflecting on your experiences in order to deepen your understanding. What enriches you may be robbing others.

▬ If you want a home away from home, why travel?

Staying in local inns is not always an option for everyone – using a squat toilet is no fun if you have arthritis. Here are some suggestions from the Center for Responsible Tourism that you can still follow:

■ If you travel in a group, keep it small.

■ Allow plenty of time in each place. It's better to visit a few places leisurely than several places in a rush.

■ Plan visits to local markets rather than the tourist shops.

■ Try to eat local foods rather than retreating to international cuisine in hotels and restaurants.

■ Wherever and whenever possible, use local transport.

■ Try to spend as much time in rural areas as in cities.

* *

Don't assume, by the way, that eating in local restaurants puts you in danger of food poisoning. Some experienced Third World travellers insist that it's actually safer to eat in moderately priced local restaurants. However, depending on the area, there are particular types of food you should avoid. For more information you can consult one of the many guides to healthy travelling, such as *Travelling in Tropical Countries* by Jacques Hébert (Hurtig, 1986) or *How to Stay Healthy Abroad* by Richard Dawood (Oxford, 1989).

Other ways to get to know a country without exploiting it include studying a language or some other subject or helping in a development project. *The Directory of Alternative Travel Resources* lists hundreds of such options around the world (**One World Family Travel Network**, P.O. Box 3417, Berkeley, CA, 94703, USA).

The burgeoning business of travel has become a threat not only to local cultures and economies but also to the environment. Thanks to tourism, parks are created and cultural monuments preserved that might otherwise be destroyed. But the trend of easy access to world-famous but environmentally sensitive sites recently caused Sir Edmund Hillary to comment that Mount Everest is "in danger of becoming a rubbish dump." A stampede of camera safaris to "capture" wildlife in its natural habitat has put increasing pressure on many of the world's most singular and treasured ecosystems.

The ecologically fragile Galapagos Islands, where Darwin uncovered many of the basic rules of evolution, is evolving into a "must see" world tourist attraction. Although a yearly limit of 12,000 visitors had been set, this was quickly upped to 25,000 to take advantage of tourist dollars. By 1986, visitors numbered in excess of 30,000.

In Nepal, where locals rely on wood for fuel, the influx of trekkers has resulted in serious deforestation, as trees are burned to provide visitors with heat, baths, boiled water for drinking, and Western-style meals that take longer to cook. Deforestation has resulted in loss of topsoil, dangerous landslides, and the disappearance of local wildlife.

On tropical islands, the clearing of swamps to build tourist facilities increases soil erosion. The soil washes onto the coral reefs, killing the coral; without the coral reefs to act as breakwaters, the local shorelines are eroded, and the beaches that attracted the tourists in the first place are washed away. The tourists move on, but the local ecosystem is destroyed.

Mount Everest is in danger of becoming a rubbish dump.

Inform yourself about species that are on the endangered list in your destination.

However, there are tour companies that have made an effort to limit and even counteract the environmental damage. For example, **Worldwide Adventures** was the first Western tour company to carry kerosene on its Nepalese treks as an alternative to burning wood. The company, which offers everything from a trip up the Amazon to a sail around grizzly-bear birthing grounds, also invests in conservation projects in the areas it visits and gives a thorough briefing on environmental and cultural do's and don'ts to its clients. If you're considering a travel package, check to see that the tour company has a sound environmental policy.

Tourists also cause environmental problems in their shopping. Although the United Nations Convention on International Trade in Endangered Species (CITES) prohibits the export of endangered animal and plant life, that doesn't mean you won't find those items for sale in tourist markets and shops. Inform yourself about species that are on the endangered list in your destination. Many airports have displays about CITES, and you can also get information from the **Canadian Wildlife Service**, Environment Canada, Ottawa, ON, K1A 0H3.

****

The impact of tourism within Canada is increasing, too. Tourism brought in over $21 billion (4% of our GNP) in 1987 and is creating jobs faster than any other industry.

Prime destinations for both Canadian travellers and overseas visitors are Canada's 33 national parks and other wilderness areas. More than 21 million people visited them in 1987.

Unfortunately, an increase in visitors is happening just as governments are cutting park funding. That puts more responsibility on all of us as individual visitors to make sure our parks are maintained as natural paradises where humans can continue to seek refuge in harmonious co-existence with plants and animals. The important word to remember is "low-impact"; when you visit a park, whether you're just stopping for a few hours or staying for several days, no one should see any evidence that you've been there.

The Woodsman's Code, developed by the Conservation Council of Ontario and the Canadian Camping Association, tells you how to be a "low-impact" user of our parks and wilderness areas. It was written for campers, but many of the rules apply equally to hikers and other daytime visitors.

Planning

1 Keep the group size small to reduce the impact on campsites.

2 Prepare carefully:

▬ Research the trip: become familiar with the geography of the area and learn the local fishing, forestry, and wildlife laws and regulations.

▬ Discuss the trip thoroughly with all group members, including emergency plans. Become familiar with the Woodsman's Code.

▬ Make sure to carry enough food for the whole trip. Don't rely on the environment for emergency food.

▬ Carry proper equipment, including good shelter, clothing, rain gear, etc.

Travelling

3 Stay on existing trails and portages. Following wildlife trails is better than cutting new trails.

4 Use switchbacks on trails. Don't cut a new trail just to save a few metres of walking; you might be creating a severe erosion problem. Walk *through* puddles to avoid widening trails.

5 Don't wear ridge-soled boots unless it's absolutely necessary. These boots destroy moss cover and other vegetation, which leads to erosion. Running shoes are much better.

Campsites and Shelters

6 Use existing campsites. Keep your heavy-use areas small, to minimize soil compaction. Very few plants can grow back where soil has been compacted. Don't expand the campsite.

7 If you have to choose a new campsite, choose one that will disturb trees or shrubs as little as possible. If your tent is pitched on top of live vegetation, move it after one or two days.

8 Don't "improve" the site by pulling vegetation, building walls, or digging trenches around your tent.

9 Use a floored tent. Don't make shelters or bedding out of branches or other natural material. A lightweight plastic tarp with ropes can provide extra protection from wind and rain.

Fire

10 Use camp stoves whenever possible. The new ones are convenient, reliable, and easy to carry. This will reduce fire hazards, save wood, and give you a chance to do some stargazing!

11 If a fire is necessary, keep it small and use existing fire pits.

12 Where there is no fire pit, build your fire on bedrock or pure sand, preferably close to water. Where this is not possible, dig a pit down to the mineral (clay) layer of the soil. Pick a spot that avoids roots, overhanging trees, needles, leaves, and other forest litter.

13 Use only dead wood for the fire.

14 Drown your fire thoroughly with water. Stir the ashes. Add more water. Leave unused firewood for the next campers. Pack out all the unburned bits of garbage, such as aluminum foil, cans, etc. In wilderness sites, eliminate all traces of the campfire.

Smoking

15 Sit down to have a smoke, so you can be careful with your ashes.

16 Remember that cigarette butts are garbage and should be packed out. They won't degrade naturally. A small metal cough-drops box is a good way of storing them. You can count them at the end of the trip!

Human Waste

17 Use existing outhouses or latrines wherever possible.

18 Where necessary, dig a small hole 15 to 20 cm deep in soil, at least 35 m from any open water. Soil can act as a filter for nutrients and bacteria, and can protect lakes and streams from pollution by human waste. Use single-ply white toilet paper, and bury everything completely.

Other Waste

19 Carry out everything you carried in! The rule is: BURN IT OR BASH IT, THEN BAG IT, *AND BRING IT BACK.*

20 Wash dishes, clothes, and yourself in a dishpan, *not* in the lake or stream. Rinse away from open water. Dump waste water in a hole located at least 35 m from open water. Use liquid or bar soaps instead of detergents.

21 Fish guts attract swarms of flies, which can ruin a campsite for following users. After cleaning and gutting fish, collect the waste and bury it in soil far from the campsite. You can also paddle it out to a rock island, where birds will eat it.

Wildlife and Natural Food

22 Remember, you are a guest in someone else's home. Avoid disturbing wildlife, especially young animals or nesting birds.

23 Avoid overfishing and overhunting. Remember that all plants and animals are protected in provincial parks.

24 Obey all fish, game, and forestry regulations. Talk to a conservation officer about them if you have questions.

25 Avoid picking edible wild foods except where they are abundant. Wildlife depends on this food. Collect wild mushrooms only if you are an expert: many common mushrooms are deadly poisonous.

26 Never feed wildlife: this interferes with their natural habits, and you may be bitten by a nervous or rabid animal. Guard your food and garbage carefully from wildlife, and keep all food out of your tent. In bear country, seal all food and garbage in your pack overnight, and hang your pack at least 6 m high on a rope between two trees. Bears that develop a taste for handouts eventually have to be shot.

In bear country, seal all food and garbage in your pack overnight, and hang your pack at least 6 m high on a rope between two trees.

Clean Up Others' Mistakes

27 Pack out any garbage that you find.

28 Cover up fire pits and latrines that are in poor locations.

29 Tell the local parks or natural resources officials about any major problems that you find.

Certain parks provide organized sports, such as horseback riding, guided nature tours, rafting, and scuba diving. For further information about facilities, activities, and rules of the various national parks, contact the Inquiry Centre of **Environment Canada** (Hull, PQ, K1A 0H3). For information on provincial parks, get in touch with the appropriate ministry in your province.

Not all "parks" are wilderness areas. Several of Canada's national and provincial parks, such as L'Anse-aux-Meadows, location of a Viking settlement, and Fort Louisbourg, are important historic sites, and certain river systems have been designated Canadian Heritage Rivers. These should be treated with the same care and respect as wilderness parks. Information on historic parks is also available from Environment Canada. To find out more about the Heritage River program, contact **Canadian Heritage Rivers**, Parks Canada, Ottawa, ON, K1A 1G2.

✳✳

cottaging

There are roughly 568,000 cottages in Canada. No one has a better chance to observe the effects of pollution than cottagers, who return to the same bit of nature every year. But the causes of pollution are varied and sometimes complicated, and many cottagers are unsure how they can avoid contributing to the problem.

In cottage areas, pollutants and raw waste are reaching the surface water and groundwater. The pollutants interfere with the ecosystems of lakes and rivers. The raw and untreated waste introduces unwanted nutrients into the water, which causes excess growth of algae and imbalance in the ecosystem and the food chain. Beer cans tossed overboard, motor oil and antifreeze spills from powerboats, shampoo and soaps, dishwasher detergent – all contribute to the growing mess. In addition, human wastes can transmit viruses such as hepatitis, polio, and intestinal flu.

In order to avoid contributing to the problem, consult the information on environment-friendly household products in Chapter 3 and on gardening and pesticides in Chapter 6. Since cottages are almost invariably close to water, it's even more important to avoid using polluting chemicals there. If you have a recycling program at home, bring back the recyclables from your cottage garbage.

An additional problem is the wood preservatives used on buildings, docks, and birdhouses. Many contain

pentachlorophenol, a highly toxic pesticide that kills insects that burrow into wood. The following mixture, tested by the U. S. Department of Agriculture, can be used as an alternative:

ALTERNATIVE WOOD PRESERVATIVE

750 mL exterior varnish
30 mL paraffin wax
enough mineral spirits or turpentine to make 4 L

Dip the wood into the mixture for two or three minutes if possible. If not, use a brush, making sure the board ends and joints are generously coated. The treated surface can be painted after two or three days of dry weather.

Since your cottage is probably not attached to a municipal sewage system, there's also the question of how you're going to dispose of wastes. One common solution is the septic tank.

The septic tank holds about 2,700 to 4,500 L of human waste underground. Water and lime stimulate the production of bacteria within the waste solution, starting the process of decomposition. The result, called "septage," is filtered and leached through a tile or gravel bed and absorbed into the ground.

Some septic tanks do not use water. Because much of the waste remains as solids in the tank, these must be inspected for clogging and pumped out regularly, and the waste taken to municipal treatment sites. The sludge can also be composted to produce rich fertilizer.

However, septic tanks are not the perfect solution. They should not be used in areas that experience high fluctuations in the water table. This increases the chance of untreated waste entering the surface water or groundwater.

An alternative to septic tanks for human waste is the biological toilet. Body wastes and toilet tissue are turned into water by the continuous action of enzymes and bacteria. The recycled waste becomes a clear and odourless liquid containing no pathogenic organisms. There is no residue, no sludge to be removed. Once a week a package of freeze-dried bacteria and enzymes is added to the toilet, and every two years the charcoal filters must be replaced.

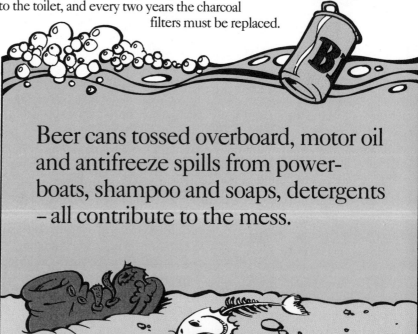

Beer cans tossed overboard, motor oil and antifreeze spills from power-boats, shampoo and soaps, detergents – all contribute to the mess.

BUG REPELLENT

At best, black flies, mosquitoes, and other biting insects are an irritation. At worst, they can cause serious illnesses, such as meningitis, Rocky Mountain fever, and Lyme Disease. However, some bug repellents contain dangerous chemicals. Fortunately, you can protect yourself to a certain extent by wearing proper clothing and using natural repellents.

Clothing should be loose and light-coloured, covering as much exposed skin as possible. Watch out for small openings, and keep collars and shirt and pant cuffs tightly closed. If you must use repellents, at least you can restrict them to the hands and face by keeping yourself well-covered.

A natural bug repellent is citronella, the oil extracted from citrus fruits, which is available at drugstores.

Some people believe that you can also eat your way to protection by consuming lots of garlic (mosquitoes supposedly don't like the smell any better than we do), avoiding refined sugar and flour, and taking extra B vitamins or brewer's yeast.

Once bitten, you can relieve the itching by rubbing the bite with raw garlic, lime or lemon juice, damp salt, or Vitamin C powder.

PROVINCIAL MINISTRIES of TOURISM and RECREATION

are the most comprehensive sources of information on leisure activities across Canada. You can also check with conservation groups, many of which publish their own newsletters and magazines. See page 152 for some addresses.

All-Terrain Vehicles

This sport can cause serious damage to the ecosystems that are favourite spots for ATV drivers – shallow rivers, gravel bars, stream beds, sand dunes, and deserts. ATVs can scar the land, kill wildlife, and destroy vegetation, creating noise pollution as they go.

* * * * * * * * * * * * * * * * * *

Aquariums

Aquariums can be fun and educational, and many promote the conservation message. However, animal rights activists have some serious concerns about their treatment of marine animals: whales, porpoises, dolphins, and others suffer undue stress during their capture; they may be kept in holding tanks that are far too small; many are seasonally transported from one aquarium to another.

* * * * * * * * * * * * * * * * * *

Beaches

There's already enough garbage in our water and washing up on our shores without tourists adding to it, so don't litter when you go to the beach. Garbage on the beach has always been considered an eyesore, but recently environmental workers have recognized that it's a serious threat to marine life. Plastic is a particular problem; seals, seabirds, marine turtles, and other wildlife, some of them endangered species, have died from eating plastic or becoming entangled in it. Sea turtles, for instance, eat plastic bags because they mistake them for jellyfish, which are among their natural prey.

Birdwatching

Check with your provincial tourism ministry or naturalists' society for bird-watching opportunities. While this is an easy and enjoyable solitary activity, there are also birdwatching clubs, competitions, and tours.

* * * * * * * * * * * * * * * *

Canadian Environment Week

Celebrated in a multitude of locations across the country in early June, this festival offers a good chance to learn about the environment through displays, demonstrations, and a variety of activities, such as tree-planting, concerts, and games.

* * * * * * * * * * * * * * * * * *

Canoeing, Kayaking, Sailing, Windsurfing

All these boating activities have the advantage of using little or no fuel. When using large sailboats with motors and toilets, be careful not to spill any fuel, oil, or sewage while on the water.

* * * * * * * * * * * * * * * * * *

City Farms

Many urban children grow up with no experience of animals other than household pets, and little idea of where eggs, milk, and other animal foods come from. Fortunately, some cities have petting zoos and farms where urban dwellers can get to know domestic animals.

Be aware of toxicity levels in the area where you are fishing.

Cycling

Environmentally speaking, this is one of the most respectable leisure activities around. As well as cycling at home, you can take cycle vacations abroad, and outfitters in vacation spots across Canada will rent cycles by the day or hour. Follow the road rules, however, and don't ride in heavy traffic unless you're experienced. Careless cyclists in some major cities have caused accidents and are beginning to give the sport a bad name.

* * * * * * * * * * * * * * * * * * *

Farm Holidays

Staying on a farm is another way of enjoying nature and educating the family. While participation is not mandatory, many farms encourage guests to get involved in farming activities. You can get a list of farm accommodations from your provincial ministry of tourism.

* * * * * * * * * * * * * * * * * * *

Field Studies

As well as the outdoor activities that come easily to mind, there are a host of more unusual possibilities that you can learn about from your provincial ministry, such as maple sugaring, seal-watching, and guided tours of woodlots. As an alternative, the Foundation for Field Research links volunteers from the public with scientists whose projects are funded by the foundation and who need research assistance. Expeditions can last anywhere from a weekend to a month. For more information, write to the **Foundation for Field Research**, P.O. Box 2010, Alpine, CA 92001-0020, USA.

Fishing

According to the Angler's Code, created by the Ontario Ministry of Natural Resources, a good angler:

■ respects private property and the rights of others

■ knows and obeys the fishing regulations

■ does not damage fish habitat

■ puts safety first in the use of his equipment and the enjoyment of the sport

■ takes pride in his skill

■ helps others to understand the recreation of fishing

■ leaves the environment as clean as he found it; he does not litter.

A good angler has respect for his quarry, before and after catching it, and knows there is much more to fishing than taking his limit. Be sure to follow fishing regulations in your province and be aware of toxicity levels in the area where you're fishing.

* * * * * * * * * * * * * * * * * * *

Giardiasis

Contrary to popular belief, Montezuma's revenge is not restricted to foreign climes. Canadians can contract giardiasis – also known as "beaver fever" – from contact with human or animal feces or drinking water contaminated by feces. The giardia parasite lodges in the digestive tract, causing diarrhea, vomiting, and other flu-like symptoms. Giardiasis can be treated, but prevention is easier. Since the parasite tends to be found in lakes, ponds, and inadequately treated water, campers and cottagers should be particularly careful. If you're using untreated water, boil it for at least five minutes. Don't swim in beaver ponds, and keep your own waste well clear of water.

Hostelling

There are more than 5,000 hostels worldwide offering cheap accommodation in everything from an ancient jail to a sailing ship. The Canadian Hostelling Association has 60 hostels that offer year-round accommodation, outdoor recreational programs led by environment-conscious volunteers, and travel talks and films. To stay in a hostel, you'll need a membership, which also entitles you to budget travel information and a bi-monthly newsletter. Students get a Student ID card entitling them to discounts on admission to museums, galleries, and events around the world. For information on Canadian and international hostelling, write to the **Canadian Hostelling Association**, 1600 James Naismith Drive, Suite 608, Gloucester, ON, K1B 5N4.

* * * * * * * * * * * * * * * * * *

Houseboats

Although floating down lakes and rivers on a houseboat sounds like the perfect natural vacation, critics are concerned about "grey water," the discharge from sinks and showers that all too often ends up in said lakes and rivers. Houseboat discharges are not currently regulated and may contain concentrations of fecal and food bacteria as well as phosphates from detergents.

* * * * * * * * * * * * * * * * * *

Lead Weights and Shot

Anglers should never use lead lures and weights, and hunters should use steel rather than lead shot, to avoid poisoning birds and fish. A single pellet can kill a bird, and lead poisoning is not a pleasant way to die. The problem is compounded when poisoned animals are eaten by predators.

Currently about 3,600 tonnes of lead ammunition falls on North America's fields and wetlands every year. It's difficult to estimate just how much wildlife is affected by this lead, but the U.S. Fish and Wildlife Service has put the number of birds alone at 1.5 to 3 million in the U.S.

* * * * * * * * * * * * * * * * * *

Outdoor Equipment

There are many good outdoor equipment stores across the country. A particularly interesting one is **Mountain Equipment Co-op**, which sells its equipment at "the lowest reasonable cost" and funds conservation projects with its profits. Since the company is owned and directed by its members, you have to purchase a membership card for a nominal fee if you want to shop there.

* * * * * * * * * * * * * * *

Pets

Four-legged family members may enjoy a vacation as much as the rest of us, but don't let them run wild in natural areas, where they may injure or be injured by the local animals. Make sure your pet has all its shots, and if you're planning to travel outside the province or country, have the documentation to prove it. Find out the location of the veterinary clinic closest to your destination, in case of emergencies.

The Canadian Hostelling Association has 60 hostels that offer year-round accommodation.

"GREEN ROVER"

A GREEN DEVELOPMENT

Where you decide to have your photos developed these days is an environmental choice.

While most large photo processors have found ways to recycle their chemicals and reclaim silver from film, photographic paper, and waste water, others have been less responsible.

The main culprits are the so-called "mini-labs" that can develop your films right before your eyes in two hours. The problem with mini-labs is that most lack the facilities to recycle their chemicals and waste water. Instead they are diluted and flushed down the drain. Since these effluents often contain silver (a heavy metal) and ferrocyanide (which converts to cyanide in the presence of sunlight and oxygen) as well as phosphates, nitrates, and other chemicals that are not eliminated by water treatment systems, dumping them into the water systems is not a good idea. So every time you get your films processed at a mini-lab, chances are you're contributing to pollution.

Two large Canadian firms have been leaders in the field of recycling. The first to take recycling seriously was **Winnipeg Photo**, a developing and printing company with several stores of its own and laboratory facilities serving more than 2,000 small outlets from coast to coast. Winnipeg Photo was the first

CONTINUED ON PAGE 151

Photography

For the most part, photography is a wonderful way to enjoy nature without doing any damage. But have regard for the feelings of your subject: both people and animals can be annoyed by the over-eager photographer. Owls, for example, are confused and frightened by the flashes used by nighttime photographers. Their feeding patterns can be so disturbed that the birds starve.

* * * * * * * * * * * * * * * * * *

Powerboats

Though powerboats are an important method of transportation for many Canadians, they do contribute to the pollution of our waters. The Allied Boating Association cites three major problem areas in powerboat use:

▬ Leaded gasoline: the association has been pushing for its abolition.

▬ Anti-fouling paint, used on the bottoms and sides of boats to protect them from marine life such as algae and barnacles. This paint usually contains tributyl tin (TBT), which has been called the most toxic substance ever introduced into the aquatic environment. It may also be used in fungicides used on air conditioners, pipes, and fishnets, and has been banned in many jurisdictions, including France and the U.K. As an alternative, you may be able to find a non-toxic wax, which does not kill the algae but instead inhibits their ability to stick to boats.

▬ Maintenance: Some boat owners start their motors in the lake for the first time each summer to clean them out and get them prepped for summer use. This often results in blowing antifreeze and engine residue into the water.

The association recommends that all maintenance work be done on shore and that you use "plumber's antifreeze," which is available at hardware stores and is less toxic.

* * * * * * * * * * * * * * * * * *

Rail Travel

Rail passes for Canada and Europe can provide you with an ecologically sound and relatively cheap way to travel. Eurail passes must be purchased before you leave Canada, through the Canadian Hostelling Association or by writing to **Eurail Pass Distribution Centre**, Box 300, Succursale R, Montreal, PQ, H2S 3K9. There are also passes available for some individual countries. Canadian passes can be purchased from the Canadian Hostelling Association or from any VIA agent.

* * * * * * * * * * * * * * * * * *

Safaris

Although poachers continue to threaten the survival of many species, cameras have taken the place of guns for many tourists. But even they can sometimes be a problem when placed in the hands of over-eager safari-goers. After rescuing a pride of lions that had been surrounded by tourists in jeeps, one exasperated park warden in Kenya suggested that if tourists were going to take liberties with the lions, maybe the lions should be allowed to take liberties with the tourists. If you plan to take a safari, make sure your tour company has a respectful attitude towards wildlife.

* * * * * * * * * * * * * * * * * *

Skiing

Downhill skiing may seem to be passive recreation, but the creation and clearing of slopes can be damaging to mountain ecosystems. Cross-country skiing or snowshoeing is a good alternative; it's best to stay on marked trails, for your own safety and that of the environment.

Snowmobiling

A brilliant Canadian invention, the snowmobile has made life and work easier and safer for people living in areas with heavy snowfalls. However, snowmobilers should stick to existing trails whenever possible, to avoid damaging the environment and frightening wildlife. For more information on using your snowmobile safely and wisely, write to the **Canadian Council of Snowmobile Organizations**, 98 Marshall Street, Barrie, ON, L4N 4L5.

* * * * * * * * * * * * * * * *

Whalewatching

Whalewatching trips that range from one-day cruises to week-long study trips have become an effective way of raising concern about preserving the whales. They have also become a $12-million industry, and observers are now concerned that the number of whalewatchers may be having a harmful effect on the whales, driving them away from their natural feeding grounds. One tour organizer and researcher, Ned Lynas of **St. Lawrence Whale Watching** (based in Ajax, Ont.), will be studying the effects of tours on the whales. In the meantime, make sure that any whalewatching group you join has a responsible attitude towards the wildlife you'll be watching.

* * * * * * * * * * * * * * * *

Wildlife

Nine out of ten Canadians take part in some form of wildlife recreation, such as birdwatching or photography; about 3.6 million every year take trips specifically for that purpose. Despite our collective concern, however, there are currently 147 species of wild plants and animals on the endangered list, and 16 species that no longer exist in Canada.

This doesn't mean that you should attempt to rescue every animal in trouble yourself. If you come across an injured animal, it's usually best to leave it where it is, unless you are able to follow through properly by taking it to an appropriate treatment centre right away. Often the stress of removing the animal from its natural surroundings is enough to kill it. Removing an animal from a trap is illegal.

Young animals may sometimes appear to have been abandoned by their mothers, but in most cases they have not, so it's best to leave them alone. The mother may indeed abandon them if she finds they've been handled by humans.

* * * * * * * * * * * * * * * *

Zoos

Animal rights activists have raised serious questions about zoos. Capturing the specimens causes considerable stress, and the animals may be killed or injured in the process. Once an animal is removed from its natural habitat, especially if it is caged, its behaviour changes. It may show signs of psychological damage, such as pacing, attacking other animals, and self-mutilation. Its life expectancy may also decrease.

Some zoos are definitely better than others. Obviously animals should be well fed and have as much space as is appropriate and possible. But good zoos also spend sizeable proportions of their budgets on research, preservation of animals' natural habitats, and re-releasing programs.

Canadian company to recycle its bleach, fixer, and developing fluid. And it's still the only firm in Canada that recycles film developer. Along the way, they've also found that recycling contributes to company profits. Unfortunately, the outlets that use Winnipeg Photo don't advertise the fact, so you'll have to ask.

Blacks Camera stores are the next best choice. They recycle all their chemicals except the film developer used on negatives. As a result, they've been able to reduce the amount of chemicals they buy by 75% to 90%; their new recycling equipment paid for itself in a year.

So ask your photo processing shop whether they recycle their chemicals and reclaim their silver. If they say they do, ask them to show you. If they don't, take your films elsewhere.

FOR MORE INFORMATION

Many of these groups have provincial affiliates.

Canadian Association of Nature and Outdoor Photographers
19 Mercer Street
Suite 301
Toronto, ON
M5V 1H2

Canadian Camping Association
1806 Avenue Road
Suite 2
Toronto, ON
M5M 3Z1

Canadian Nature Federation
(publisher of *Nature Canada* magazine)
453 Sussex Drive
Ottawa, ON
K1N 6Z4

Canadian Parks and Recreation Association
333 River Road
Vanier, ON
K1L 8B9

Canadian Parks and Wilderness Society
(publisher of *Borealis* magazine)
160 Bloor Street East
Suite 1150
Toronto, ON
M4W 1B9

Canadian Wildlife Federation
1673 Carling Avenue
Ottawa, ON
K2A 1C4

Wilderness Canoe Association
Box 496
Station K
Toronto, ON
M4P 2G9

World Wildlife Fund
60 St. Clair Avenue East
Toronto, ON
M4T 1N5

* *

PROVINCIAL TOURISM DEPARTMENTS

Travel Alberta
Box 2500
Edmonton, AB
T5J 2Z4

TravelArctic
Yellowknife, NT
X1A 2L9

Tourism British Columbia
Parliament Buildings
Victoria, BC
V8V 1X4

Travel Manitoba
7th floor
155 Carlton Street
Winnipeg, MB
R3C 3H8

Tourism New Brunswick
P.O. Box 12345
Fredericton, NB
E3B 5C3

Tourism Branch Newfoundland Department of Development and Tourism
P.O. Box 2016
St. John's, NF
A1C 5R8

Nova Scotia Department of Tourism and Culture
P.O. Box 456
Halifax, NS
B3J 2R5

Ontario Ministry of Tourism and Recreation
Queen's Park
Toronto, ON
M7A 2E5

Prince Edward Island Visitor Services
P.O. Box 940
Charlottetown, PE
C1A 7M5

Tourisme Québec
P.O. Box 20,000
Quebec City, PQ
G1K 7X2

Tourism Saskatchewan
1919 Saskatchewan Drive
Regina, SK
S4P 3V7

Tourism Yukon
P.O. Box 2703
Whitehorse, YT
Y1A 2C6

ADVENTURE TOURS for the GREEN TOURIST

Canada has thousands of tour operators of all sizes and philosophies. Federal and provincial tourism departments will be glad to fill your mailbox with thorough lists of them.

The small sampling below is the result of a telephone survey in June 1989 of wildlife and naturalist groups across the country, who were asked to name a few operators with especially good reputations in the conservation community. There are many other reputable operators, but space does not allow for a complete listing.

TOUR OPERATOR	TYPE OF HOLIDAY	DESTINATIONS	POLICIES
Athabasca Trail Trips Box 6117 Hinton, AB T7V 1X5 (403) 865-7549	horse-assisted hiking and camping	Willmore Wilderness Park (north of Jasper, Alberta)	Contributes to Friends of the Earth and Pollution Probe; member of Alberta Wilderness Association and Canadian Parks and Wilderness Society. Small groups, vegetarian meals; horses are used to carry gear only.
The Adventure Centre 17 Hayden St. Toronto, ON M4Y 2P2 (416) 922-7584	camping, cycling tours, trekking, overlanding	Africa, Canada, China, Galapagos Islands, Himalayas, India, South America	Supports WWF; promotes low-impact tourism.
Black Feather 1341 Wellington St. Ottawa, ON K1Y 3B8 (613) 722-9717	canoeing, hiking, kayaking, whitewater rafting	Arctic, Baffin Island, British Columbia, Greenland, Northern Quebec, NWT	Helped to formulate the revised Woodsman's Code; works with Parks Canada on environmental policy; promotes environmental protection and low-impact tourism.

TOUR OPERATOR	TYPE OF HOLIDAY	DESTINATIONS	POLICIES
Canadian Himalayan Expeditions 721 Bloor St. W. Toronto, ON M5G 1L5 (416) 537-2000	adventure trekking	Africa, India, Nepal	Supports a variety of educational and environmental projects. All tours are conducted to minimalize environmental impact; for example, kerosene stoves are used instead of wood to reduce deforestation.
Canadian Nature Tours 335 Lesmill Road Don Mills, ON M3R 2W8 (416) 444-8419	birdwatching, canoeing, cycling tours, nature tours, scientific research expeditions, whalewatching	mostly Canada	Operated by the Federation of Ontario Naturalists. Proceeds from tours go to the Federation, which supports wetlands preservation and other conservation causes.
Canadian Wilderness Trips 171 College St. Toronto, ON M5T 1P7 (416) 977-3703	birdwatching, camping, canoeing, hiking, outdoor school	Algonquin Park (Ontario)	Contributes to Temagami Wilderness Society; member of Canadian Nature Federation. All camping is low-impact.
Drum Travel 121 Harbord St. Toronto, ON M5S 1G9 (416) 964-3388	adventure holidays, trekking	worldwide	Supports a variety of Third World organizations; no tours to South Africa.
East Wind Arctic Tours and Outfitters Box 2728 Yellowknife, NWT X1A 2R1 (403) 873-2170	archaeological tours, backpacking, birdwatching, boating, hiking, photography tours, wildlife tours	Keewatin Zone, Mackenzie and Nahanni Rivers, Thelon Game Sanctuary, Yellowknife	Contributes to WWF; supports Sierra Club, member Canadian Nature Federation. Some excursions are research trips led by biologists; lay tourists are welcome to participate in the scientific work.
Eco Summer Expeditions 1516-AG Duranleau St. Granville Island, BC V6H 3S4 (604) 669-7741	nature trips, photography tours, sailing, sea kayaking, whalewatching	Queen Charlotte Islands, Vancouver Island	Member of Canadian Wildlife Federation; promotes low-impact tourism; educates clients in environmental responsibility.
Mingan Islands Cetacean Study 285 Green St., St. Lambert, PQ J4P 1T3 (514) 465-9176 (winter) (418) 949-2845 (summer)	trips to watch and study whales, dolphins, and other marine mammals	Gulf of St. Lawrence	Research is supported by fees from tourist passengers. Tourists are welcome to participate in the scientific work.

TOUR OPERATOR	TYPE OF HOLIDAY	DESTINATIONS	POLICIES
Ocean Search Tours P.O. Box 129 Grand Manan, NB E0G 2M0 (506) 662-8144	birdwatching, sailing, whalewatching	Bay of Fundy (New Brunswick)	Non-profit research station; tours are guided by a marine biologist and preceded by an educational presentation. Promotes sensitivity to wildlife and environment.
Passages Exotic Expeditions 296 Queen St. W. Toronto, ON M5V 2A1 (416) 593-0942	outdoor adventure holidays	Africa, Costa Rica, Peru, Thailand	Contributes to Monteverde Conservation Fund; involved in schools and development projects in villages in host countries. Tours are low-impact and non-exploitive.
Sobek International 159 Main St., Unionville, ON L3R 2G8 (416) 479-2600	adventure holidays, kayaking, rafting, research holidays, trekking	worldwide, including Antarctica	Emphasizes conservation and environmental responsibility with clients. Tour groups are small.
Worldwide Adventures 920 Yonge St. Suite 747 Toronto, ON M4W 3C7 (416) 963-9163	adventure holidays, birdwatching, gorillawatching, rafting, sailing, trekking, whalewatching	Africa, Canada, Central and South America, China, India, Nepal	Supports a variety of conservation and environment causes, with donations in host countries. All trekkers are given comprehensive cultural and environmental briefings before starting out.

FURTHER READING

*I*n addition to books and papers referred to in the text, the authors have found the following works helpful. Many of them will interest readers who wish to learn about the larger issues surrounding our environmental problems.

* *

- Bahro, Rudolf. *Building the Green Movement*. Philadelphia: New Society, 1986.
  An anthology of writings by one of the founders of the Green Party in West Germany.

- Bertell, Rosalie. *No Immediate Danger? Prognosis for a Radioactive Earth*. Toronto: Women's Press, 1985.
  Examines the risks of nuclear power and nuclear weapons testing.

- Bookchin, Murray. *The Ecology of Freedom: The Emergence and Dissolution of Hierarchy*. Palo Alto, CA: Cheshire Books, 1982.
  Bookchin is a leading figure in the "social ecology" movement, which examines the relationship between environment and politics. This is his most comprehensive and insightful book.

- Brown, Lester R. et al. *State of the World 1989: A Worldwatch Institute Report on Progress Toward a Sustainable Society*. New York and London: Norton, 1989.
  An annual report on the global environment, highlighting key issues each year.

- Campbell, Monica E., and William M. Glenn. *Profit from Pollution Prevention*. Toronto: Pollution Probe Foundation, 1982.

- Carson, Rachel. *Silent Spring*. Boston: Houghton Mifflin, 1962.
  The book that started it all, more than 25 years ago.

- Caufield, Catherine. *In the Rainforest*. New York: Knopf, 1985.

- Devall, Bill. *Simple in Means, Rich in Ends*. Salt Lake City, UT: Gibbs Smith, 1988.
  Devall is a leading thinker in the "deep ecology" school, which stresses the primacy of nature over human society. This book is intended as a practical guide.

- Fukuoka, Masanobu. *The One-Straw Revolution: An Introduction to Natural Farming*. Emmaus, PA: Rodale, 1978.
  A proposal for a new approach to farming, still more radical than organic farming.

- *The Gaia Atlas of Planet Management*. London: Pan, 1985.

- Gorz, André. *Ecology as Politics*. Montreal: Black Rose, 1980.
  Attempts to reconcile socialism with an ecological ethic, in order to produce a new politics.

- Harrison, Paul. *The Greening of Africa: Breaking Through in the Battle for Land and Food*. London and Toronto: Paladin, 1987.
  Success stories in the effort to rehabilitate collapsing ecosystems in Africa.

- Kazis, Richard, and Richard L. Grossman. *Fear at Work: Job Blackmail, Labor and the Environment*. New York: Pilgrim Press, 1982.
  Discusses efforts by business to pit environmental concerns against labour concerns; shows that environmental regulation will actually mean more jobs.

- Keating, Michael. *To the Last Drop: Canada and the World's Water Crisis*. Toronto: Macmillan, 1986.

- Lovelock, J.E. *Gaia: A New Look at Life on Earth*. Oxford and New York: Oxford University Press, 1979.
  Develops the famous "Gaia hypothesis," which posits that the earth can be thought of as a single organism.

- Lovins, Amory B. *Soft Energy Paths: Toward a Durable Peace*. New York: Harper & Row, 1979.
  The definitive explanation of why we will have to change our energy supply, technology, use, and efficiency if we are to survive.

- Mackenzie Valley Pipeline Inquiry [Berger Commission]. *Northern Frontier, Northern Homeland*. 2 vols. Ottawa: Supply and Services, 1977.
  Beyond its study of the impact of building pipelines in the North, this report examines fundamental questions of land use and native land claims in Canada.

- May, John. *The Greenpeace Book of the Nuclear Age: The Hidden History, The Human Cost*. Toronto: McClelland & Stewart, 1990.

- Moore-Lappé, Frances. *Diet for a Small Planet*, rev. ed. New York: Ballantine, 1982.
  A critical look at current agricultural practices, with proposals for possible alternatives.

- Nicholson-Lord, David. *The Greening of the Cities*. London: Routledge and Kegan Paul, 1987.
  Discusses the shape of the sustainable city.

- Odum, Eugene P. *Basic Ecology*. Philadelphia and Montreal: Saunders College Publishing, 1983.
  An excellent introduction to the science of ecology.

- Peterson, Roger Tory, ed. *The Peterson Field Guide Series*. Boston: Houghton Mifflin.
  An excellent series of more than 35 guides to wildlife.

- Pollution Probe Foundation. *Probe Post: Canada's Environmental Magazine*. (quarterly).
  Discusses topical environmental issues in Canada.

- Schumacher, E.F. *Small Is Beautiful*. New York: Harper & Row, 1973.
  The revolutionary book that provided the first examination of sustainable economics.

- Seymour, John, and Herbert Girardet. *Blueprint for a Green Planet*. New York: Prentice Hall, 1987.

- Swift, Jamie. *Cut and Run: The Assault on Canada's Forests*. Toronto: Between the Lines, 1983.

- World Commission on Environment and Development [Brundtland Commission]. *Our Common Future*. Oxford and New York: Oxford University Press, 1987.

- Worldwatch Institute. *Worldwatch Papers* (series).
  Papers on environmental issues.

ENVIRONMENTAL ORGANIZATIONS

Your local environmental group needs your help. Refer to this list for a group in your community, or start your own.

* *

Canadian Coalition on Acid Rain
112 St. Clair Avenue West
Suite 401
Toronto, ON
M4V 2Y3

Canadian Environmental Law Association
517 College Street
Suite 401
Toronto, ON
M6G 4A2

Canadian Environmental Network
P.O. Box 1289
Station B
Ottawa, ON
K1P 5R3

Canadian Wildlife Federation
1673 Carling Avenue
Ottawa, ON
K2A 1C4

Concerned Citizens of Manitoba
592 Walker Avenue
Winnipeg, MB
R3L 1C4

Conservation Council of New Brunswick
180 St. John Street
Fredericton, NB
E3B 4A9

Ecology Action Centre of Nova Scotia
3115 Veith Street
3rd Floor
Halifax, NS
B3K 3G9

Energy Probe
225 Brunswick Avenue
Toronto, ON
M5S 2M6

Environmental Resource Centre of Alberta
10511 Saskatchewan Drive
Edmonton, AB
T6E 4S1

Friends of the Earth
251 Laurier Avenue West,
Suite 701
Ottawa, ON
K1P 5J6

Great Lakes United
24 Agassiz Circle
Buffalo, NY
14214 USA

Greenpeace
580 Bloor Street West
Toronto, ON
M6G 1K1

Manitoba Environmentalists, Inc.
Box 3125
Winnipeg, MB
R3C 4E6

Pollution Probe
12 Madison Avenue
Toronto, ON
M5R 2S1

Saskatchewan Environmental Society
Room 205
219 - 22nd Street East
Saskatoon, SK
S7K 0G4

Société pour vaincre la pollution
P.O. Box 65
Succ. Place d'armes
Montreal, PQ
H2Y 3E9

West Coast Environmental Law Association
Room 1001
207 West Hastings Street
Vancouver, BC
V6B 1H7

World Wildlife Fund Canada
60 St. Clair Avenue East
Suite 201
Toronto, ON
M4T 1N5

Yukon Conservation Society
Box 4163
Whitehorse, YT
Y1A 3T3

ACKNOWLEDGEMENTS

At Pollution Probe, the spring of 1989 was far from silent. Hundreds of individual citizens called to ask what steps they could take in their daily lives to help solve the environmental crisis. And Doug Gibson of McClelland & Stewart was calling to see if Pollution Probe would be interested in producing a guide for consumers concerned about the environment.

In Britain, John Elkington and Julia Hailes had overwhelming success in recruiting consumers to environmental activism with their groundbreaking Green Consumer Guide. The readiness of our supporters to take individual action convinced us that the time was right to accept Gibson's proposal.

After Warner Troyer and Glenys Moss had made their contributions, scores of staff, volunteers, and experts in the field were enlisted to bring together the details you need for "responsible shopping that won't cost the earth." Gord Perks and Barbara Czarnecki teamed up to co-ordinate the researchers and writers behind The Canadian Green Consumer Guide. We thank them all for their participation and enthusiasm.

In particular, the authors wish to thank the following people and organizations for their assistance in researching, writing, and producing this book:

Brenda Ackerman

Vanessa Alexander

Linda Biesenthal

Bill Bradley

Dave Bruer

Kathy Cooper

Rick Coronado

Marina Dickson

Joan Evans

Cindy Eves

Diane Forrest

Friends of the Earth

John Geeza

Marcus Ginder

Stephen Hall

Molly Harrington

Don Huff

Colin Isaacs

Steven Johnston

Se Keohane

Michi Komori

Dee Kramer

Colin Lamont

Fran MacDonald

Pamela Millar

Diane Mossman

Ito Peng

Linda Pim

John Rahme

Paul Raugust

R.E.I.C. Ltd.

Don Reynolds

Richard Rice

Peter Rickwood

Rocky Mountain Institute, Colorado

Rodale Press

Jill Troyer

The Watt Group

Hugh Westrup

Toronto Humane Society

Transport 2000

Katharine Vanderlinden

Michael Wainwright

A&P, 47
acetone, 49, 50, 63
acid rain, 20-21, 23-24, 26, 27, 32, 59, 67, 78, 103, 104, 116, 118, 123
acrylic, 58
additives in food, 31, 47
aerosol sprays, 48, 49, 54, 61, 62, 63, 64
affinity credit cards, 137
agriculture: chemical, 31-32; city farms, 147; farm holidays, 148; live-stock farming, 33, 40-41; monocrop, 22, 31, 33; organic, 33-35, 58
air conditioning, 82-83, 122
air fresheners, 49-50
air pollution, 20, 23, 27, 31, 59, 103-104, 116, 118-122, 123; indoor, 74, 85-89; *see also* acid rain; green-house effect
air-vapour barriers, 68
airplanes, 125
Alachlor, 35
Alar, 30-31, 45
all-purpose cleaners, 50
all-terrain vehicles, 147
allergies, 86
Alternatives in Diapering, 62
aluminum, 9, 87, 105, 109
aluminum foil, 39
ammonia, 49, 50, 54, 55
angling, *see* fish and shellfish
animal products, 28; in cosmetics, 60-61, 63
animal welfare, 27-29, 33, 41, 59-60, 147; injured animals, 151
anti-fouling paint, 150
antibiotics in foods, 33, 40, 41, 43, 44
antifreeze, 150
antiperspirants, 61
apples, 30-31, 45, 96
appliances, 66, 78-83
aquaculture, *see* fish and shellfish
aquariums, 147
arsenic, 42
asbestos, 69, 86
atmosphere, *see* greenhouse effect; ozone layer; air pollution
automatic dishwasher detergents, 52, 80
automobiles, *see* cars
Avalon Dairy Ltd., 112
Avon Canada, 60

baby care products, 61-62
Bacillus thuringiensis, 100
badger bristles, 64
baking soda, 49, 50, 53, 54, 55
basking sharks, 28, 60-61
bath products, 62
bathroom cleaners, 50
baths, 75
batteries, 89, 113-114

beaches, 27, 141, 147
beaver fever, 148
Becker's, 112
beef, 32, 41
beer, 46-47
beeswax, 53
Benomyl, 35
benzene, 76, 116, 125
beverages, 39, 45-47, 107, 108-109, 110
bicycles, 124-125, 131, 148
biodegradable plastics, 39, 111-112
biomass fuels, 24, 79, 120
birds, 98; birdwatching, 29, 147
Blacks Camera, 151
bleach, 48, 49, 50, 55, 113-114, 151
blister packages, 115
Blue Box, 39, 108, 109-110
boating, 147, 149, 150
Body Shop, 63
bonfires, 94
borax, 49, 52, 54, 55, 71
bottled water, 46
bottles, 39, 44, 109, 112
boxboard, 130
Brazil nuts, 39
bread, 44
Brundtland, Gro Harlem, 8, 9, 11-12, 127
bulk foods, 34, 108
buses, 123, 124, 125
business, environmental responsibili-ties of, 126-135
butter, 44

cabinetry, 87
cadmium, 39, 42, 89, 104, 125
cafeterias, 131
camping, 142-145, 152
Canadian Council on Animal Care, 28
Canadian Environment Week, 147
Canadian Federation of Humane Societies, 28
Canadian Organic Growers, 33, 92, 98, 101
canoeing, 147
cans, 26, 39, 105-106
Captan, 35
carbamates, 98
carbon dioxide, 19, 24, 66, 67, 74, 103, 104, 116, 119, 120
carbon disulphide, 62
carbon filtration, 76
carbon monoxide, 74, 116, 118, 119, 120
cardboard, 38, 95, 109
carnauba wax, 53
carpeting, 88
cars, 21, 116-122, 124, 125, 131
catalytic converters, 119
caulking, 67-68, 70
cedar, 86, 87
cedar oil, 71

cellulose insulation, 69, 70
Center for Responsible Tourism, 140, 141
CFCs (chlorofluorocarbons), 13, 17-18; as aerosol propellants, 17, 49, 61, 62, 64; as coolants, 17, 79, 80, 82, 122; in dry cleaning, 17, 57; in foam plastics, 17, 88, 115; in insulation, 17, 69
cheese, 44
chemicals, *see* fertilizers; pesticides
chlordane, 42
chlorobenzenes, 103
chlorofluorocarbons, *see* CFCs
chlorothalonil, 35
chromium, 42
citronella, 146
city farms, 147
cleaners, 48-57, 131
climate change, *see* greenhouse effect
clothes washers, 75, 78, 82
clothing, 55, 58-59
club soda, 46, 54
coal, 20, 23-24
coffee, 45
compact fluorescent lightbulbs, 83-84, 131
composting, 33, 91-93, 107, 108, 109, 110, 131
condoms, 62
Consumers Association of Canada, 41, 46
Contours, 139
contraceptives, 62
Convention on International Trade in Endangered Species (CITES), 142
cooking tips, 40, 42, 81
cornmeal, 54
cornstarch, 54, 55
corporations, environmental respon-sibilities of, 126-135; investment in, 134-137
cosmetics, 59-65; cruelty-free, 60; homemade, 63
cottaging, 145-146
cotton, 55, 58, 62
credit unions, 134
cresol, 50
cruelty-free toiletries, 60
cyanide, 59, 150
cycling, 124-125, 131, 148

dairy products, 44
decorating materials, 87-89
deforestation, 19, 20, 21-22, 39, 41, 45, 59, 61, 88-89, 104, 141, 142; and loss of species, 21, 88, 141
degradable plastics, 111-112
deodorants, 61
deodorized kerosene, 55
depilatories, 62

INDEX

diapers, 61-62, 107
diatomaceous earth, 100
diesel-powered cars, 119, 120
dimmer switches, 84-85
dioxins and furans, 5, 26, 42, 103; in bleached papers, 44, 45, 61; in foods, 44
dish detergents, 52
dishwashers, 52, 75, 76, 78, 80
dolphins, 42, 147
Dominion, 47
dormant oil spray, 100
drain openers, 52-53
drinking boxes, 39, 45, 115
driving tips, 121-122
dry cleaning, 57
dryers, 78, 82
dyes in foods, 42, 44

Eco-Tech Inc., 127
Ecumenical Coalition on Third World Tourism, 139, 140
eggs, 44, 115
electricity, 19, 20, 64, 78-84, 120
endangered species, 21, 27-28, 59, 60-61, 63, 142, 151
Energuide, 78-79, 80, 81, 82
energy conservation and efficiency, 14, 21, 23, 25; in appliances, 78-83; by mode of transportation, 123, 124, 125; furnaces, 71-72; in house design, 66, 78; in lighting, 83-85; in space heating, 67-74; in water heating, 75-76
energy consumption, 14, 23; agricultural, 32, 45; domestic, 19, 66-85; industrial, 66; in transportation, 66, 116, 117, 121, 122, 123, 124
energy sources, 23-25; diesel, 119, 120; electricity, 19, 20, 64, 78-84, 120; firewood, 19, 32, 141, 142; fossil fuels, 19, 20, 23-24, 32, 66, 67; garbage incineration, 103, 104; nuclear, 23, 24, 25, 37, 38; renewable, 24-25, 78, 79, 120-121
environmental technologies, 127, 134, 135
enzymes in detergents, 52, 56
ethanol, 120
ethical investing, 134-137
ethylene dibromide, 116
exhaust emissions, 118-121

fabric softeners, 53
facials, 62-63
fans, 83
farming, see agriculture
farmland, disappearing, 22, 36, 40, 104
fat in foods, 41, 45
faucets, 77, 78, 131

Federation of Canadian Municipalities, 107
ferrocyanide, 150
fertilizers: chemical, 32, 91, 131; natural, 33, 95
field studies, 148
film processing, 113-114, 150-151
filters for coffee, 45
fireplaces, 68
fires, at campsites, 143-144, 145
firewood, 19, 32, 141, 142
fish and shellfish, 20, 26, 27, 32, 41-44, 59, 104; fish farming, 41-44; sport fishing, 20, 144, 148, 149
floor polishes, 53, 113-114
flooring, 87
fluorocarbons, 57
food and drink, 30-47; contaminants in, 30-31, 33, 35, 40-47, 99, 103; cooking tips, 40, 42, 81; organic, 34-35; retailers, 34, 35, 38; storing, 39; wastes for composting, 92-93, 131; when travelling, 141; wild foods, 144; world food supplies, 32
forests, see deforestation; paper
formaldehyde, 50, 62, 69, 74, 86, 87, 88
fossil fuels, 19, 20, 23-24, 32, 66, 67; see also acid rain; greenhouse effect; oil
Fraser River, 27
freezers, 78, 80
Friends of the Earth, 78, 101, 117
fruits and vegetables, 30-31, 39-40, 99; juices, 45; residues in, 30-31, 35, 44, 47
fuel-efficient cars, 117, 118, 122, 127
fuels, see energy sources
furans, see dioxins and furans
furnaces, 67, 71-72
furniture, 87, 88, 131; polishes, 53, 113-114

Galapagos Islands, 141
garbage crisis, 25-26, 102, 106-109; see also packaging; waste management
garbage disposals, 81
gardening, 90-101, 131
garlic, 146
gas, see gasoline; natural gas
gasohol, 120
gasoline, 118, 119, 124, 150; alternatives to, 120-121
giardiasis, 148
glass, recycling, 39, 44, 109
glass cleaners, 55
global warming, see greenhouse effect
gloves, work, 85
glues, 85

gold, 59
Good Woods, 87-88
grains, 44; fed to livestock, 32, 41; global stocks, 22, 32
Great Lakes, 26-27
greenhouse effect, 18-19, 21, 23-24, 26, 32, 67, 103, 104, 105, 116, 119, 120, 123
Greenpeace, 42, 43
grocery stores, 34, 35, 38
ground almonds, as facial scrub, 62
ground cover, 94-95
groundwater contamination, 32, 36, 48, 57, 61, 145, 146
Guelph, Ontario, 109, 110

hair spray, 63
Halifax harbour, 27
handkerchiefs, 64
Harrowsmith, 96
hazardous materials in workplace, 131-132
hazardous wastes, 49, 57, 87, 113-114, 125, 131
heat exchangers, 72, 74
heat loss, prevention of, 66, 67-74
heat pumps, 73-74, 83
heat recovery ventilators, 74
heat traps, 76
heating systems: integrated, 72; space, 66, 67-74; water, 66, 75-76, 78
heavy-duty cleaners, 50
heritage seeds, 96, 101
hiking, 142-145
H.J. Heinz, 31
hormones in foods, 40-41, 44
hostelling, 149
hot-water tanks, 76
houseboats, 149
household hazardous waste, 49, 113-114
humus, 32, 33, 93
hunting, 144, 149
hybrid seeds, 95-96
hydrocarbons, 116, 118, 119, 120
hydrogen chloride, 104
hydrogen peroxide, 50, 55
hydroponic gardening, 90

incineration, of garbage, 103-104
Inco Ltd., 127
industry, environmental responsibilities of, 126-135
inorganic insulating materials, 69
insect repellent, 146
insecticides, 31, 71, 98, 99, 100
insulation, 68-71, 76, 78, 86
integrated heating systems, 72
Integrated Pest Management, 34
investment, 128, 134-137
irradiation of food, 36-38

ivory in brush handles, 64

James Bay power project, 27
jewellery, 59
juices, 45

kayaking, 147
kerosene, 55, 142
ketone, 49
kettles, 75

labelling, 13, 34, 44, 63
labour unions, 128
lakes, *see* water pollution
land loss, 21-22, 36, 116, 117; *see also* soil
landfill sites, 25-26, 57, 61, 104-105
laundry detergents, 51, 52
lawn care, 97, 98, 131
lead, 39, 42, 76, 89, 91, 99, 116, 119, 120, 125, 149
lighting, 66, 83-85, 107, 131
linen, 58
liquor, 46
livestock, 33, 40-41
Loblaws, 34, 41, 47, 51, 95, 125
low-impact camping, 142-145
lumber, 86-88

makeup, 63
manure, 32, 33, 92, 93, 95
maple syrup industry, 20
Marks & Spencer, 60
meat and poultry, 40-41, 44
medicines, 113-114
mercury, 27, 42, 76, 89, 103-104
metal polishes, 113-114
metering water, 77
methane, 105, 120
methanol, 120
methoprene, 71
mice, in gardens, 94
micro-breweries, 47
microwave ovens, 40, 81, 115
milk, 44, 112
mineral water, 46
Miracle Foodmart, 38, 51
moisturizers, 63
Montreal Protocol, 17-18
moth repellents, 53
motor oil, 109, 113-114, 125
mulch, 94-95
mushrooms, wild, 144
musk, 63
mutual funds, 135-136
nail care products, 63
naphtha, 53
natural gas, 23, 61, 71, 81, 82, 120
natural versus synthetic products, 1-3, 55, 58, 85, 87, 88-89
Nepal, 141, 142
Neunkirchen, Austria, 109, 110
newspapers, 26, 55, 95, 109

nitrates, 76, 150
nitrogen, in fertilizers, 32, 92, 93, 94
nitrogen oxides, 20-21, 24, 74, 104, 116, 118, 119, 120, 121
nitrous oxide, 32, 49
nuclear power, 23, 24, 25, 37, 38
nuts, Brazil, 39

oatmeal, as facial scrub, 62
oil, 23, 71-72, 118, 123; motor oil, 109, 113-114, 125; source of textiles, 58
oils, vegetable, 44, 45
Ontario Advanced House, 66-67
open-pollinated seeds, 96
organic agriculture and food, 33-35, 44, 45, 46, 47, 58; gardening, 90-101; suppliers, 33, 35
organic polymer insulation, 69
organophosphates, 98
outdoor equipment, 149
oven cleaners, 54
ovens, 78, 81; microwave, 40, 81, 115
ozone, as greenhouse gas, 118
ozone layer, 16-18, 57; *see also* CFCs (chlorofluorocarbons)

packaging, 38-39, 44, 59, 61, 64; laws and regulations, 110-111; and microwave ovens, 81, 115; and waste management, 26, 105-113, 115
paint, 88-89, 113-114
paper: consumption of, 14, 21, 25, 38; dioxins in, 26, 44, 45, 61; garbage, 38, 64, 106-107; recycling, 38, 64, 109, 129, 130; waxed, 39
paper towels, 53, 59
parabolic-aluminized reflector lamps, 84
parks, Canadian, 142, 145
particulates, 119, 120
PCBs (polychlorinated biphenyls), 26, 42, 103
pearls, 59
peat extraction, 22, 46
Peel Region, Ontario, 108
pentachlorophenol, 146
perchlorethylene, 57
perennials, 94, 96
perfumes, 49, 55, 59, 63
pesticides: in agriculture, 31-32, 35, 45, 58; chemical, 98, 113-114, 131, 146; commercial, 100; natural, 98-99; residues in food, 30-31, 35, 40, 44, 47
petroleum, *see* oil
pets, 149
phenols, 50
phosphates, 51, 52, 55, 56, 80, 149, 150
photo processing, 113-114, 150-151
photocells, 84, 85

photodegradable plastics, 39, 111-112
photography, 150, 152
plants as energy sources, 24, 120; *see also* biomass fuels
plastics: bags, 26, 34, 39, 107, 108, 111-113, 147; degradable, 39, 111-112; in diapers, 61; foamed, 38, 39, 45, 70, 115; food containers, 39, 44, 45, 108, 112; food wrap, 39; as ground cover, 95; recycling, 105, 109, 111-112; threat to marine life, 38, 111, 147
polishes, 53, 54, 113-114
pollution, *see* air pollution; soil contamination; water pollution
Pollution Probe, 15, 20, 34, 95
polyaromatic hydrocarbons, 103
polynuclear aromatic hydrocarbons, 125
pool chemicals, 113-114
potpourri, 49
pottery, glazed, 39
poultry, 40-41
powerboats, 150
propane, 120
Protect Yourself, 52
Provigo, 47
public transportation, 123-125
pyrethrum, 100

quarternary ammonium compounds, 55

R-2000 houses, 66, 78
radial tires, 121
rags for cleaning, 53, 59
rail travel, 116, 125, 150
rainforests, *see* deforestation
ranges, 78, 81
rayon, 55, 58, 62
razors, disposable, 64, 107
RBW Graphics, 127
re-refined motor oil, 125
recycling, 39, 107, 108-110, 127; at work, 34, 129-131; degradable plastics, 111-112; energy and resource savings from, 21, 104, 105, 106, 109; recycled products, 38, 39, 64, 125, 150-151; versus manufacturing, 105-106
red pepper, as insecticide, 71
refrigerators, 78, 79-80, 80
renewable energy sources, 24-25, 78, 79, 120-121
renovation, 85-89
rentals, 108, 122
repairs, 108
re-refined motor oil, 125
reuse, 39, 58-59, 107, 108
reverse osmosis, 76
Ryley, Alberta, 109, 110
roofing, 86

INDEX

re-refined motor oil, 125
reuse, 39, 58-59, 107, 108
reverse osmosis, 76
Riley, Alberta, 109, 110
roofing, 86
rotenone, 100
rug cleaners, 54, 113-114

safaris, 29, 141, 150
Safeway, 47
sailing, 147
salmon, 41-42, 43
salt, 53, 54, 71
sanitary pads, 64
schools, 131
Science Council of Canada, 80
scotch whisky, 46
scouring powder, 55
sea turtles, 147
sealants, 68, 70
seaweed, 92, 93, 94, 95
seeds, 95-96
septic tanks, 146
sewage treatment, 27, 48, 49, 64, 81;
    at camps and cottages, 144, 145,
    146, 148; on boats, 147, 149
shades and blinds, 70, 83
shampoos, 63
shark, basking, 28, 60-61
shaving aids, 64
shellfish, 42-43
showers, 75, 77
siding, 86-87
silk, 55, 58
silver, 54, 150, 151
skiing, 150
slow-cookers, 81
slugs, 94, 99
smog, 23, 85, 116, 118, 123; see also
    air pollution
snails, 99
snowmobiles, 151
snowshoeing, 150
soap, 49, 51, 52, 55, 64, 144
sodium bisulphide, 55
sodium hydroxide, 52
soil: contamination, 31, 36, 61, 103-
    104; erosion, 21-22, 32, 33, 36,
    59, 141; for gardening, 91-95
solar energy, 16, 24, 78, 79, 121
solvents, 49, 68, 85, 88-89
space heating, 66, 67-74
sponges, 53, 64
sports, 145, 147-151
spot removers, 54
spring water, 46
squalene, 61
starch, 55
static cling, 53, 55
steel, 25, 26, 105-106
Steinberg, 35, 38, 47
stocks and bonds, 134-137
stoves, 78, 81

St. Lawrence River, 26
subways, 123
sulphites, 46
sulphur dioxide, 20-21, 24, 59, 67,
    104, 119, 120, 127
sulphur oxides, 118
supermarkets, 34, 35, 38
sustainable development, 8, 12, 126,
    127

tampons, 64
Tanglefoot, 100
taps, 77, 78, 131
taxis, 122
tea, 45
Tetra-Paks, 115
textiles, 58
thermostats, 73
Third World, travelling in, 138-142
3M, 70, 127
three Rs, 13, 107-109
timers for lights, 84, 85
tires, radial, 121
tissues, 64, 130
titanium dioxide, 65
toilet paper, 64
toiletries, 59-65; cruelty-free, 60
toilets, 77, 131; biological, 146;
    cleaners, 55
toluene, 50, 63, 116
toothpaste, 65
Toronto Department of Public
    Health, 44, 103
tour operators, 142, 153-155
tourism, 138-142, 147-155; provin-
    cial departments, 152
trains, 116, 125, 150
transportation, 116-125; public, 123-
    125
travel, 138-155
trees, 19, 61, 83, 96, 100, 104, 118;
    see also deforestation; paper
tributyl tin (TBT), 150
trihalomethanes, 76
tropical forests, see deforestation
tropical hardwoods, 86, 87-88, 131
trucks, 116
tub and tile cleaners, 55
tuna fleets, 42
tungsten halogen bulbs, 84
turtles, 147
2,4-D, 32, 98

unions, 128
untreated seeds, 96
upholstery, 88, 113-114
urban planning, 123, 124, 125

varsol, 57
vegetables, see fruits and vegetables
veneers, 88
ventilation, 74

venture capital, 134
Via Rail, 125
vinegar, 49, 50, 53, 54, 55, 71

washcloths, 53, 62, 64
washers (clothes), 75, 78, 82
washing soda, 49, 50, 51, 52, 53
waste management, 61-62, 87, 102-
    115, 144, 145, 146
water heating, 66, 75-76, 78
water pollution, 26-27, 76; agricul-
    tural, 31, 32, 36, 42, 43, 45, 91,
    96, 98; from cleaners, 48, 49, 50,
    51, 57, 80; from leisure activities,
    91, 98, 144, 145, 149; industrial,
    46, 53, 57, 59, 103-104, 105, 150-
    151; see also acid rain;
    groundwater contamination
water treatment, 26-27, 48, 76, 148;
    bottled water, 46
water use, 59, 75, 76, 77-78, 80, 81,
    97-98
waxed paper, 39
weatherstripping, 67-68
weedkillers, see pesticides
wetlands, 22
whales, 26, 28-29, 60, 63, 147;
    whalewatching, 151
whistle-blowing, 132-133
wildlife, 88, 141, 144; injured ani-
    mals, 151; recreation, 144,
    147-151
wind power, 24, 78, 79
windows, 68, 70-71, 78, 83, 86;
    cleaners, 55; condensation on, 74
windsurfing, 147
wines, organic, 45, 46
Winnipeg Photo, 150-151
wood: cleaners, 50, 53; firewood, 19,
    32, 141, 142; for home renova-
    tion, 86-88; preservatives,
    145-146
Woodsman's Code, 142-145
wool, 55, 58
workers, environmental responsibil-
    ities of, 128-133
Workplace Hazardous Materials
    Information System (WHMIS),
    131-132
World Commission on Environment
    and Development, 8, 11-12, 23
World Resources Institute, 25
Worldwatch Institute, 19, 32

xylene, 50, 116

yogurt, 44

zinc stearate, 50
zoos, 151